ESSENTIALS OF

software
engineering

THIRD EDITION

Frank Tsui

Orlando Karam

Barbara Bernal

All of Southern Polytechnic State University

JONES & BARTLETT
LEARNING

World Headquarters
Jones & Bartlett Learning
5 Wall Street
Burlington, MA 01803
978-443-5000
info@jblearning.com
www.jblearning.com

Jones & Bartlett Learning books and products are available through most bookstores and online booksellers. To contact Jones & Bartlett Learning directly, call 800-832-0034, fax 978-443-8000, or visit our website, www.jblearning.com.

Substantial discounts on bulk quantities of Jones & Bartlett Learning publications are available to corporations, professional associations, and other qualified organizations. For details and specific discount information, contact the special sales department at Jones & Bartlett Learning via the above contact information or send an email to specialsales@jblearning.com.

Production Credits
Executive Publisher: Kevin Sullivan
Senior Developmental Editor: Amy Bloom
Director of Production: Amy Rose
Production Assistant: Eileen Worthley
Marketing Manager: Lindsay White
V.P., Manufacturing and Inventory Control: Therese Connell
Composition: Northeast Compositors, Inc.
Cover and Title Page Design: Kristin E. Parker
Cover and Title Page Image: © Kushch Dmitry/ShutterStock, Inc.
Printing and Binding: Edwards Brothers Malloy
Cover Printing: Edwards Brothers Malloy

Library of Congress Cataloging-in-Publication Data
Tsui, Frank F.
  Essentials of software engineering. -- Third edition / Frank Tsui, Orlando Karam, Barbara Bernal.
     pages cm
  Includes bibliographical references and index.
  ISBN 978-1-4496-9199-8 (pbk.) -- ISBN 1-4496-9199-4 (pbk.)
1. Software engineering. I. Karam, Orlando. II. Bernal, Barbara. III. Title.
  QA76.758.T78 2014
  005.1--dc23
                          2012029913

6048
Printed in the United States of America
17 16 15 14 13   10 9 8 7 6 5 4 3 2

Preface

Essentials of Software Engineering was born from our experiences in teaching introductory material on software engineering. Although there are many books on this topic available in the market, few serve the purpose of introducing only the core material for a one-semester course that meets approximately three hours a week for 16 weeks. With the proliferation of small web applications, many new information technology personnel have entered the field of software engineering without fully understanding what it entails. This book is intended to serve both new students with limited experience as well as experienced information technology professionals who are contemplating a new career in the software engineering discipline. The complete life cycle of a software system is covered in this book, from inception to release and through support.

The content of this book has also been shaped by our personal experiences and backgrounds—one of us with more than 25 years in building, supporting, and managing large and complex mission-critical software with companies such as IBM®, BlueCross BlueShield, MARCAM, and RCA and another with extensive expertise in constructing smaller software with Agile methods.

Although new ideas and technology will continue to emerge and some of the principles introduced in this book may have to be updated, we believe that the underlying and fundamental concepts we present here will remain.

Preface to the Third Edition

For this third edition, our goal is, again, to improve the text without growing it beyond the original intent, which was to include only the essential topics such that they can be covered within a one-semester introduction to software engineering course. The flow of the text has also been kept constant throughout the different editions.

Thanks to feedback from many readers and students, we have made numerous corrections and small commentary changes. We have proactively solicited input from those who have used this as a textbook in their classes and have incorporated many of their suggestions. As such, we have been joined by a third author, Barbara Bernal, who has used this book as the text in her introduction to software engineering classes for several years.

This third edition includes the following main modifications and additions:

- Addition of Scrum method and elimination of some lesser-used processes in Chapter 5
- Expanded UI design discussion that includes an example of HTML-Script-SQL design and implementation in Chapter 7
- Inclusion of "essential samples" for Team Plan, Software Development Plan, Requirements Specification, Design Plan, and Test Plan, presented in new appendices
- Retitled Chapter 14 from "Epilogue" to "Epilogue and Some Contemporary Issues" to briefly relate some current issues within software engineering

The first and second editions of this book have been used by numerous colleges and universities, and we thank them for their patience and input. We have learned a lot in the process. We hope the third edition will prove to be a better one for all future readers.

Organization of the Book

Chapters 1 and 2 demonstrate the difference between a small programming project and the effort required to construct a mission-critical software system. We purposely took two chapters to demonstrate this concept, highlighting the difference between a single-person "garage" operation and a team project required to construct a large "professional" system. The discussion in these two chapters delineates the rationale for studying and understanding software engineering. Chapter 3 is the first place where software engineering is discussed more formally. Included in this chapter is an introduction to the profession of software engineering and its code of ethics.

The traditional topics of software processes, process models, and methodologies are covered in Chapters 4 and 5. Reflecting the vast amount of progress made in this area, these chapters explain in extensive detail how to evaluate the processes through the Capability Maturity Models from the Software Engineering Institute (SEI).

Chapters 6, 7, 9, 10, and 11 cover the sequence of development activities from requirements through product release at a macro level. Chapter 8, following the chapter on software design, steps back and discusses design characteristics and metrics utilized in evaluating high-level and detail designs. Chapter 11 discusses not only product release, but the general concept of configuration management.

Chapter 12 explores the support and maintenance activities related to a software system after it is released to customers and users. Topics covered include call management, problem fixes, and feature releases. The need for configuration management is further emphasized in this chapter. Chapter 13 summarizes the phases of project management, along with some specific project planning and monitoring techniques. It is only a summary, and some topics, such as team building and leadership qualities, are not included. The software project management process is contrasted from the development and support processes. Chapter 14 concludes the book and provides a view of some of the future topics in our field.

The new appendices for this third edition give readers and students insight into possible results from major activities in software development. An often-asked question is what a requirements document or a test plan should look like. To help answer this question and provide a starting point, we have included sample formats of possible documents resulting from the four activities of Planning, Requirements, Design, and Test Plan. These are provided as follows:

- Appendix A Essential Software Development Plan (SDP)
- Appendix B Essential Software Requirements Specifications (SRS)
  - Example 1: Essential SRS—Descriptive
  - Example 2: Essential SRS—Object Oriented
  - Example 3: Essential SRS—IEEE Standard
  - Example 4: Essential SRS— Narrative Approach
- Appendix C Essential Software Design
  - Example 1: Essential Software Design—UML
  - Example 2: Essential Software Design—Structural
- Appendix D Essential Test Plan

Many times in the development of team projects by novice software engineers there is a need for specific direction on how to document the process. The four new appendices were developed to give the reader concrete examples of the possible essential outlines. Each of the appendices gives an outline with explanations. This provides the instructor with concrete material to supplement class activities, team project assignments, and/or independent work.

The topical coverage in this book reflects those emphasized by the IEEE Computer Society-sponsored *Software Engineering Body of Knowledge* (SWEBOK) and by the *Software Engineering 2004 Curriculum Guidelines for Undergraduate Degree Program in Software Engineering*. The one topic that is not highlighted but is discussed throughout the book concerns quality—a topic that needs to be addressed and integrated into all activities. It is not just a concern of the testers. Quality is discussed in multiple chapters to reflect its broad implications and cross activities.

Suggested Teaching Plan

All the chapters in this book can be covered within one semester. However, some instructors may prefer different emphasis:

- Those who want to focus on direct development activities should spend more time on Chapters 6 through 11.
- Those who want to focus more on indirect and general activities should spend more time on Chapters 1, 12, and 13.

It should be pointed out that both the direct development and the indirect support activities are important. The combined set forms the software engineering discipline.

There are two sets of questions at the end of each chapter. For the Review Questions, students can find answers directly in the chapter. The Exercises are meant to be used for potential class discussion, homework, or small projects.

Supplements

PowerPoint Lecture Outlines, Answers to End-of-Chapter Exercises, and sample Test Questions are available for free instructor download. To request access, please visit go.jblearning.com/Tsui3e or contact your account representative.

Acknowledgments

We would first like to thank our families, especially our wives, Lina Colli and Teresa Tsui. They provided constant encouragement and understanding when we spent more time with the manuscript than with them. Our children—Colleen and Nicholas; Orlando and Michelle; and Victoria, Liz, and Alex—enthusiastically supported our efforts as well. We would also like to thank Han Reichgelt, Dean of the School of Computing and Software Engineering at Southern Polytechnic State University, and Lisa Rossbacher, President of Southern Polytechnic State University, for providing us with a supportive and conducive environment for manuscript research and writing.

In addition, we would like to thank the reviewers who have improved the book in many ways. We would like to specifically thank the following individuals:

- Brent Auernheimer, California State University–Fresno
- Ayad Boudiab, Georgia Perimeter College
- Kai Chang, Auburn University
- David Gustafson, Kansas State University
- Theresa Jefferson, George Washington University
- Dar-Biau Liu, California State University–Long Beach
- Bruce Logan, Lesley University
- Jeanna Matthews, Clarkson University

- Michael Oudshoorn, Montana State University

- Frank Ackerman, Montana Tech

- Mark Hall, Hastings College

- Dimitris Papamichail, University of Miami

- Dr. Jody Paul, Metro State Denver

We continue to appreciate the help from Tim Anderson, Amy Bloom, Eileen Worthley, and others at Jones & Bartlett Learning.

Any remaining error is solely the mistake of the authors.

—Frank Tsui
—Orlando Karam
—Barbara Bernal

Contents

CHAPTER 1

Writing a Program

OBJECTIVES

- Analyze some of the issues involved in producing a simple program:
  - Requirements
  - Design constraints
  - Testing
  - Effort estimation
  - Implementation details
- Understand the sequence of activities involved in writing even a simple program.
- Preview many additional software engineering topics found in the later chapters.

1.1   A Simple Problem

In this chapter we will analyze the tasks involved in writing a relatively simple program. This will serve as a contrast to what is involved in developing a large system, which is described in Chapter 2.

Assume that you have been given the following problem: "Given a collection of lines of text (strings) stored in a file, sort them in alphabetical order, and write them to another file." This is probably one of the simplest problems you will be involved with. You have probably done similar assignments for some of your introduction to programming classes.

1.2   Decisions, Decisions

A problem statement such as the one above does not completely specify the problem. You need to clarify the requirements in order to produce a program that better satisfies the real problem. You need to understand all the **program requirements** and the **design constraints** imposed by the client on the design, and you need to make important technical decisions. A complete problem statement would include the requirements, which state and qualify what the program does, and the design constraints, which depict the ways in which you can design and implement it.

> **Program requirements**   Statements that define and qualify what the program needs to do.
>
> **Design constraints**   Statements that constrain the ways in which the software can be designed and implemented.
>
> **Functional requirements**   What a program needs to do.
>
> **Nonfunctional requirements**   The manner in which the functional requirements need to be achieved.

The most important thing to realize is that the word *requirements* is not used as it is in colloquial English. In many business transactions, a requirement is something that absolutely must happen. However, in software engineering many items are negotiable. Given that every requirement will have a cost, the clients may decide that they do not really need it after they understand the related cost. Requirements are often grouped into those that are "needed" and those that are "nice to have."

It is also useful to distinguish between **functional requirements**—what the program does—and **nonfunctional requirements**—the manner in which the program must behave. In a way, a function is similar to that of a direct and indirect object in grammar. Thus the functional requirements for our problem will describe what it does: sort a file (with all the detail required); the nonfunctional requirements will describe items such as performance, usability, and maintainability. Functional requirements tend to have a Boolean measurement where the requirement is either satisfied or not satisfied, but nonfunctional requirements tend to apply to things measured on a linear scale where the measurements can vary much more. Performance and maintainability requirements, as examples, may be measured in degrees of satisfaction.

Nonfunctional requirements are informally referred as the "ilities," because the words describing most of them will end in "-ility." Some of the typical characteristics defined as nonfunctional requirements are performance, modifiability, usability, configurability, reliability, availability, security, and scalability.

Besides requirements, you will also be given design constraints, such as the choice of programming language, platforms the system runs on, and other systems it interfaces with. These design constraints are sometimes considered nonfunctional requirements. This is not a very crisp or easy-to-define distinction (similar to where requirement analysis ends and design starts); and in borderline cases, it is defined mainly by consensus. Most developers will include usability as a nonfunctional requirement, and the choice of a specific user interface such as graphical user interface (GUI) or Web-based, as a design constraint. However, it can also be defined as a functional requirement as follows: "the program displays a dialog box 60 by 80 pixels, and then …"

Requirements are established by the client, with help from the software engineer, while the technical decisions are often made by the software engineer without much client input. Oftentimes, some of the technical decisions such as which programming languages or tools to use can be given as requirements because the program needs to interoperate with other programs or the client organization has expertise or strategic investments in particular technologies.

In the following pages we will illustrate the various issues that software engineers confront, even for simple programs. We will categorize these decisions into functional and nonfunctional requirements, design constraints, and design decisions. But do keep in mind that other software engineers may put some of these issues into a different category. We will use the simple sorting problem presented in Section 1.1 as an example.

1.2.1 Functional Requirements

We will have to consider several aspects of the problem and ask many questions prior to designing and programming the solution. The following is an informal summary of the thinking process involved with functional requirements:

- *Input formats:* What is the format for the input data? How should data be stored? What is a character? In our case, we need to define what separates the lines on the file. This is especially critical because several different platforms may use different separator characters. Usually some combination of new-line and carriage return may be considered. In order to know exactly where the boundaries are, we also need to know the input character set. The most common representation uses 1 byte per character, which is enough for English and most Latin-derived languages. But some representations, such as Chinese or Arabic, require 2 bytes per character because there are more than 256 characters involved. Others require a combination of the two types. With the combination of both single- and double-byte character representations, there is usually a need for an escape character to allow the change of mode from single byte to double byte or vice versa. For our sorting problem, we will assume the simple situation of 1 byte per character.

- *Sorting:* Although it seems to be a well-defined problem, there are many slightly and not so slightly different meanings for sorting. For starters—and of course, assuming that we have English characters only—do we sort in ascending or descending order? What do we do with nonalphabetic characters? Do numbers go before or after letters in the order? How about lowercase and uppercase characters? To simplify our problem, we define sorting among characters as being in numerical order, and the sorting of the file to be in ascending order.

- *Special cases, boundaries, and error conditions:* Are there any special cases? How should we handle boundary cases such as empty lines and empty files? How should different error conditions be handled? It is common, although not good practice, to not have all of these requirements completely specified until the detailed design or even the implementation stages. For our program, we do not treat empty lines in any special manner except to specify that when the input file is empty the output file should be created but empty. We do not specify any special error-handling mechanism as long as all errors are signaled to the user and the input file is not corrupted in any way.

1.2.2   Nonfunctional Requirements

The thinking process involved in nonfunctional requirements can be informally summarized as follows:

- *Performance requirements:* Although it is not as important as most people may think, performance is always an issue. The program needs to finish most or all inputs within a certain amount of time. For our sorting problem, we define the performance requirements as taking less than 1 minute to sort a file of 100 lines of 100 characters each.
- *Real-time requirements:* When a program needs to perform in real-time, which means it must complete the processing within a given amount of time, performance is an issue. The variability of the running time is also a big issue. We may need to choose an algorithm with a less than average performance, if it has a better worst-case performance. For example, Quick Sort is regarded as one of the fastest sorting algorithms; however, for some inputs, it can have poor performance. In algorithmic terms, its expected running time is on the order of $n \log(n)$, but its worst-case performance is on the order of n squared. If you have real-time requirements in which the average case is acceptable but the worst case is not, then you may want to choose an algorithm with less variability, such as Heap Sort or Merge Sort. Run-time performance analysis is discussed further in Main and Savitch (1997).
- *Modifiability requirements:* Before writing a program, it is important to know the life expectancy of the program and whether there is any plan to modify the program. If the program is to be used only once, then modifiability is not a big issue. On the other hand, if it is going to be used for 10 years or more, then we need to worry about making it easy to maintain and modify. Surely, the requirements will change during that 10-year period. If we know that there are plans to extend the program in certain ways, or that the requirements will change in specific ways, then we should prepare the program for those modifications as the program is designed and implemented. Notice that even if the modifiability requirements are low, this is not a license to write bad code, because we still need to be able to understand the program for debugging purposes. For our sorting example, consider how we might design and implement the solution if we know that down the road the requirement may change from descending to ascending order or may change to include both ascending and descending orders.

1.2.3   Design Constraints

The thinking process related to design constraints can be summarized as follows:

- *User interface:* What kind of **user interface** should the program have? Should it be a command-line interface (CLI) or a graphical user interface (GUI)? Should we use a web-based interface? For the sorting problem, a web-based interface doesn't sound appropriate because users would need to upload the file and download the sorted one. Although GUIs have become the norm over the past decade or so, a command-line interface can be just as appropriate for our sorting problem, especially bacuase it would make it easier to invoke inside a script, allowing for automation of manual processes and reuse of this program as a module for future ones. This is one of those design considerations that also involves user interface. In Section 1.5, we will create several implementations, some CLI based and some GUI based. Chapter 7 also discusses user-interface design in more detail.

> **User interface**   What the user sees and hears from the system.

- *Typical and maximum input sizes:* Depending on the typical input sizes, we may want to spend different amounts of time on algorithms and performance optimizations. Also, certain kinds of inputs are particularly good or bad for certain algorithms; for example, inputs that are almost sorted make the naive `Quick Sort` implementations take more time. Note that you will sometimes be given inaccurate estimates, but even ballpark figures can help anticipate problems or guide you toward an appropriate algorithm. In this example, if you have small input sizes, you can use almost any sorting algorithm. Thus you should choose the simplest one to implement. If you have larger inputs but they can still fit into the random access memory (RAM), you need to use an efficient algorithm; if the input does not fit on RAM, then you need to choose a specialized algorithm for on-disk sorting.

- *Platforms:* On which platforms does the program need to run? This is an important business decision that may include architecture, operating system, and available libraries and will almost always be expressed in the requirements. Keep in mind that, although cross-platform development has become easier and there are many languages designed to be portable across platforms, not all the libraries will be available in all platforms. There is always an extra cost on explicitly supporting a new platform. On the other hand, good programming practices help achieve portability, even when not needed. A little extra consideration when designing and implementing a program can minimize the potentially extensive work required to port to a new platform. It is good practice to perform a quick cost-benefit analysis on whether to support additional platforms and to use technologies and programming practices that minimize portability pains, even when the need for supporting new platforms is not anticipated.

- *Schedule requirements:* The final deadline for completing a project comes from the client, with input from the technical side on feasibility and cost. For example, a dialogue on schedule might take the following form: Your client may make a request such as "I need it by next month." You respond by saying, "Well, that will cost you twice as much than if you wait two months" or "That just can't be done; it usually takes three months; we can push it to two, but no less." The client may agree to this, or could also say, "If it's not done by next month, then it is not useful" and cancel the project.

1.2.4   Design Decisions

The steps and thoughts related to design decisions for the sorting problem can be summarized as follows:

- *Programming language:* Typically this will be a technical design decision, although it is not uncommon to be given as a design constraint. The type of programming needed, the performance and portability requirements, and the technical expertise of the developers often heavily influence the choice of the programming language.

- *Algorithms:* When implementing systems, there are usually several pieces that can be influenced by the choice of algorithms. In our example, of course, there are a variety of algorithms we can choose among to sort a collection of objects. The language used and the libraries available will influence the choice of algorithms. For example, to sort, the easiest solution would be to use a standard facility provided by the programming language rather than to implement your own. Thus, use whatever algorithm that implementation chooses. Performance will usually be the most important influence in the choice of an algorithm, but it needs to be balanced with the effort required to implement it, and the familiarity of the developers with it. Algorithms are usually design decisions, but they can be given as design constraints or even considered functional requirements. In many business environments there are regulations that mandate specific algorithms or mathematical formulas to be used, and in many scientific applications the goal is to test several algorithms, which means that you must use certain algorithms.

1.3   Testing

It is always a good idea to test a program, both while it is being developed and after it is completed. This may sound like obvious advice, but it is not always followed. There are several kinds of testing, including acceptance testing, which refers to testing done by clients, or somebody on their behalf, to make sure the program runs as specified. If this testing fails, the client can reject the program. The developers should run their own tests, prior to the client acceptance testing, to determine if the program works.

Although there are many types of testing performed by the development organization, the most important kind of testing for the individual programmer is unit testing—a process followed by a programmer to test each piece or unit of software. When writing code, you must also write tests to check each module, function, or method you have written. Some methodologies, notably Extreme Programming, go as far as saying that programmers should write the test cases before writing the code; see the discussion on Extreme Programming in Beck (1999). Inexperienced programmers often do not realize the importance of testing. They write functions or methods that depend on other functions or methods that have not been properly tested. When a method fails, they do not know which function or method is actually failing.

Another useful distinction is between black-box and white-box testing. In black-box testing, the test cases are based only on the requirement specifications, not on the implementation code. In white-box testing, the test cases can be designed while looking at the design and code implementation. While doing unit testing, the programmer has access to the implementation but should still perform a mixture of black-box and white-box testing. When we discuss implementations for our simple program, we will perform unit testing on it. Testing will be discussed more extensively in Chapter 10.

1.4   Estimating Effort

One of the most important aspects of a software project is estimating how much effort it involves. The effort estimate is required to produce a cost estimate and a schedule. Before producing a complete effort estimate, the requirements must be understood. An interesting exercise illustrates this point.

Try the following exercise:

> Estimate how much time, in minutes, it will take you, using your favorite language and technology, to write a program that reads lines from one file and writes the sorted lines to another file. Assume that you will be writing the sort routine yourself and will implement a simple GUI like the one shown in Figure 1.21, with two text boxes for providing two file names, and two buttons next to each text box. Pressing one of the two buttons displays a File Open dialog, like the one shown in Figure 1.22, where the user can navigate the computer's file system and choose a file. Assume that you can work only on this one task, with no interruptions. Provide an estimate within 1 minute.

Step 1.
Estimated ideal time: _____

Is the assumption that you will be able to work straight through on this task with no interruptions realistic? Won't you need to go to the restroom or drink some water? Can you spend the time on this task? If you were asked to do this task as soon as reasonably possible, starting right now, can you estimate when would you be finished? Calculate the number of minutes between now and the time you would be finished.

Step 2.
Estimated calendar time: _____

Now, let's divide the task into several subtasks. Assume you will create a class, called StringSorter, with three public methods: Read, Write, and Sort. For the sorting routine, assume that your algorithm involves finding the largest element, putting it at the end of the array, and then sorting the rest of the array using the same mechanism. Assume you will create a method called IndexOfBiggest that returns the index of the biggest element on the array. Using the following chart, estimate how much time it will take you to do each task (and the GUI).

Step 3.

Ideal Time	Calendar Time
IndexOfBiggest	
Sort	
Read	
Write	
GUI	
Testing	
Total	

How close is this estimate to the previous one you did? What kind of formula did you use to convert from ideal time to calendar time?

Now implement your solution.

Step 4.

Keep track of the time you actually spend on each task as well as the interruptions you experience. Compare these times with your estimates. How high or low did you go? Is there a pattern? How accurate is the total with respect to your original estimate?

If you performed the activities in this exercise, chances are that you found the estimate was more accurate after dividing it into subtasks. You will also find that estimates in general tend to be somewhat inaccurate, even for well-defined tasks. Project estimation and effort estimation is one of the toughest problems in software project management and software engineering. This topic will be revisited in detail in Chapter 13. For further reading on why individuals should keep track of their development time, see Humphrey (1996). Accurate estimation is very hard to achieve. Dividing tasks into smaller ones and keeping data about previous tasks and estimates are usually helpful beginnings.

It is important that the estimation is done by the people who do the job, which is often the programmer. The client also needs to check the estimates for reasonableness. One big problem with estimating is that it is conceptually performed before the project is done, but in reality a lot of information, possibly up to design, is needed in order to be able to provide a good estimate. We will talk more about estimating in Chapter 13.

1.5   Implementations

In this section we will discuss several implementations of our sorting program, including two ways to implement the sort functionality and several variations of the user interface. We will also discuss unit testing for our implementations. Sample code will be provided in Java, using JUnit to aid in unit testing.

1.5.1   A Few Pointers on Implementation

Although software engineering tends to focus more on requirements analysis, design, and processes rather than implementation, a bad implementation will definitely mean a bad program even if all the other pieces are perfect. Although for simple programs almost anything will do, following a few simple rules will generally make all your programming easier. Here we will discuss only a few language-independent rules, and point you to other books in the Suggested Readings section at the end of this chapter.

- The most important rule is to be consistent—especially in your choice of names, capitalization, and programming conventions. If you are programming alone, the particular choice of conventions is not important as long as you are consistent. You should also try to follow the established conventions of the programming language you are using, even if it would not otherwise be your choice. This will ensure that you do not introduce two conventions. For example, it is established practice in Java to start class names with uppercase letters, and variable names with lowercase letters. If your name has more than one word, use capitalization to signal the word boundaries. This results in names such as `FileClass` and `fileVariable`. In C, the convention is to use lowercase almost exclusively and to separate with an underscore. Thus, when we program in C, we follow the C conventions. The choice of words for common operations is also dictated by convention. For example, printing, displaying, showing, or echoing a variable are some of the terminologies meaning similar actions. Language conventions also provide hints as to default names for variables, preference for shorter or longer names, and other issues. Try to be as consistent as possible in your choice, and follow the conventions for your language.

- Choose names carefully. In addition to being consistent in naming, try to make sure names for functions and variables are descriptive. If the names are too cumbersome or if a good name cannot be easily found, that is usually a sign that there may be a problem in the design. A good rule of thumb is to choose long, descriptive names for things that will have global scope such as classes and public methods. Use short names for local references, which are used in a very limited scope such as local variables, private names, and so on.

- Test before using a function or method. Make sure that it works. That way if there are any errors, you know that they are in the module you are currently writing. Careful unit testing, with test cases written before or after the unit, will help you gain confidence in using that unit.

- Know thy standard library. In most modern programming languages, the standard library will implement many common functions, usually including sorting and collections of data, database access, utilities for web development, networking, and much more. Don't reinvent or reimplement the wheel. Using the standard libraries will save extra work, make the code more understandable, and usually run faster with fewer errors, because the standard libraries are well debugged and optimized. Keep in mind that many exercises in introductory programming classes involve solving classic problems and implementing well-known data structures and algorithms. Although they are a valuable learning exercise, that does not mean you should use your own implementations in real life. For our sample programming problem, Java has a sorting routine that is robust and fast. Using it instead of writing your own would save time and effort and produce a better implementation. We will still implement our own for the sake of illustration but will also provide the implementation using the Java sorting routine.

- If possible, perform a review of your code. Software reviews are one of the most effective methods for reducing defects in software. Showing your code to other people will help detect not just functionality errors but also inconsistencies and bad naming. It will also help you learn from the other person's experience. This is another habit that does not blend well with school projects. In most such projects, getting help from another student might be considered cheating. Perhaps the code can instead be reviewed after it is handed in. Reviews are good for school assignments as well as for real-world programs.

1.5.2   Basic Design

Given that we will be implementing different user interfaces, our basic design separates the sorting functionality from the user interface, which is a good practice anyway, because user interfaces tend to change much faster than functionality. We have a class, called StringSorter, that has four methods: (1) reading the strings from a file, (2) sorting the collection of strings, (3) writing the strings to a file, and (4) combining those three, taking the input and output file names. The different user interfaces will be implemented in separate classes. Given that StringSorter would not know what to do with exceptional conditions, such as errors when reading or writing streams, the exceptions pass through in the appropriate methods, with the user interface classes deciding what to do with them. We also have a class with all our unit tests, taking advantage of the JUnit framework.

1.5.3   Unit Testing with JUnit

JUnit is one of a family of unit testing frameworks, the J standing for Java. There are variations for many other languages—for example, cppUnit for C++; the original library was developed in Smalltalk. Here we discuss JUnit in a very basic way; JUnit is discussed further in Chater 10. We just need to create a class that inherits from junit.framework.TestCase, which defines public methods whose names start with test. JUnit uses Java's reflection capabilities to execute all those methods. Within each test method, assertEquals can be used to verify whether two values that should be equal are truly equal.

1.5.4   Implementation of StringSorter

We will be presenting our implementation followed by the test cases. We are assuming a certain fundamental background with Java programming, although familiarity with another object-oriented programming language should be enough to understand this section. Although the methods could have been developed in a different order, we present them in the order we developed them, which is Read, then Sort, then Write. This is also the order in which the final program will execute, thus making it easier to test.

We import several namespaces, and declare the StringSorter class. The only instance variable is an ArrayList of lines. ArrayList is a container that can grow dynamically, and supports indexed access to its elements. It roughly corresponds to a vector in other programming languages. It is part of the standard Java collections library and another example of how using the standard library saves time. Notice we are not declaring the variable as private in **Figure 1.1**, because the test class needs access to it. By leaving it

```
import java.io.*; // for Reader(s), Writer(s),
import java.util.*; // for List, ArrayList, Iterator
public class StringSorter {
     ArrayList lines;
```

Figure 1.1 Class declaration and `Import` statements.

```
public void readFromStream(Reader r) throws
IOException
{
     BufferedReader br=new BufferedReader(r);
     lines=new ArrayList();
     while(true) {
          String input=br.readLine();
          if(input==null)
               break;
          lines.add(input);
     }
}
```

Figure 1.2 The `readFromStream` method.

with default protection, all classes in the same package can access it because Java has no concept like friend classes in C++. This provides a decent compromise. Further options will be discussed in Chapter 10. Our first method involves reading lines from a file or stream, as seen in **Figure 1.2**. To make the method more general, we take a `Reader`, which is a class for reading text-based streams. A stream is a generalization of a file. By using a `Reader` rather than a class explicitly based on `Files`, we could use this same method for reading from standard input or even from the network. Also, because we do not know how to deal with exceptions here, we will just let the `IOException` pass through.

For testing this method with `JUnit`, we create a class extending `TestCase`. We also define a utility method, called `make123`, that creates an `ArrayList` with three strings—one, two, and three—inserted in that order in **Figure 1.3**.

```
public class TestStringSorter extends TestCase {
     private ArrayList make123() {
          ArrayList l = new ArrayList();
          l.add("one");
          l.add("two");
          l.add("three");
          return l;
     }
```

Figure 1.3 `TestStringSorter` declaration and `make123` method.

```
public void testReadFromStream() throws
IOException{
             Reader in=new
FileReader("in.txt");
             StringSorter ss=new
StringSorter();
             ArrayList l= make123();
             ss.readFromStream(in);
             assertEquals(l,ss.lines);
}
```

Figure 1.4 testReadFromStream.

We then define our first method, testReadFromStream, in **Figure 1.4**. In this method we create an ArrayList and a StringSorter. We open a known file, and make the StringSorter read from it. Given that we know what is in the file, we know what the internal ArrayList in our StringSorter should be. We just assert that it should be equal to that known value.

We can run JUnit after setting the classpath and compiling both classes, by typing java junit.swingui.TestRunner. This will present us with a list of classes to choose from. When choosing our TestStringSorter class, we find a user interface like the one shown in **Figure 1.5**, which indicates that all tests are implemented and successfully run.

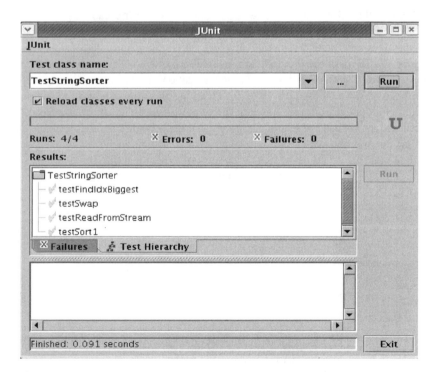

Figure 1.5 JUnit GUI.

```
static void swap(List l, int i1, int i2) {
     Object tmp=l.get(i1);
     l.set(i1, l.get(i2));
     l.set(i2, tmp);
}
```

Figure 1.6 The code for swapping two integers.

Pressing the `run` button will rerun all tests, showing you how many tests were successful. If any test is unsuccessful, the bar will be red rather than green. Classes are reloaded by default, so you can leave that window open, modify, recompile, and just press `run` again.

After we verify that our test is successful, we can begin the next method—building the sorting functionality. We decided on a simple algorithm: find the largest element in the array, then swap it with the last element, placing the largest element at the end of the array, then repeat with the rest of the array. We need two supporting functions, one for swapping the two elements in the array and another for finding the index of the largest element. The code for a swap is shown in **Figure 1.6**.

Because swap is a generic function that could be reused in many situations, we decided to build it without any knowledge of the `StringSorter` class. Given that, it makes sense to have it as a static method. In C++ or other languages, it would be a function defined outside the class and not associated with any class. Static methods are the closest technique in Java. We get as parameters a `List`, where `List` is the generic interface that `ArrayList` implements, and the indexes of the two elements. The test for this method is shown in the `testSwap` method of `TestStringSorter` class in **Figure 1.7**.

The next method is the one that returns the index of the largest element on the list. Its name is `findIdxBiggest`, as shown in **Figure 1.8**. `Idx` as an abbreviation of index is ingrained in our minds. We debated whether to use `largest`, `biggest`, or `max`/`maximum` for the name (they are about equally appropriate in our minds). After settling on `biggest`, we just made sure that we did not use the other two for naming the variables.

We use the `compareTo` method of `Strings`, that returns –1 if the first element is less than the second, 0 if they are equal, and 1 if the first is largest. In this method we use the fact that the elements in the `ArrayList` are strings. Notice that Java (as of version 1.4) does not have support for generics (templates in C++), so the elements have to be explicitly casted to `Strings`. The test is shown in **Figure 1.9**.

```
public void testSwap() {
     ArrayList l1= make123();
     ArrayList l2=new ArrayList();
     l2.add("one");
     l2.add("three");
     l2.add("two");
     StringSorter.swap(l1,1,2);
     assertEquals(l1,l2);
}
```

Figure 1.7 The `testSwap` method.

```
static int findIdxBiggest(List l, int from, int to) {
     String biggest=(String) l.get(0);
     int idxBiggest=from;
     for(int i=from+1; i<=to; ++i) {
          if(biggest.compareTo((String)l.get(i))<0) {// it is bigger
               biggest=(String)l.get(i);
               idxBiggest=i;
          }
     }
     return idxBiggest;
}
```

Figure 1.8 The `findIdxBiggest` method.

```
public void testFindIdxBiggest() {
     ArrayList l = make123();
     int i=StringSorter.findIdxBiggest(l,0,l.size()-
   1);
     assertEquals(i,1);
}
```

Figure 1.9 The `testFindIdxBiggest` method.

   With `swap` and `findIdxBiggest` in place, the `sort` method, shown in **Figure 1.10**, becomes relatively easy to implement. The test for it is shown in **Figure 1.11**. Note that if we knew our standard library, we could have used a much easier implementation, using the `sort` function in the standard Java library, as shown in **Figure 1.12**. We would have also avoided writing `swap` and `findIdxBiggest`! It definitely pays to know your standard library.

   Now on to writing to the file; this is shown in **Figure 1.13**. We will test it by writing a known value to the file, then reading it again and performing the compare in **Figure 1.14**. Now all that is needed is the `sort` method taking the file names as shown in **Figure 1.15**. Given that we have already seen how to do it for the test cases, it is very easy to do. The test for this method is shown in **Figure 1.16**.

```
public void sort() {
   for(int i=lines.size()-1; i>0; --i) {

     int big=findIdxBiggest(lines,0,i);
     swap(lines,i,big);
   }
}
```

Figure 1.10 The `sort` method.

```
public void testSort1() {
     StringSorter ss= new StringSorter();
     ss.lines=make123();
     ArrayList l2=new ArrayList();
     l2.add("one");
     l2.add("three");
     l2.add("two");
     ss.sort();
     assertEquals(l2,ss.lines);
}
```

Figure 1.11 The `testSort1` method.

```
void sort() {
   java.util.Collections.sort(lines);
}
```

Figure 1.12 The `sort` method using Java's standard library.

```
public void writeToStream(Writer w) throws IOException {
     PrintWriter pw=new PrintWriter(w);
     Iterator i=lines.iterator();
     while(i.hasNext()) {
            pw.println((String)(i.next()));
     }
}
```

Figure 1.13 The `writeToStream` method.

```
public void testWriteToStream() throws IOException{
     // write out a known value
   StringSorter ss1=new StringSorter();
     ss1.lines=make123();
     Writer out=new FileWriter("test.out");
     ss1.writeToStream(out);
     out.close();
     // then read it and compare
     Reader in=new FileReader("test.out");
     StringSorter ss2=new StringSorter();
     ss2.readFromStream(in);
     assertEquals(ss1.lines,ss2.lines);
}
```

Figure 1.14 The `testWriteToStream` method.

```
public void sort(String inputFileName, String
   outputFileName)
                    throws IOException
{

     Reader in=new FileReader(inputFileName);
     Writer out=new FileWriter(outputFileName);
     StringSorter ss=new StringSorter();
     ss.readFromStream(in);
     ss.sort();
     ss.writeToStream(out);
     in.close();
     out.close();
}
```

Figure 1.15 The `sort` method (taking file names).

```
public void testSort2() throws IOException{
     // write out a known value
     StringSorter ss1=new StringSorter();
     ss1.sort("in.txt","test2.out");
     ArrayList l=new ArrayList();
     l.add("one");
     l.add("three");
     l.add("two");
     // then read it and compare
     Reader in=new FileReader("test2.out");
     StringSorter ss2=new StringSorter();
     ss2.readFromStream(in);
     assertEquals(l,ss2.lines);
}
```

Figure 1.16 The `testSort2` method.

1.5.5   User Interfaces

We now have an implementation of `StringSorter` and a reasonable belief that it works as intended. We realize that our tests were not that extensive; however, we can go on to build a user interface, which is an actual program that lets us access the functionality of `StringSorter`. Our first implementation is a command-line, not GUI, version, as shown in **Figure 1.17**. It takes the names of the input and output files as command parameters. Its implementation is as shown in the figure.

We would use it by typing the following command:

```
java StringSorterCommandLine abc.txt abc_sorted.txt
```

Do you believe this is a useful user interface? Actually, for many people it is. If you have a command-line window open all the time or if you are working without a GUI, then it is not that hard to type the command. Also, it is very easy to use this command inside

```
import java.io.IOException;
public class StringSorterCommandLine {
   public static void main(String args[]) throws IOException
   {
     if(args.length!=2) {
          System.out.println("Use: cmd inputfile
   outputfile");
     } else {
          StringSorter ss=new StringSorter();
          ss.sort(args[0],args[1]);
     }
   }
}
```

Figure 1.17 The `StringSorterCommandLine` class, which implements a command-line interface for `StringSorter` functionality.

a script, to sort many files. In fact, you could use a script to more thoroughly test your implementation. Another important advantage, besides scriptability, is how easy it is to build the interface. This means less effort, lower costs, and fewer errors.

However, for some people this would not be a useful interface. If you are accustomed to only using GUIs or if you do not usually have a command window open and are not going to be sorting many files, then a GUI would be better. Nevertheless, GUI is not necessarily a better interface than a Command Line Interface (CLI). It depends on the use and the user. Also, it is extremely easy to design bad GUIs, such as the implementation shown in **Figure 1.18**. The code in this figure would display the dialog box shown in **Figure 1.19**. After the user presses OK, the dialog box in **Figure 1.20** would be shown.

```
public class StringSorterBadGUI {
   public static void main(String args[]) throws IOException
   {
     try {
          StringSorter ss=new StringSorter();
          String inputFileName=JOptionPane.showInputDialog
               ("Please enter input file name");
          String outputFileName=JOptionPane.showInputDialog
               ("Please enter output file name");
          ss.sort(inputFileName, outputFileName);
     } finally {
          System.exit(1);
     }
   }
}
```

Figure 1.18 `StringSorterBadGUI` class, which implements a hard-to-use GUI for `StringSorter` functionality.

Figure 1.19 An input file name dialog box for a hard-to-use GUI.

Figure 1.20 An output file name dialog for a hard-to-use GUI.

This does not involve much more effort than the command-line version, but it is very inefficient to use. Although it is a GUI, it is worse than the CLI for almost every user. A better interface is shown in **Figure 1.21**. Although it is not a lot better, at least both inputs are in the same place. What makes it more useful is that the buttons on the right open a dialog box as shown in **Figure 1.22** for choosing a file.

This would at least be a decent interface for most GUI users. Not terribly pretty, but simple and functional. The code for this GUI is available on the website for this book. We are not printing it because it requires knowledge of Java and Swing to be understood. We will note that the code is 75 lines long in Java, a language for which GUI building is one of its strengths, and it took us longer to produce than the StringSorter class! Sometimes GUIs come with a heavy cost. We will discuss user-interface design in Chapter 7.

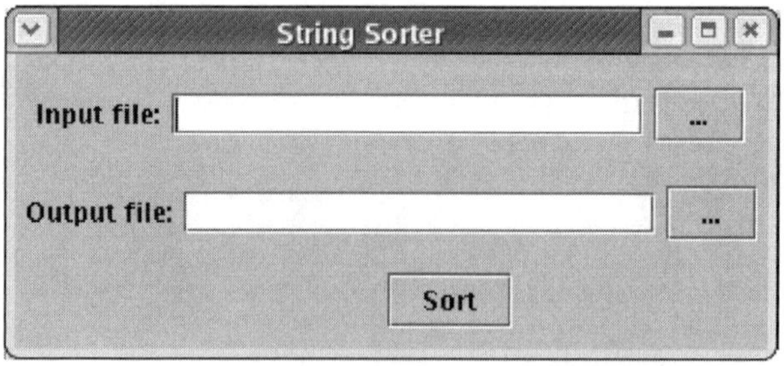

Figure 1.21 Input and Output file name dialog for GUI.

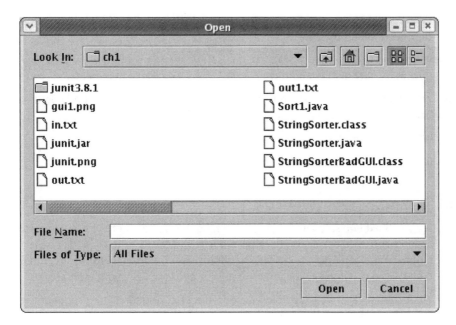

Figure 1.22 File Open dialog for GUI.

1.6   Summary

In this chapter we have discussed some of the many issues involved in writing a simple program. By now, you should have realized that even for simple programs there is much more than just writing the code. One has to consider many of the following items:

- Requirements
- Design
- Code implementation
- Unit testing
- Personal effort estimation
- User interface

Much of that material belongs to software engineering, and in this text we will provide an overview of it.

1.7   Review Questions

1. What are statements that define and qualify what the program needs to do?

2. What are statements that constrain the ways in which the software can be designed and implemented?

3. Which type of requirement statement defines what the program needs to do?

4. What requirements qualify as functional requirements? Specify in what manner they need to be achieved.

5. Which decisions are those taken by the software engineer about the best ways (processes, techniques, and technologies) to achieve the requirements?

6. What type of testing refers to testing done by the clients (or somebody on their behalf) to make sure the program runs as specified?

7. What is GUI? What is CLI?

8. List three of the typical kinds of nonfunctional requirements.

1.8   Exercises

1. For your next two software projects (assuming that you are getting programming assignments; otherwise consider a program to find the `max` and the `min` of a set of rational numbers) estimate how much effort they would take before doing them, then keep track of the actual time spent. How accurate were your estimates?

2. What sequence of activities did you observe in considering the programming effort discussed in this chapter?

3. Discuss whether you think a programming language constraint may be viewed as a requirement. Explain why you think so.

4. Download the programs for this chapter, and add at least one more test case for each method of the `StringSorter` class.

5. In the discussion of the simple program in this chapter, what were the items considered for "basic" design? Would you have written down these considerations and perhaps reviewed them with a trusted person before the actual coding?

6. Consider a command-line interface that, rather than taking the file names as parameters, asks for them from the keyboard (e.g., it displays "Input file name:" then reads it from the keyboard). Would this be a better user interface? Why or why not?

7. Consider a new user interface for our sorting program that combines the command-line interface and the GUI. If it receives parameters in the command line, it does the sort; if it does not, it displays the dialog. Would this be a better interface? What would be its advantages and disadvantages compared with other interfaces?

1.9   Suggested Readings

K. Beck, *Extreme Programming Explained: Embrace Change* (Reading, MA: Addison-Wesley, 1999).

N. Dale, C. Weems, and M. R. Headington, *Programming and Problem Solving with Java* (Sudbury, MA: Jones and Bartlett, 2003).

W. Humphrey, *Introduction to the Personal Software Process* (Reading, MA: Addison-Wesley, 1996).

A. Hunt and D. Thomas, *Pragmatic Unit Testing in Java with JUnit* (Sebastopol, CA: Pragmatic Bookshelf, 2003).

B. W. Kernighan and R. Pike, *The Practice of Programming* (Reading, MA: Addison-Wesley, 1999).

M. Main and W. Savitch, *Data Structures and Other Objects Using C++* (Reading, MA: Addison-Wesley, 1997).

Steve McConnell, *Code Complete 2* (Redmond, WA: Microsoft Press, 2004).

C. T. Wu, *Introduction to Objected Oriented Programming with Java*, 3rd ed. (New York: McGraw-Hill, 2004).

CHAPTER 2

Building a System

OBJECTIVES

- Characterize the size and complexity issues of a system.
- Describe the technical issues in development and support of a system.
- Describe the nontechnical issues of developing and supporting a system.
- Demonstrate the concerns in the development and support activities of a large application software, using a payroll system example.
- Describe the coordination efforts needed for process, product, and people; these software engineering topics are expanded in later chapters.

2.1   Characteristics of Building a System

The previous chapter focused on the environment and the conditions under which a single program may be developed by one person for, perhaps, just a few users. We have already seen multiple items that must be considered even when one person is writing a single program. In this chapter we will describe the problems and concerns associated with building a system that contains multiple components—anything from just a few components to maybe hundreds or thousands of components. The increase in number of components and complexity is what requires us to study and understand the various aspects, principles, and techniques of software engineering that will be discussed in the later chapters. This discussion introduces the rationale for software engineering as a discipline, especially for large and complex projects that require a team of people.

2.1.1   Size and Complexity

As software becomes ubiquitous, the development of systems involving software is also becoming more complex. Software engineers are asked to solve both simple and complex problems and to deal with the distinct differences between them. The complex problems come in multiple levels of breadth and depth. The breadth issue addresses the sheer numbers involving the following:

- Major functions
- Features within each functional area
- Interfaces to other external systems
- Simultaneous users
- Types of data and data structures

The depth issue addresses the linkage and the relationships among items. The linkages may either be through the sharing of data or through the transfer of control, or both. These relationships may be hierarchical, sequential, loop, recursive, or some other form. In developing solutions to these complex problems, software engineers must design with possibly yet another set of relationships different from that of the problem. **Figure 2.1** shows the effect of introducing both (1) the size in terms of breadth and (2) the complexity in terms of depth and number of interactions. Although you can get a natural "feel" of the difference by just viewing the diagram, it would be worth taking the time to analyze the differences. The simple case in this figure has three major segments: (1) start process, (2) perform three normal tasks, and (3) stop process. In Figure 2.1(b), the number of normal tasks has increased from three to five with the addition of the "wait for signal" and "perform task A2." There is also a new decision task, represented by the diamond-shaped figure in the center. The decision task has greatly increased the number of paths or choices, and thus it causes the increase of complexity. In addition, the complexity is further exacerbated by introducing a loop relationship with the decision task. There are many more interactions involved in a loop or repeat relationship, which is more complex than the straight sequential relationship among the tasks portrayed in Figure 2.1(a).

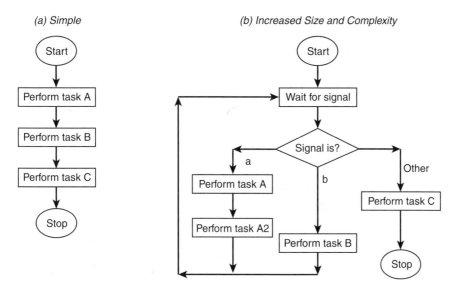

Figure 2.1 Size and complexity.

As shown in Figure 2.1, a relatively minor increase in the number of tasks and decisions has greatly increased the complexity. As is the case for a single programming module, when both size and complexity are magnified several times in a software system problem, the solution to those problems also involves a comparable expansion in size and complexity.

2.1.2   Technical Considerations of Development and Support

In the following three sections we will discuss a variety of technical issues related to developing and supporting a system.

Problem and Design Decomposition   When we move from a simple to a complex situation of building software systems, there are some technical issues that we must consider. The basic issue is how to handle all the pieces, parts, and relationships. One common solution is based on the concept of divide and conquer. This has its roots in the modularization concept first presented by Parnas (1972). Modularization will be further discussed in Chapter 7. The natural question—how we divide a large, complex problem and its solution into smaller parts—is more difficult than it sounds. We first need to simplify the large, complex problem by addressing the problem in smaller segments. After we have successfully completed that process, our next step is to decide whether we should design and decompose the software system solution along the dividing lines of the problem segments. Thus, if the problem description, or the requirement, is segmented by function and feature, should we architect and design the solution along the same function and feature segments? Alternatively, should we choose another decomposition method for the solution, perhaps along the line of "objects"? (Further discussions on objects can be found in Chapter 7.) The key to attacking large and complex problems is to consider some form of simplification through the following types of activities:

- Decomposition
- Modularization
- Separation
- Incremental iterations

This notion is further expanded in Section 2.2.2, which discusses the design of a payroll system.

Technology and Tool Considerations   Aside from the important issue of decomposing a problem and its solution, there are problems related to technology and tool considerations that will also need to be addressed. If you are not writing a program alone for a limited set of users, the choice of the specific programming language may become an issue. A large, complex system requires more than one person to develop the software solution. While all the developers involved may know several languages, each individual usually comes with different experience. This diversity in background and experience often results in personal biases for or against a certain programming language and the choice of development tool. A common development language and development environment needs to be picked. Beyond the programming language and the development tools, there are further considerations of other technical choices related to the following:

- Database
- Network
- Middleware
- Other technical components such as code version control

These must be agreed upon by all parties involved in building and supporting a complex software system.

Process and Methodology   We alluded to methodology and process earlier when we discussed the need for simplification and decomposition. When there is only a single person developing the solution, there is still a need to understand the problem or requirements. There is often a need to take the time to put together or design the solution and then implement it. The testing of the solution may be performed by the same person and, possibly, with a user. Under such conditions, there is very little communication among people. No material, such as a design document, is passed from the author to another person. There still may be a need to document the work performed because even a single developer forgets some of the rationale behind the decisions made. There is usually no need to coordinate the work items because there may not be that many parts. The specific methodology used in performing any of the tasks does not need to be coordinated when only one or two people are involved.

In a large, complex development situation, the problem is decomposed and is worked on by many different experts. A **software development process** is needed to guide and coordinate the

> **Software development process**   The set of tasks, the sequence and flow of these tasks, the inputs to and the outputs from the tasks, and the preconditions and postconditions for each of the tasks involved in the production of a software.

group of people. Simple items, such as the syntax for the expression of a design, need to be agreed upon by all the developers so that they can all review, understand, author, and produce a consistent and cohesive design. Each method used for a specific task along with the entire development process must be agreed to by the group of people involved in the project. Software development and support processes were invented to coordinate and manage complex projects involving many people. The process is greatly facilitated when a group of people can be converted into a cooperating team of individuals. Although continuous improvements and new proposals are constantly being made, no one has yet proposed the complete elimination of process or methodology. Regardless of what is believed about software processes, it is commonly accepted that some process must exist to help coordinate a complex and successful software project. Traditional software process models and emerging process models, including the currently popular Agile methods, will be discussed in Chapters 4 and 5.

Consider the simple scenario of depicting the five major tasks shown in **Figure 2.2**. These are the common tasks often performed in software development and support. Each task appears as an independent item, and each one begs the questions of what is expected and how we perform it. For example, is there a methodology to gathering requirements? If there is more than one person performing the requirements-gathering task, how that task should be broken down needs to be defined. Similarly, we might ask what constitutes user support and what problems must be fixed.

The tasks in Figure 2.2 are displayed independently. When several individuals are involved in software development and support, there has to be a clear understanding of the sequence, overlap, and starting conditions. For example, the designers and coders may be one group of people that is different from the requirements analysts who are working with the customers. At what point should the designers and coders start their tasks? How much can these tasks overlap? How should the completed code be integrated and tested? The process definition should answer these questions and help in coordinating the various tasks and in ensuring that they are carried out according to previously agreed-upon methodologies.

Figure 2.3 represents one approach that employs the concept of incremental development and continuous integration. Continuous integration has been practiced since the 1970s, when large systems were first being built (see Tsui and Priven 1976). Recently, because of the widespread use of incremental development and Agile methodologies, continuous integration is gaining general popularity. The methodologies involved in

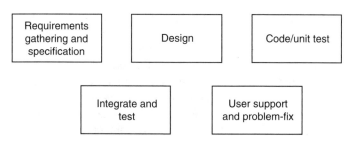

Figure 2.2 Independent tasks.

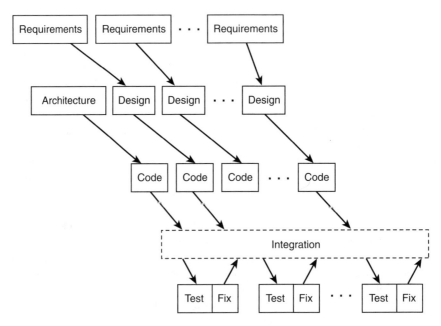

Figure 2.3 One possible process approach.

incremental development must all be agreed to and practiced by the entire development team. The seemingly simple boxes depicting the test–fix–integrate cycle in Figure 2.3 is extremely deceptive. That simple cycle requires a description of a methodology that answers the following questions:

- Is there a separate and independent test group?
- When a problem is found, how and to whom should it be reported?
- How much information must accompany a problem description?
- Who decides the severity level of a problem?
- How is a problem-fix returned to the tester?
- Should all problem-fixes be retested?
- How are the problem-fixes integrated back into the code?
- What should be done with the problems that are not fixed?

These are just some of the questions that must be determined and worked out for a portion of the process depicted in Figure 2.3. We will expand on the specifics relating to testing and integration methodologies and process in Chapters 10 and 11. The process also assumes that incremental development is utilized and that both the problem and the design can be decomposed into increments. Figure 2.3 does not include the support and customer problem-fix activities. We must not forget that software products need usage support, problem-fixes, and enhancements. Process plays a vital part in defining and coordinating the activities for large, complex systems development and support.

2.1.3 Nontechnical Considerations of Development and Support

In addition to technical implications, large and complex systems also require a cognizance of nontechnical issues. We will discuss two such issues here.

Effort Estimation and Schedule For a small and fairly simple software project that involves a team of one to three people, the effort estimation and scheduling of the project is relatively easy. Both the functional and nonfunctional requirements of the project are fewer in number and complexity. Even then, as you have seen in Chapter 1, it is still not a trivial task. For complex and large systems, capturing and understanding the requirements alone can be overwhelming. Estimating the total effort and coming up with a reliable project schedule under this difficult condition is one of the main reasons behind so many software project failures; see Jorgensen (2004) for more details. The inaccurate effort estimates and schedules for large, complex systems are often extremely optimistic and aggressive; this places unrealistic expectations on both the customers and the suppliers of these systems.

As an example, consider a relatively simple software project that requires three major functions with a total of 12 features. The effort estimation of this project requires a good understanding of all the functional features and the productivity of the individuals in the small team who will be working on these 12 features. For a large, complex software system, the number of major functions is often in the tens or hundreds. The total number of features within these major functions may easily be in the hundreds and thousands. The number of people needed to develop such a system may easily be in the hundreds. Under such circumstances, the probability of understanding all the requirements well and of knowing the productivity of all the individuals accurately is very low. The sorting of the number of combinations of individuals assigned to the design and coding of such a large number of features alone can be a daunting task. The resulting effort estimation and the schedule is often a good "guess" and far from being accurate. The software industry has long recognized this problem and has been confronting this issue. In Chapter 13 we will address some of the techniques that have been developed and are now available.

Assignments and Communications We touched on the problem of assigning people to designing and coding the different functional features when the number of features increases and the corresponding number of developers increases. Furthermore, there are other activities that require people resources. The assignment of different people to different tasks such as testing, integration, or tool support requires more understanding of the skills of the people involved and the specific tasks they have to perform. The assignment of the most effective and properly skilled people to the right tasks requires a deeper level of granularity and a finer level of scheduling.

Another related problem with the increase in personnel is the problem of communications. For a small project involving two or three people, the number of communications paths is one between two people and three among three people. **Figure 2.4** illustrates how maximum communication paths increase as the number of participants increases.

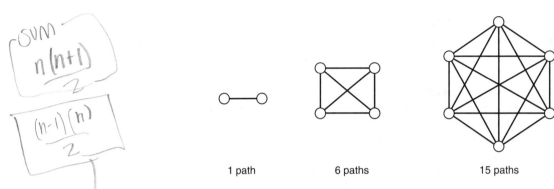

1 path   6 paths   15 paths

Figure 2.4 Maximizing communication paths.

The nodes in this figure represent the people, and the lines represent the communication paths. The number of possible communications paths more than doubled when the number of team members increased from four to six.

In general, the number of communication paths for n people is SUM(n-1), where SUM is the arithmetic sum function of 1, 2, . . ., n. Thus a modest increase from a 4-person team to a 12-person team would increase the potential number of communication paths from 6 to 66. A tripling of a small team would increase the potential communication paths by more than ten times!

Associated with this increase in the sheer number of communication paths is the chance of an error in communications. Consider, for example, that the chance of communicating correctly a particular message between any two people is 2/3. The probability that we will communicate properly from one person to another and then from that second person to a third person would be $(2/3 \times 2/3) = 4/9$. In general, for n people where n is 2 or more, the probability of correctly communicating this message would be $(2/3)^{n-1}$. Thus for this message, there is only a 16/81 chance of correctly passing it from the first person to the fifth person in the team. Suddenly, we have reduced a 2/3 chance of correctly communicating a message to less than 1/4. Such a low probability of correct communication among team members may be a serious problem, especially if the message is critical. Organizational structures of people need to be put in place to reduce the complexity and increase the chance of correct communications.

2.2   Building a Hypothetical System

In this section we will use a hypothetical payroll system to illustrate some of the problems introduced in Section 2.1. The discussion here will cover the major tasks of developing such a system and of supporting the system once it is released to users. The intent of this section is to provide only a glimpse of the different problems and concerns that arise in building our system but not to delve into all the details of constructing and supporting this system.

2.2.1   Requirements of the Payroll System

Everyone has some idea of what a payroll system is. Take a moment to think about what you would consider as the major functional and the nonfunctional requirements of a payroll system. The following functional capabilities represent only some of the tasks a payroll system should be able to perform. This list is far short of what a real payroll system would need.

- Add, modify, and delete the names and associated personal information of all employees.
- Add, modify, and delete all the benefits associated with all employees.
- Add, modify, and delete all the tax and other deductions associated with all employees.
- Add, modify, and delete all the gross income associated with all employees.
- Add, modify, and delete all the algorithms related to computing the net pay for each employee.
- Generate a paper check or an electronic direct bank deposit for each employee.

Each of these functional requirements may be expanded to several levels of more details. For example, just for the first item of names and associated personal information, one would need to understand what the associated information is. This is a simple question, but would require the software engineer to solicit the input for this. Where and who would the software engineer ask? Should the software engineer ask the users, some designated official requirements person, or the project leader? Once the question is answered, should the answer be documented? The next functional requirement in the preceding list speaks to all the benefits. What are all the benefits? What does having a benefit mean to an employee's payroll? Is there a list of all possible benefits? It does not take much to realize that the requirements solicitation, gathering, documentation, analysis, and validation of a payroll system will need a considerable effort. In order to properly handle the application side of the payroll system requirement, we may need to understand something about benefits, tax laws, and other domain-specific knowledge.

In addition, the payroll system must be able to generate the paychecks and direct deposits several times a month. What is the allowable payroll cycle? In other words, if the checks and deposits must be completed by the middle and end of the month, when must the inputs to the cycle, such as salary increase, be closed? Here we are interested in understanding the payroll-processing-cycle window that is allowable within the business environment and what performance capability the system must have to satisfy that processing window. The answer to this question will require the software engineer to know the volume of payroll transactions and the speed of processing each payroll transaction. To analyze and handle this type of requirement, we may need to know the hardware and operating system environment capability on top of which the payroll system will be running. Some of the payroll system requirements will require, in addition to payroll domain knowledge, the knowledge of technical system and interface information.

There also needs to be an understanding of how the actual payroll run process works at the user/customer site. For example, if there is a bad record, how should that person's paycheck be reprocessed? Does this imply that there is a requirement to rerun the payroll system several times? There may also be some requirements that the users/customers may not even remember to provide. In Chapter 6 we discuss how we may handle these late requirements.

Once the requirements information of a payroll system is documented, the complexity of such a system will most likely necessitate a review with the users/customers prior to having the requirements specification passed forward to the design and coding phase. These reviews may be conducted gradually as the requirements are incrementally analyzed and documented or all at once when all the requirements are analyzed and specified together. Either situation will require a coordination of effort between the users/customers and the requirements analysts.

It is thus clear that the total number of activities needed to complete a payroll system requirement phase alone may be extremely high as well as time consuming. Not just a single requirements analyst but a team of requirements analysts—individuals having diverse skills spanning everything from payroll domain-specific knowledge to IT and systems development expertise—may be needed. From a quality perspective, it has also been pointed out by Jones (1992) that approximately 15% of software defects are due to requirements errors. The activities related to completing a requirements specification for a system, such as that in our payroll example, are difficult and have significant impact on all downstream activities and on the final product. Complete books have been written on just this single topic. (See the Suggested Readings section at the end of this chapter.)

2.2.2   Designing the Payroll System

Once the requirements of the payroll system are understood and agreed to, the system must still be designed. Put aside the fact that the payroll system requirements expressed in Section 2.2.1 are just an example and are incomplete. For example, we might naturally ask whether all the "add, update, and delete" functional requirements should be grouped together into a single component called "payroll administrative functions." We might then ask if all the processing functions such as the calculations of all the deductions and the net pay amount should be grouped together into a component called "payroll processing." Certainly, we must be prepared to handle errors and exceptions. So, those functions dealing with errors and exceptions processing may be aggregated into an exceptions-processing component. In addition, the payroll system must interface with external systems such as direct bank deposits or batch transmissions to remote sites for local check printing. We may decide to place all the interface functions into a component called "payroll interfaces." This grouping of related functions into components has several advantages:

- Provides some design cohesiveness within the component
- Matches the business flow and the payroll processing environment
- Provides a potential assignment of work by components
- Allows easier packaging of the software by components

There may be some drawbacks to this approach. It is conceivable that there are still heavy interactions or coupling among these components. The coupling, in this case, may arise from extensive usage of a common data file or a common table in a relational database. Even at this high level, designers need to look at both the characteristics of design cohesiveness and coupling. The concepts related to these topics are discussed extensively in Chapter 8.

There are also nonfunctional specific, but common-service, needs that must be designed. For example, the help service or the message service must be designed for

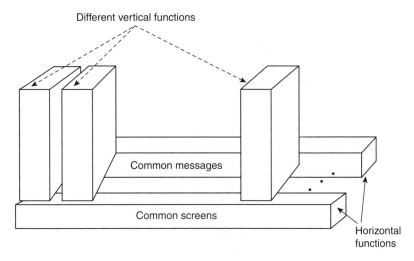

Different vertical functions

Common messages

Common screens

Horizontal functions

Figure 2.5 Vertical and horizontal design entities.

all the functional components. These services may all be placed in one component called the *services component*. The combination of functional components and common services is shown in **Figure 2.5** as horizontal and vertical design entities. The horizontal entities are the common service functions such as the error handler that crosses all the individual application features. The vertical entities are the different application domain-specific functions such as the tax and benefits deduction function in a payroll system. The interaction, or coupling, of the various functional components with these common services is a key design concern.

It is during design that the screen interface layout is finalized. In the case of a payroll system, this is a heavily batch-oriented system rather than an interactive system. User interface in terms of screen architecture is thus not a prime design concern. Nevertheless, it needs to be addressed. The database tables and search keys, however, are important and would be a significant design concern for a large batch-processing application.

Although there are many ways to perform high-level and detailed design, the design of a payroll system requires a broad set of skills because of the breadth and depth of the system. From the breadth perspective, the design skills needed require complex knowledge: database, network, and transmission interfaces; printing interfaces; operating system interfaces; development tools environment; and the payroll application domain. From a depth perspective, the designer needs to understand and appreciate the specifics of a payroll system, such as performance and error processing. Although it is a batch-processing system, the sheer volume of payroll records for large enterprises often requires special design concerns that would make the seemingly simple process of error handling into a complex task. The design must not only catch erroneous information or conflicting information but must also consider what should happen to the people whose records cannot be processed. If these records are not dealt with immediately and allowed to accumulate until the end of the payroll cycle, there is no time to react. These records must be handled so that they can be converted to a paycheck within the payroll processing cycle. The designer must consider the payroll environment and the possibility of having to hand code the paychecks for a small number of unfortunate people. Thus the designer must design the system to include hand-processing exits from the system and the reconciliation of these hand-processed records back into the automated payroll system. The depth of error processing in a large system such as payroll can be a challenge for even the most experienced designers.

The payroll design mentioned here utilizes functional decomposition and synthesis techniques within each of the components. In addition to the intercomponent interactions, the various pieces within a component must be clearly divided and the intracomponent interaction between the pieces must also be designed. Clearly, designing a complex system is quite different from designing a single programming module and will require greater discipline and additional guiding principles as well as the possibility of several more team members.

2.2.3   Code and Unit Testing the Payroll System

The high-level design or architecture for the payroll system needs to be further refined and converted into running code. Within each design component, the individual, interacting, functional unit needs to be designed and converted into code. This activity is familiar to most people who enter the IT and computing field. The first course often taught to students entering software engineering or computer science involves a small problem that must be solved with a detailed functional design and code. At times, when the solution is small enough, the detail design is not even recorded and only the source code of the module is available.

For each of the functional units, the programmer must address and develop the following material:

- Precise layout of the screen interface in some language
- Precise functional processing logic in some programming language
- Precise data access and storage logic in some language
- Precise interface logic in some language

Furthermore, if there are many of these programming units, some common standards must be set. An example would be a naming convention for each of the modules that would uniquely identify each as the module of a specific component. Conventions may also need to be set for different database records such that all elements from a specific relational table have the same prefix. There may be conventions set to document some of the detail design such as providing comments on the conditions under which this module may be entered and exited. The comments may also describe the data that are vital to the processing and a short description of the intended function. A very important part is the design, code, and the documentation of how to handle the various error conditions. The error messages displayed from the different program modules need to be consistent; thus each program unit must follow the error message standard.

After the program module has been completed, the individual who performed the task should test the module to confirm that it performs the intended tasks. The first step in this unit-testing task is to set the conditions of the module and to choose the appropriate input data. The next step is to execute or run the module and observe the behavior of the module, mainly through checking the output from the module, to ensure that it is performing what it is intended to do. Finally, if there is any problem discovered through unit testing, it must be fixed and retested. When all the problems are fixed, the module is ready for integration into a larger unit such as a functional unit or into a component if the module itself is a functional unit.

The programming or coding and unit testing of a module is usually performed by one individual. For a large system, such as a payroll system, there may be hundreds of modules that need to be coded and unit tested. Thus, programming is a heavily human resource intensive activity. When the number of programmers increases to a large figure, then the coordination and integration of all the programming efforts become a manage-ment challenge. Once again, principles of software engineering management need to be brought in to alleviate the situation.

2.2.4 Integration and Functionally Testing the Payroll System

As the modules are completed and unit tested, they have to be formally collected from the individual programmers. The collection activity is known as *integration*, which is a part of a larger control mechanism known as *configuration management*. Configuration management will be mentioned throughout this text but will be formally discussed in Chapter 11. A simple reason for the integration step is that if the completed modules are left with the individual programmers, the programmers tend to make changes to an already unit-tested module and get confused about which is indeed the latest version. To ensure that the latest unit-tested modules do work together as a functional unit, these modules need to be compiled and linked together. A functional unit, in the case of the payroll system, may be a part of the previously mentioned administrative component that performs the add, modify, and delete functions of all the federal deduction laws, which almost always change annually. The integrated set of modules is then tested with functional test cases generated by a more objective group than the programmers who coded the modules.

Functional testing usually uncovers some problems that will require fixing by the programmers. The cycle of problem detection to problem-fix needs to be coordinated between the testers and the code fixers. The fix code must be integrated into the func-tional unit and be retested to ensure that all the fixes as a group have not impacted each other negatively. As a set of modules in a functional unit completes the functional test, it is electronically labeled as such and is locked from further changes. These functional units need to be managed by the configuration management mechanism as do the mod-ule units. In the case of a simple one or two module situation, there is not much need for an integration and configuration management mechanism. In a very large software system construction such as a payroll system, there is usually a tool, such as PVCS from Serena Software, used to help automate the configuration management mechanism. The people and skills required to tackle the integration and functional testing of a payroll system are usually different from those needed for coding, designing, or requirements gathering. However, test scenarios and test scripts often require the knowledge of the requirements and the design.

2.2.5   Release of the Payroll System

After the functional units are tested and integrated into components, these components must be tested together to ensure that the complete system works as a whole. This is important to ensure that all the interfaces across components actually do work. Also, the various fixes for the functional units and components may impact some other previously working functional units and components. Even after the entire payroll system is tested through all the user scenarios in the context of the user business environment, the system cannot be released unless no problem was found. At least all the major problems and showstoppers must be fixed before the system can be considered releasable to the users. Once again, the tested payroll system must be managed and protected from further changes.

Even if the payroll system is totally error free, the users must still be educated in the usage of the system—a process that for a large system cannot be an afterthought and must be planned and orchestrated. The development of the educational material alone for such a system is a nontrivial task. The effort may take several people and several months. The delivery of user education may require some different skills from technical design or coding. The emphasis would be presentation and communication skills. The people who develop the educational material content may be different from those who deliver the education.

Another area of preparation prior to releasing the payroll system would be the preparation of user support personnel. It would be rare that the users can master all the details of a payroll system just through education. Furthermore, it is also rare that a large and complex system will be totally error free. The support personnel themselves must be preeducated on the payroll system, user environments, and tools needed for supporting customers.

Once the system test is complete, the users have been trained, and the support group is trained and established, the payroll system is then ready for release to the users. Who should be the person that makes the final call of a product release? Should this be a group decision? And what criteria should that person use in making the determination for release? These topics fall under the umbrella of software project management, discussed further in Chapter 13.

2.2.6   Support and Maintenance

For a small, one- or two-module software product that is utilized by a few people, the support effort is not a major concern. For a large system such as a payroll, the postrelease support of the users and customers may be a very complex set of tasks. Who does the user call for help, after consulting the user manual, when the payroll system stalls and pops up a message with several possible choices for the user before the payroll system can continue processing? Who does the user call when the direct deposit interface on the bank side has changed and the existing payroll system interface needs to be modified? Who does the user call when the payroll system shows a different behavioral problem after applying a previous problem-fix? These are just a few of the many questions that will arise after the payroll system is released. Several assumptions must be made and be included in the calculation of the expected payroll system support effort. Many of the following decision factors will play a role:

- Number of expected users and customers
- Number and type of known problems that existed at release time
- Projected number of problems that will be discovered by users
- Amount of user training
- Amount of support personnel training
- Number of development personnel committed to support the system
- Expected number of problem-fix releases and future functional releases

Based on these factors, the number of postrelease people required to support and maintain the payroll system must be estimated and allocated. Clearly distinct skills will be needed to support such a complex environment, and it will be necessary to consider at least two sets of support personnel:

- A group to answer and handle system usage and simple problem work-arounds
- A group to fix difficult problems and implement future enhancements

The first group does not have to include any program coding personnel. They must, however, possess good communication skills as well as payroll system and usage knowledge. The second group often needs to include designers and coders. If there is an expected long product life for the payroll system, then the support personnel must be prepared for several releases of functional enhancements. The support personnel in this group may thus resemble a complete development team. The important concept here is that large, complex systems such as a payroll system will require a support organization that may be comparable in size and complexity to the original development team. Chapter 12 will cover the postrelease support and maintenance subject in more detail.

2.3 Coordination Efforts

The payroll example demonstrates the need for many of the software engineering activities. A critical concern for large, complex systems is the upward scaling of the needed process, of the design structure and contents of the product, and of the required personnel. In the opposite direction is the concern of downward scaling of the same parameters for simpler systems. In this section we will introduce these concerns and discuss the details of process, product design, and personnel management in later chapters.

2.3.1 Process

We have already discussed the notion of a process. As both applications and systems software became large and complex in the 1980s and 1990s, the number of serious and costly problems skyrocketed. Often in the past, more and more hurdles—usually in the form of more reviews, more inspections, more testing, and more meetings—have been inserted as a part of the process. Large corporations signed up for expensive quality assurance and measurement efforts. These efforts were designed to prevent, detect, and correct problems, thereby improving the quality of software and increasing the productivity of the software developers. Extensive metric programs were put in place to measure quality and productivity; see the article on the Motorola measurement program by Daskalantonakis (1992). The development and support processes became heavily weighted toward risk aversion. In recent years there has been a movement to simplify the process as speed and cost started to take center stage in the software industry (Beck 1999; Cockburn 2001). There is no single process that fits all occasions. Some are more appropriate for large, complex systems that require extensive coordination, and others are much simpler and are appropriate for small and quick software projects. We will cover the topic of software processes in detail in Chapters 4 and 5.

2.3.2   Product

A software product is often thought of as only containing the executable code. However, in developing and supporting software, many more artifacts have to be produced, ranging from requirements documents to functional test scenarios. Many sophisticated users and customers require user manuals, user education, and product support as part of the product. Simply delivering a package of executable code is not enough in many cases.

The payroll system considered in this chapter is an example of a system where the customers and users will be demanding much more than just the executable code. Besides the artifacts required in developing the final product, they may ask for the design document and the source code so that future modifications may be carried out by their own personnel. Of course, once the product source code is modified by the users and customers, that portion of the product will have to be maintained and supported by the users and customers themselves. The software product, large or small, which is expected to have a long life span, will need to be designed for changes and easy maintenance. The coordination of the software components and artifacts through a long and lengthy period of changes, updates, and maintenance is a complex endeavor. A large software product may initially be designed to be high in functional cohesiveness within each part and minimal in interactions or coupling among the parts. It is very difficult to maintain a high degree of internal cohesion and a low amount of coupling as the large software product evolves through many cycles of modifications. A software product needs to be protected from design drift and erosion (Taylor, Medvidovic, and Dashofy 2009). The design of the software product and the notion of cohesion and coupling will be further covered in Chapters 7 and 8.

As both the design and product increase in complexity, so do the testing efforts. The coordination of test preparation, testing, fixing, and integration are covered more extensively in Chapters 9, 10, and 11.

2.3.3   People

As the payroll system example has already demonstrated, for a large software system we need a team of people with an assortment of skills and experience to develop and support the system. The human element is a crucial component in the development and support of software. In many ways, the software industry is still labor intensive. Thus the study of software engineering must include the issues of coordinating people's activities and management skills.

Part of the discussion on coordinating software engineers' activities is embedded in the process discussion. A large and vital part of coordinating software personnel lies in the organizational structure and the strength of communications among the various constituencies. Chapter 13 will cover some people-management issues as they relate to different phases of a software project.

2.4 Summary

In this chapter, we have described the growth in the breadth and depth of complex software problems and the associated software solutions. Both the technical and nontechnical issues—from design decomposition and communications to process, tools, and methodology—were introduced. A typical payroll system in a large business was used as the basis for introducing and demonstrating the real problems in large software development and in supporting such products. Large software projects require the control of the process, the product, and the people involved. The field of software engineering is vital to the development and support of these large and complex systems.

2.5 Review Questions

1. Define the depth versus the breadth issue in software complexity.

2. Describe a way to simplify a complex problem.

3. List two technical concerns in developing large systems.

4. What is the maximum number of communication paths for a team of 20 people?

5. List four factors that should be considered in deciding how many postrelease people will be needed.

2.6 Exercises

1. (a) Give an example of an increase in software size. (b) Give an example of an increase in complexity. (c) Discuss which type of increase, in your view, is more difficult to handle.

2. Discuss the difference between vertical and horizontal functions and the potential interactions between the two sets.

3. What is meant by integration and why is it important to manage this effort for large systems?

4. What are the major tasks in developing and supporting a software system?

5. (a) Write a program that reads 11 numbers, divides the sum of the first 10 numbers by the 11th number, and displays the result. (b) List all the questions you had in the process of programming part (a) of this question. (c) Discuss, in your view, what type of skills are needed to collect and specify the requirements of a system.

6. Discuss the three areas that need to be coordinated in a large software engineering project. Is any one of them more important than the others? Explain your conclusion.

2.7   Suggested Readings

K. Beck, *Extreme Programming Explained: Embrace Change* (Reading, MA: Addison-Wesley, 1999).

A. Cockburn, *Agile Software Development* (Reading, MA: Addison-Wesley, 2001).

M. K. Daskalantonakis, "A Practical View of Software Measurement and Implementation Experiences within Motorola," *IEEE Transactions on Software Engineering* 18, no. 11 (November 1992): 998–1010.

T. Gilb and D. Graham, *Software Inspection* (Reading, MA: Addison-Wesley, 1993).

C. Jones, *Critical Problems in Software Measurement*, Version 1.0 (Burlington, MA: Software Productivity Research, Inc., 1992).

M. Jorgensen, "Realism in Assessment of Effort Estimation Uncertainties: It Matters How You Ask," *IEEE Transactions on Software Engineering* 30, no. 4 (April 2004): 209–217.

D. Leffingwell and D. Widrig, *Managing Software Requirements: A Use Case Approach*, 2nd ed. (Reading, MA: Addison-Wesley, 2003).

L. Maciaszek, *Requirements Analysis and System Design*, 2nd ed. (Reading, MA: Addison-Wesley, 2004).

D. Parnas, "On Criteria to Be Used in Decomposing Systems into Modules," *Communications of the ACM* 15, no. 12 (December 1972): 1053–1058.

Serena Software Inc., www.serena.com.

R. N. Taylor, N. Medvidovic, and E. M. Dashofy, *Software Architecture: Foundations, Theory, and Practice* (Hoboken, NJ: John Wiley & Sons, 2009).

F. Tsui and L. Priven, "Implementation of Quality Control in Software Development," *AFIPS Conference Proceedings* (1976), 443–449.

CHAPTER 3

Engineering of Software

OBJECTIVES

- Understand the rationale behind the need to establish a discipline in software engineering.
- Analyze the main causes of software project failures.
- Give an example of software product failures.
- Understand the term *software engineering* as it was introduced at the 1968 NATO conference.
- Define the concepts of software engineering and of professionalism.
- Review the software engineering code of ethics.
- Discuss the sets of principles and foundations of software engineering put forward by Alan Davis, Walker Royce, and Anthony Wasserman.

3.1 Examples and Characteristics of Software Failures

There are many differences between a one-person programming effort and a large software system effort, as discussed in Chapters 1 and 2. The degree of complexities between these two approaches have caused many project managers and software engineers to realize the need to bring more discipline into the field. Another strong motivation to establish the software engineering discipline is the number of failures in software projects and defects encountered in the software products. This section will explore some of these failures.

3.1.1 Project Failures

A quick search on the Internet today for software project failures will quickly result in pages of examples. The Chaos Report, published in 1995 by the Standish Group, suggests that many of the mistakes in software projects are not well investigated and that the same mistakes continue to be repeated. Their research included large, medium, and small companies across most of the major industries—banking, manufacturing, retail, state and local government, health, and so on. Using a sample size of 365 respondents, researchers found that only about 16% of the software projects were completed on time and on budget, with all the features and functions as initially specified. The report goes on to profile the success and failure factors. The four most important reasons for project success are the following:

1. User involvement
2. Executive management support
3. Clear requirement statements
4. Proper planning

These four factors form 52.4% of the responses to the question of contributors to project success. A software project has a dramatically higher chance of success if these four factors are performed properly. As the article "They Write the Right Stuff" from FastCompany (2005) indicates, factors such as clear requirements and user involvement are also among the reasons attributed to the success between NASA and Lockheed Martin Corporation in developing the space shuttle software.

The Chaos Report also listed the three top failure factors for software projects. The study defined "challenged" projects as those that are completed and operational but over budget or over the time estimate, or those lacking some functional features from the original specification. The top three reasons of failure for these challenged projects are as follows:

1. Lack of user input
2. Incomplete requirements and specifications
3. Changing requirements and specifications

These reasons form approximately 37% of the survey participants' responses for software projects that are classified as "challenged."

The following reasons are cited for failure of the projects that are impaired and ultimately cancelled:

1. Incomplete requirements
2. Lack of user involvement
3. Lack of resources

These three factors form about 36% of the responses for reasons for the ultimate cancellations of software projects.

The Chaos Report looked further into two cancelled software projects and two successful projects. The two cancelled projects were the California DMV's driver's license and registration applications and American Airlines' car rental and hotel reservation system. Both projects had little user involvement and unclear requirements. The American Airlines project was a joint enterprise with Budget Rent-A-Car, Marriot Corporation, and Hilton Hotels, thus involving many people, which increased the project complexity.

The two successful projects were the Hyatt Hotels' reservation system and the Banco Itamarati's banking system. The Hyatt Hotel reservation system had both user involvement and clear requirements. The Banco Itamarati project did not have clear requirement statements, but it did have heavy user involvement. In his book, *Assessment and Control of Software Risks*, Capers Jones (1994) also lists "creeping user requirements" as the top risk factor for management information systems.

It is not surprising that user involvement and user requirements are listed as top reasons for both software project successes and failures. Without understanding what is to be developed, there is very little chance of success for any project. Software projects are especially difficult to specify because many aspects of the work involved are nontangible. Requirements elicitation, analysis, and specification activities form a key component of software engineering. Requirements engineering activities are introduced in Chapter 6.

3.1.2 Software Product Failures

Software project failures include many types of problems, such as cost or schedule overruns. Software product failure is one of the types of project failure. Capers Jones (1996) has also studied software product failures and the origins of those bugs. He illustrates the distribution of software product errors by different origins. The average percentages of bugs by different origins are as follows:

- Requirements errors: 12.50%
- Design errors: 24.17%
- Code errors: 38.33%
- Documentation errors: 13.33%
- Bad-fix errors: 11.67%

These numbers, by themselves, would indicate that more errors are caused by coding. But it hides the cost issue behind problem-fixes. An error introduced during the requirements phase may propagate into design and coding. It may not be discovered until after the product's release. Furthermore, one requirement error may turn into several design and coding problems. Thus, fixing a requirement error that escaped into design or code is generally more expensive than fixing a coding error. Therefore, even though the percentage of errors originated from the requirements phase is only 12.5%, the cost of fixing those problems is usually the most expensive. It would seem that more problem-preventive activities should be applied to the requirements phase of software development than some of the later phases. Unfortunately, requirements gathering and specification is often hurried through.

Both requirements specification and design specification are not directly executable. A prototype may be built to test them. However, for the most part, errors in requirements specification or design document are detected through reviews and formal inspections. The more often these errors are found prior to coding, the less impact they will have on coding, testing, and on user guide development and other documentation activities.

3.1.3   Coordination and Other Concerns

Many software project failures are blamed on bad code, but the causes are often not rooted in programming efforts or the software alone. Rather, as a recent Associated Press report stated, "As systems grow more complicated, failures instead have far less technical explanations: bad management, communications or training." They cite multiple examples. In 2004, a southern California system that controls communications between commercial jets and air traffic controllers malfunctioned due to a lack of proper software maintenance.

To reduce risks, many corporations are moving toward buying established enterprise software products such as SAP, Oracle, and PeopleSoft. (PeopleSoft has been acquired by Oracle at the writing of this book.) Some are engaged in using consultants and in outsourcing the implementation of these large, complex enterprise resource management systems. The problems surrounding these types of projects are usually not the software product themselves. These large endeavors involve complex factors:

- Executive commitments and leadership
- Thorough planning of both business and technical processes
- Skilled and experienced consultants
- Relentless management focus and monitoring of the project
- Willingness to change and make adjustments when required

In a March 2004 U.S. General Accounting Office report to the Committee on Armed Services of the U.S. Senate, three basic management strategies were cited as key to ensuring the delivery of high-quality software on time and within budget:

1. Focused attention on the software development environment(s)
2. Disciplined development processes
3. Methodical usage of metrics to gauge cost, schedule, and performance targets

These three characteristics were demonstrated in leading companies visited by the U.S. Department of Defense (DOD).

The DOD is an acquisition office, and its focus is on acquisition process. Thus the DOD must properly train its personnel on managing the acquisition of needed software. It is vital for the DOD acquisition managers to be able to recognize signs of successful software organizations from which they source their software. They must be able to differentiate those that are practicing good software engineering from those that are not.

3.2   Software Engineering

3.2.1   What Is Software Engineering?

So far, we have used the term *software engineering* and relied on each reader's intuitive feel for what software engineering is. We have discussed and given examples of activities that are part of software engineering. We have characterized attributes of both simple and complex software products and software projects. We have cited examples of software project and product failures. We have provided glimpses of what may be needed to succeed. Software engineering has many aspects, and we have hitherto delayed any formal definition because we wanted readers to take in the wide scope of this discipline. It is a young field, still evolving and growing, that has its origin in computer science and programming. Thus it is difficult to define, and its definition will also continue to evolve.

The term *software engineering* was first introduced in a 1968 North Atlantic Treaty Organization (NATO) conference held in Germany. During the late 1960s, the computing field was starting to face a software "crisis." Computer hardware had made great leaps in computing power and storage capacity. This ushered in an era that saw the beginning of developing large and complex software that required a large number of programmers. The first wave involved system-level software such as operating systems, file systems, and access methods. With the recognition of the huge potential of business automation, large and complex business applications software also started to emerge shortly afterward. Early experiences with writing programs proved to be insufficient for these large, complex projects. As a result, many software projects were delayed, and some were never completed. Others were completed but experienced excessive budget overruns. The final software product often demonstrated unsatisfactory quality and performance. The users of these software systems were often subjected to incomprehensible manuals that were written by programmers who never met the users. These software releases needed continual support and maintenance that the original programmers were not trained to handle. The attendees of the 1968 NATO conference recognized the need for a discipline much like the other engineering disciplines and thus formalized the concept of software engineering. In the past 30 years, great strides and improvements have been made in the software industry and in academia. But many more improvements are still needed for software engineering.

3.2.2   Definitions of Software Engineering

One of the earlier definitions of software engineering may be attributed to David Parnas, who stated that software engineering is a multiperson construction of multiversion software (see Hoffman and Weiss 2001). This definition certainly brings out some of the aspects of software engineering that have been discussed.

Ian Sommerville (2004) states that "software engineering is an engineering discipline whose focus is the cost-effective development of high-quality software systems." He further explains that software is "abstract and intangible" and defines software engineering as "an engineering discipline that is concerned with all aspects of software production from the early stages of system specification to maintaining the system after it has gone into use." This definition certainly captures the software life cycle from inception to product sunset.

> **Software engineering**   A broad field that touches on all aspects of developing and supporting a software system:
> - Technical and business processes
> - Specific methodologies and techniques
> - Product characteristics and metrics
> - People, skills, and teamwork
> - Tools and training
> - Project coordination and management

Shari Pfleeger (2001) uses the relationship between chemistry and chemical engineering as an analogy to discuss the relationship between computing and software engineering. She states that in computing we can focus on the "computers and programming languages themselves or we can view them as tools to be used in designing and implementing a solution to a problem. Software engineering takes the latter view." According to her view, software engineering is the application of computing tools to solving problems.

The Software Engineering 2004 Curriculum Guidelines for Undergraduate Degree Programs in Software Engineering published by the Association of Computing Machinery (ACM) and IEEE Computer Society recognizes the broad scope of the field and highlights three definitions from different sources:

- From F. L. Bauer: "The establishment and use of sound engineering principles (methods) in order to obtain economically software that is reliable and works on real machines."
- From CMU/SEI-90-TR-003: "Software engineering is that form of engineering that applies the principles of computer science and mathematics to achieving cost-effective solutions to software problems."
- From IEEE std 610-1990: "The application of a systematic, disciplined, quantifiable approach to the development, operation, and maintenance of software."

The *Curriculum Guidelines* goes on to further state,

> "Software engineering is about creating high-quality software in a systematic, controlled, and efficient manner. Consequently, there are important emphases on analysis and evaluation, specification, design, and evolution of software. In addition, there are issues related to management and quality, to novelty and creativity, to standards, to individual skills, and to teamwork and professional practice that play a vital role in software engineering."

It is clear that capturing **software engineering** in a single sentence is very difficult due to its breadth and its short history. In the rest of this text we will cover many of these fundamental components of software engineering.

3.2.3 Relevancy of Software Engineering and Software

Given that the field of software engineering is so broad and that today's software is intricately involved in our daily lives, it is impossible to ignore the significance of software. Our financial systems are managed by banking systems, our transportation is managed by various devices that contain embedded software, our household appliances and cars all contain embedded software, our health care is dependent on sophisticated medical systems, our manufacturing is run with large enterprise resource processing systems, and even our food supply is managed by distribution and warehouse software systems.

With our world depending so heavily on software, it is only natural that software engineering, which includes the development and support of these software systems, is gaining the attention of the software industry, academia, and the government. At the writing of the 3rd edition of this book in 2012, twenty-one U.S. universities have received accreditation in software engineering from the Accreditation Board of Engineering and

Technology (ABET). Many more are in the process of preparing for their accreditations in software engineering.

As software usage grows, so has its value. According to a 2002 Research Triangle Institute (RTI) report prepared for the U.S. National Institute of Standards and Technology, software has become an "intrinsic part of all the U.S. businesses today." It goes on to state that the total sales of software reached approximately $180 billion in 2000.

The increased value of software has also brought its share of problems, as millions of dollars of software are stolen each year, mostly in the form of illegally copied material. Software is an intellectual property. As such, it has value and needs to be protected. Many different types of violations of intellectual properties are cited in a 2004 U.S. Justice Department's *Task Force Report on Intellectual Property*. Counterfeit software is listed as a prime example of some of the intellectual property prosecutions conducted by the Justice Department. According to this same report, the department is making the enforcement of criminal intellectual property laws a high priority and has developed a specially trained team of prosecutors to focus on intellectual property crimes.

3.3 Software Engineering Profession and Ethics

The traditional engineering professions, such as civil or electrical engineering, has a designation of Professional Engineer (PE) in the United States. This title is earned, and it is certified by the local state government. The certification involves work experience, training, and examinations. In many other countries, the traditional engineers are also certified. In software engineering, however, we do not yet have such a professional certification. In 1998, the Texas Board of Professional Engineers adopted software engineering as a distinct discipline under which an engineering license may be issued. This effort is still new and is anticipated to take some time and much effort before actual licenses will be granted.

3.3.1 Software Engineering Code of Ethics

Today, software is a valuable intellectual property, and software engineering is moving toward a more disciplined profession. Software plays a key role in all dimensions of our lives. As professionals, software engineers must conduct their practices at some level of professionalism to minimally ensure that their work results in no harm to society. The IEEE-CS/ACM Version 5.2 joint task force report has recommended eight principles for ethics and professional practices in software engineering:

1. Software engineers shall act consistently with the public interest.
2. Software engineers shall act in a manner that is in the best interests of their client and employer, consistent with the public interest.
3. Software engineers shall ensure that their products and related modifications meet the highest professional standards possible.
4. Software engineers shall maintain integrity and independence in their professional judgment.
5. Software engineering managers and leaders shall subscribe to and promote an ethical approach to the management of software development and maintenance.

6. Software engineers shall advance the integrity and reputation of the profession consistent with the public interest.

7. Software engineers shall be fair to and supportive of their colleagues.

8. Software engineers shall participate in lifelong learning regarding the practice of their profession and shall promote an ethical approach to the practice of the profession.

Under each of these general principles, there are several subelements that further explain the principles. For example, the second principle of this code, which deals with client and employer, has nine more explanatory subprinciples regarding the duties of software engineers:

1. Provide service in their areas of competence, being honest and forthright about any limitations of their experience and education.

2. Not knowingly use software that is obtained or retained either illegally or unethically.

3. Use the property of a client or employer only in ways properly authorized, and with the client's or employer's knowledge and consent.

4. Ensure that any document upon which they rely has been approved, when required, by someone authorized to approve it.

5. Keep private any confidential information gained in their professional work, where such confidentiality is consistent with the public interest and consistent with the law.

6. Identify, document, collect evidence, and report to the client or the employer promptly if, in their opinion, a project is likely to fail, to prove too expensive, to violate intellectual property law, or otherwise to be problematic.

7. Identify, document, and report significant issues of social concern, of which they are aware, in software or related documents, to the employer or the client.

8. Accept no outside work detrimental to the work they perform for their primary employer.

9. Promise no interest adverse to their employer or client, unless a higher ethical concern is being compromised; in that case, inform the employer or another appropriate authority of the ethical concern.

Software engineering, to be judged as a professional engineering practice, must include the code and regulations that its members must uphold. Thus software engineering also includes directions for its members' knowledge acquisition and directions for its members' behavioral practices. This is particularly difficult because there are no government regulations and codes for software engineering similar to those for civil or chemical engineering. As mentioned earlier, there are laws for protecting intellectual properties, and software engineers can look to those for guidance. The fact that there has been a task force effort on defining the code of conduct for software engineers already indicates that significant progress has been made in software engineering toward professionalism.

3.3.2 Professional Behavior

Following the code of ethics recommended in the eight principles is certainly a good start. However, there are so many details in these eight principles. One of the authors of this book has utilized a simpler moral and ethical guide in the years of practicing software development, support, and management in the software industry. These values were heavily influenced by the earlier IBM corporate values:

- Respect others and strive for fairness
- Perform to one's best capability
- Follow the law

These seem to be simplistic guidelines, but they in fact provide a basis for a broad scope of the actions and judgments for professionals in software engineering. It is impossible to list all the potential places where a software engineer must behave ethically. However, there are plenty of opportunities where these simple guidelines would apply, including the following examples:

- Handling information privacy
- Handling quality issues and problem resolutions
- Handling project estimation and project coordination
- Handling reuse and intellectual property
- Handling security

In all of the above situations, software engineers would be well served if they would stop and consider the issue of respecting others and fairness, of performing to their best ability, and of abiding by the law prior to making a judgment or taking an action.

There are several websites that provide further information on ethics and the issues surrounding this topic. The Software Engineering Ethics Research Institute at the East Tennessee State University site maintained by Donald Gotterbarn is a current example. Gotterbarn also chaired the Executive Committee of the IEEE-CS/ACM Joint Task Force that developed the *Software Engineering Code of Ethics and Professional Practices*.

The questions dealing with code of conduct and ethical behavior eventually lead to a discussion of concepts related to terms such as *good* and *bad* or *virtue* and *evil*. Philosophical discourse on this topic is beyond the scope of this textbook, but there are many good books that deal with this subject.

Michael Quinn (2004) provides a good introduction to ethical theories and the application of those theories to information technology. Ethics as a topic has certainly been studied and analyzed by philosophers for thousands of years. For those interested in more in-depth philosophical writings by some of the leading thinkers in this area, such as Bertrand Russell, Sir David Ross, G. E. Moore, and A. C. Ewing, see the readings in ethical theory gathered by Sellars and Hospers (1952).

3.4 Principles of Software Engineering

Many students of software engineering as well as practicing software engineers have asked if there are natural laws or principles in software engineering similar to those we find in other disciplines—for example, something equivalent to laws of motion or laws of thermodynamics. We in software engineering do not have a set of laws. We do have several sets of proposed **principles of software engineering**. These principles have evolved through numerous years of past experience and many are well accepted. Because software engineering is still young and still developing, the existing principles will continue to be modified and new ones added. In this section we will introduce some of them.

> **Principles of software engineering**   The rules and assumptions in software engineering derived from extensive observations.

3.4.1   Davis's Early Principles of Software Engineering

Alan Davis (1994) is one of the earlier authorities to bring forward a set of principles that underlie software engineering. His article on the 15 principles of software engineering actually includes 30 principles. He later published a book titled *201 Principles of Software Development*. Here we will introduce only the 15 "most important principles" as Davis saw them.

1. *Make quality Number 1:* It is shortsightedness to deliver a product that is of poor quality. Quality has many definitions and means different things to different constituents. For example, to the developer, it may mean "elegant design," and to the customers it may mean "good response time." In any case, quality must be viewed as the first requirement.

2. *High-quality software is possible:* Large software systems can be built with good quality, although it may carry a high price.

3. *Give products to customers early:* It is very difficult to completely understand and capture the users' needs during the requirements phase; thus it is more effective to give the users a prototype of the product and let them play with it. Gather the feedback and then go into full-scale development of the product.

4. *Determine the problem before writing the requirements:* Before the software engineers rush to offer the solution, ensure that the problem is well understood. Then explore the potential solution and various alternatives.

5. *Evaluate design alternatives:* After the requirements are understood and agreed upon, explore a variety of design architecture and related algorithms. Ensure that the selected design and algorithms are the best match to satisfy the goals of the requirement.

6. *Use an appropriate process model:* Since there is no universal process model that applies to all projects, each project must select a process that best fits the project based on parameters such as corporate culture, project circumstances, user expectations and requirements volatility, and resource experiences.

7. *Use different languages for different phases:* No one single language is optimal for all phases of software development. Therefore select the best methodology and language for the different phases of software development. The difficulty in transition from one phase to another is not necessarily solved by using a single language across all phases.

8. *Minimize intellectual distance:* It is easier to create the solution if the distance between the real-world problem and the computerized solution to that problem is minimized. That is, the software solution structure needs to be as close as possible to the real-world problem structure.

9. *Put technique before tools:* Before using the tool, the technique needs to be well understood. Otherwise, the tool just rushes us into performing the wrong thing faster.

10. *Get it right before you make it faster:* It is essential to make the software execute correctly first and then work on improving it. Do not worry about optimization for either execution speed or code during initial coding.

11. *Inspect code:* Inspection as first proposed by IBM's Mike Fagan is a much better way to find errors than testing. Some early data in inspections showed a reduction of 50% to 90% of the time-to-test.

12. *Good management is more important than good technology:* A good manager can produce extraordinary results even with limited resources. Even the best technology cannot compensate for terrible management because it cannot motivate the people as good mangers can.

13. *People are the key to success:* Software is a labor-intensive profession, and people with experience, talent, and appropriate drive are the key. The right people can overcome many of the shortcomings in process, methodology, or tools. There is no substitute for quality people.

14. *Follow with care:* Be careful in adopting tools, process, methodology, and so on. Do not follow just because someone else is doing it or using it. Run some experiments before making a major commitment.

15. *Take responsibility:* If you developed the system, then you should take responsibility to do it right. Blaming the failure or the problem on others, on the schedule, or on the process is irresponsible.

All except two of Davis's 15 principles of software engineering address the management of and techniques of software development and support. Also note how much the 15th principle resembles the principles related to a code of conduct much like the software engineering code of ethics discussed earlier. The first two of Davis's principles address the software product quality attribute. It is interesting that quality is the only software product attribute mentioned in these principles. There is clearly a need to have more principles that address software product attributes. These product attributes might include the following:

- Maintainability
- Installability
- Usability
- Reusability
- Interoperability
- Modifiability

These attributes are still ill-defined. We must thus first clearly define them and then come to some consensus on which ones are important. As our field matures, the necessary software product attributes will gradually be developed.

3.4.2   Royce's More Modern Principles

Building on Davis's list, Walker Royce (1998) in his book proposes a more modern set. His top 10 principles for modern software management are as follows:

1. Base the process on an architecture-first approach.
2. Establish an iterative process that addresses risks early in the process.
3. Emphasize component-based development to reduce the coding effort.
4. Change management should be established to handle iterative process.
5. Enhance the iterative development process environment, called round-trip engineering, where multiple changes may occur constantly across multiple artifacts with automated tools.
6. Use model-based and machine-processable notation to capture design.
7. Establish the process for objective quality control and project progress assessment that includes the assessment of all the intermediate artifacts.
8. Use a demonstration-based approach where intermediate artifacts are transitioned to executable demonstration of the user scenario so that these artifacts can be assessed earlier.
9. Plan to have incremental releases, each composed of a group of usage scenarios, with evolving levels of detail.
10. Establish a configurable process, because no one process is suitable for all software development.

These 10 principles are heavily influenced by the assumption that the underlying development process should be iterative in nature. It is considered modern because it is becoming more evident that building a large, complex system in one iteration is extremely difficult. Simply understanding the requirements of a large system alone requires multiple iterations. A process that allows us to construct a software system iteratively and incrementally is crucial and is preferred as an alternative to the sequentially regimental phase approach such as the waterfall process model. We will discuss and expand on the different traditional and emerging software development process models in Chapters 4 and 5.

3.4.3   Wasserman's Fundamental Software Engineering Concepts

Anthony Wasserman (1996) suggested that there are eight software engineering concepts that have remained relatively constant even though the software industry has been changing. The following basic concepts thus form a foundation to the software engineering discipline:

- Abstraction
- Analysis and design methods and notation

- User interface prototyping
- Modularity and architecture
- Reuse
- Life cycle and process
- Metrics
- Tools and integrated environment

The first concept, abstraction, is a technique that is often categorized as a design technique. It is in fact a broad method that software engineers employ to aid in generalization of a concept and postponing the concerns for the details. Proper analysis and design is the second concept and is a key to successfully developing software. Analysis provides us a clear set of requirements, and design transforms the requirements to the solution structure. Many have attempted to omit or reduce these efforts, and such incomplete work has been the major cause of many software failures, as shown earlier in Section 3.1.2. In addition, the notation for analysis and design needs to be standardized to facilitate more universal communications.

Developing standard notation is crucial in order for software engineering to move toward a disciplined engineering profession. The third major concept, user interface prototyping, contributes to a vital portion of understanding requirements and user preferences. It also contributes heavily to an iterative process approach to software development. Modularity in software architecture, the fourth concept, contributes heavily to the quality and maintainability of the software. The notion and significance of modularity have been earlier stressed by David Parnas. In addition to modularity, Wasserman also focuses on design patterns and the need for standardizing architectures. Certainly, design patterns and standardization of architecture contributes heavily to the notion of reuse, which is listed as the fifth concept. Reuse is a long-standing practice in the software industry since the inception of macros in assembly language and standard math libraries. In operating systems and software tools, we find an abundance of libraries of general functions. Industry-specific components that are easily identifiable and reusable need to be developed. Software process may not appear to be as significant to software engineering as concepts such as specification and analysis because there are software projects that have been successfully completed without much discipline or organized process. It is important to recognize, however, that most of the large, complex software projects have not survived without some defined process. Thus the sixth major concept is life cycle and process. Employing metrics, the seventh concept, is an important engineering, as well as management, technique. It is impossible to measure any software attributes or software process without well-defined metrics and measurement techniques, let alone attempting to improve on these attributes and processes. Finally, tools and integrated environment, the eighth major concept, are necessary for the development and support of any large, complex software.

When each of Wasserman's ideas is viewed individually, the concepts do not appear extraordinarily exceptional. However, taken together, they certainly delineate many of the significant advances made in the software engineering field. Many of these concepts were brought out in Chapter 2, where we discussed the development and support of a payroll system as an example of a large, complex software system.

3.5   Summary

This chapter has shown examples of software project failures and has characterized some of the reasons behind the failures. A primary cause of these software failures can be traced back to poor requirements and lack of user involvement. Since the late 1960s, software developers were alarmed by the growth of software quality problems and realized a need for a more rigorous engineering discipline. This new discipline was named *software engineering*. Several definitions are provided here. This relatively new field is still growing and the value of software is increasing dramatically. The recognition of the value of software intellectual capital and the need for professionalism has resulted in the development of a *Software Engineering Code of Ethics*. Many improvements and much progress made in software engineering in recent decades have allowed us to formulate a set of principles. Although these principles will continue to evolve, three sets, from Alan Davis, Walker Royce, and Anthony Wasserman, are presented and discussed in this chapter.

3.6   Review Questions

1. List two key reasons that have caused both software project successes and failures.

2. From the definition of software engineering, list three areas that software engineering must touch upon.

3. List two of the three strategies cited by the 2004 U.S. General Accounting Office report as key to ensuring delivery of successful software.

4. When and where was the term *software engineering* first introduced?

5. What are the eight principles for software engineering code of ethics recommended by the IEEE-CS/ACM Version 5.2 joint task force report?

6. What is meant by the term *principles of software engineering*?

7. Can a software engineer become a certified Professional Engineer (PE)? Explain.

3.7   Exercises

1. Prioritize the three areas that you listed for the software engineering definition in Review Question 2. Explain your priorities.

2. What is the reason behind having a code of ethics for software engineering?

3. Use the Web or the referenced material in the list of Suggested Readings and examine the IEEE-CS/ACM's *Software Engineering Code of Ethics and Professional Practices*. List the subprinciples for the fourth principle, which addresses the maintenance of integrity and independence in professional judgment.

4. Which of the possible interpretations of the term *quality* in Davis's first principle do you think is most important?

5. Trace the three sets of software engineering principles of Davis, Royce, and Wasserman and discuss the following software engineering topics in terms of relevance and emphasis placed by them.

   a. Requirements
   b. Architecture and design
   c. Process
   d. Tools
   e. Metrics and measurement
   f. Testing and quality

6. Using the Web, explore Donald Gotterbarn's site at http://seeri.etsu.edu. Pick one of his case studies on ethics and summarize it.

3.8 Suggested Readings

A. M. Davis, "Fifteen Principles of Software Engineering," *IEEE Software* (November 1994): 94–101.

S. L. Edgar, *Morality and Machines* (Sudbury, MA: Jones and Bartlett, 2003).

FastCompany, "They Write the Right Stuff," http://www.fastcompany.com/ online/06 /writestuff.html, 2005.

D. Gotterbarn, Software Engineering Ethics Research Institute, http://seeri.etsu.edu, 2004.

D. M. Hoffman and D. M. Weiss, *Software Fundamentals: Collected Papers by David Parnas* (Reading, MA: Addison-Wesley, 2001).

IEEE Computer Society and Association of Computing Machinery, Joint Task Force on Computing Curricula, *Software Engineering 2004 Curriculum Guidelines for Undergraduate Degree Programs in Software Engineering*, http://sites.computer.org/ccse/se2004Volume .pdf, 2004.

C. Jones, *Assessment and Control of Software Risks* (Upper Saddle River, NJ: Prentice Hall, 1994).

C. Jones, *Applied Software Measurement*, 2nd ed. (New York: McGraw-Hill, 1996).

S. Pfleeger, *Software Engineering Theory and Practices*, 2nd ed. (Upper Saddle River, NJ: Prentice Hall, 2001).

M. J. Quinn, *Ethics for the Information Age* (Reading, MA: Addison-Wesley, 2004).

N. Radziwill, "An Ethical Theory for the Advancement of Professionalism in Software Engineering," *Software Quality Professional* (June 2005): 14–23.

Research Triangle Institute, "The Economic Impacts of Inadequate Infrastructure for Software Testing," RTI Project Number 7007.011 (Research Triangle Park, NC: Research Triangle Institute, 2002).

W. Royce, *Software Project Management A Unified Framework* (Reading, MA: Addison-Wesley, 1998).

W. Sellars and J. Hospers, eds., *Readings in Ethical Theory* (New York: Appleton-Century-Crofts, 1952).

I. Sommerville, *Software Engineering*, 7th ed. (Reading, MA: Pearson Addison-Wesley, 2004).

Standish Group, Chaos, http://www.projectsmart.co.uk/docs/chaos_report.pdf, 1995.

W. A. Stimson, "A Deming Inspired Management Code of Ethics," *Quality Progress* (February 2005): 67–75.

U.S. Department of Justice, *Report of the Department of Justice's Task Force on Intellectual Property*, http://www.justice.gov/olp/ip_task_force_report.pdf, October 2004.

U.S. General Accounting Office, *Defense Acquisitions: Stronger Management Practices Are Needed to Improve DOD's Software-Intensive Weapon Acquisitions*, http://www.frwebgate.access.gpo.gov/cgi_bin/multidbicgi, March 2004.

A. I. Wasserman, "Toward a Discipline of Software Engineering," *IEEE Software* (November 1996): 23–33.

CHAPTER 4

Software Process Models

OBJECTIVES

- Introduce the generic concept of software engineering process models.
- Discuss the three traditional process models:
  1. Waterfall
  2. Incremental
  3. Spiral
- Discuss the chief programming team approach.
- Describe the Rational Unified Process along with the significance of entry and exit criteria for all the processes.
- Assess processes in terms of the Capability Maturity Model (CMM) and Capability Maturity Model Integrated (CMMI).
- Discuss the need to modify and refine a standard process.

4.1   Software Processes

We have mentioned processes in earlier chapters and have indicated the significant roles they play in software engineering. The process of developing and supporting software often requires many distinct tasks to be performed by different people in some related sequences (as shown in Chapter 2). When software engineers are left to perform tasks based on their own experience, background, and values, they do not necessarily perceive and perform the tasks in the same way or in the same order. They sometimes do not even perform the same tasks. This inconsistency causes projects to take a longer time with poor end products and, in worse situations, total project failure. Watts Humphrey has written extensively on software processes and process improvement in general and has also introduced the personal software process at the individual level in his book *Introduction to the Personal Software Process* (1997).

In this chapter we will cover the traditional software processes, and leave the emerging processes, such as the Agile processes, to the next chapter. We will also cover the general evaluation and assessment of processes in this chapter.

4.1.1   Goal of Software Process Models

The goal of a software process model is to provide guidance for systematically coordinating and controlling the tasks that must be performed in order to achieve the end product and the project objectives. A process model (similar to the definition provided in Chapter 2 for software development process) defines the following:

- A set of tasks that need to be performed
- The input to and output from each task
- The preconditions and postconditions for each task
- The sequence and flow of these tasks

We might ask whether a software development process is necessary if there is only one person developing the software. The answer is that it depends. If the software development process is viewed as only a coordinating and controlling agent, then there is no need because there is only one person. However, if the process is viewed as a prescriptive roadmap for generating various intermediate deliverables in addition to the executable code—for example, a design document, a user guide, test cases—then even a one-person software development project may need a process.

4.1.2   The "Simplest" Process Model

When programmers are left alone, they naturally gravitate to what is often perceived as the single most important task, coding. Most of the people involved with the information technology field, including the software engineers, start in the profession by learning how to write code in some programming language, as indicated in Chapter 1. **Figure 4.1** shows this perhaps simple process. It depicts the tasks involved in the code–compile–unit test cycle. Because coding is usually considered the central task in this process, the model is sometimes known as the code-and-fix model. When there is a problem detected in compilation or in the unit testing, debugging, which is problem analysis and resolution, is performed. The code is then modified to reflect the problem correction

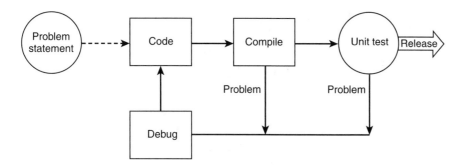

Figure 4.1 A simple process.

and recompiled. Unit testing then follows. When unit testing is completed and all the detected problems resolved, the code is released.

Two areas of Figure 4.1 deserve some attention. The first is the problem statement, the precursor to what we now call requirements specifications in software engineering. The significance of this area was neither recognized nor appreciated in the early days. The second area is testing. Unit testing the code was performed in an informal way by the author of the code. Because the problem statement was often allowed to be incomplete or unclear, the testing of the code to ensure that it met the problem statement was also itself often incomplete. The testing effort often reflected what the programmer understood the problem to be.

Even with all the shortcomings, this simple process model served many early projects. As software projects increased in complexity, more tasks, such as design and integration, were introduced. As more people participated in a software project, better coordination was introduced. The tasks in the process, the relationship among them, and the flow of these tasks become better defined.

As software engineers gained more experience, different software development models were introduced to solve different concerns. Today there is an understanding that there is no one process model that will fit all the software projects. Some of the earlier process models and associated topics will be introduced in this chapter; the more recently developed process models will be discussed in Chapter 5.

4.2 Traditional Process Models

In this section, several of the earlier software development models will be presented. Each of these models has also been adapted and modified to fit different situations. We will present the models only in their generic form.

4.2.1 Waterfall Model

The waterfall software development process model is probably the oldest publicized model. It is sometimes referred to as the classic software life cycle model. Although

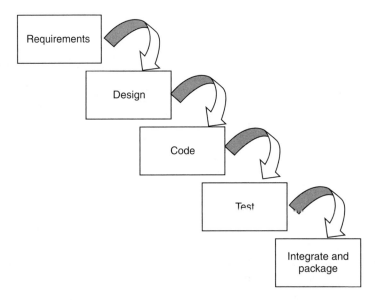

Figure 4.2 A waterfall model.

many organizations utilized this model, Royce (1970) is one of the earliest people to write about this model. The name of the waterfall model is derived from the process it represents: tasks occur sequentially one after another, with the output from one task dropping into the next task, as shown in **Figure 4.2**.

Resembling a multilayered waterfall, the model provided many advantages, especially to the software project managers in the early 1970s. It served as a tool for managing software projects and represented the software life cycle as the software went through different and distinct stages of development. It gave the project managers a way to describe the status more precisely than just saying the software is "almost complete." Although we now recognize many shortcomings to this process, the waterfall model also has many positive aspects:

- Requirements must be specified in the first step.
- Four main tasks must be completed before the software can be packaged for release: requirements, design, code, and test.
- The output from each stage is fed into the next stage in sequence.
- The software project may be tracked as it moves sequentially through specific and identifiable stages.

Because of the heavy amount of documents that were generated with requirements, design, and testing, the waterfall model also became known as the document-driven approach.

Many modifications to the basic waterfall model have been applied throughout the years since its early definition, each addressing some of its shortcomings. For example, the model was usually viewed as a single iteration model that provided very little task overlapping. Thus backward arrows were introduced in the diagram to depict the addition of iterative activities.

The waterfall model has also been criticized for its limited interaction with users at only the requirements phase and at the delivery of the software. The implementers of the waterfall model included the users and the customers in the design phase with techniques such as joint application development (JAD) and in the testing phase.

The single most important contribution of the waterfall model is probably that it gave software engineering a process upon which software development could focus its attention. As a result of this focus on process, the waterfall model, as well as software quality problems in general, started to be resolved through the years.

4.2.2 Chief Programmer Team Approach

The chief programmer team approach is a type of coordination and management methodology rather than a software process. The concept was a popular organizational idea in the mid-1970s.

In his book, *The Mythical Man Month* (1975), Fred Brooks described a small-team approach to coordinate the activities of software development. He attributed the original proposal to Harlan Mills of IBM. The proposed approach mimics a surgical team organization where there is a chief surgeon and other specialists to support the chief surgeon. Instead of a large number of people all working on smaller pieces of the problem, there is a chief programmer who plans, divides, and assigns the work to the different specialists. The chief programmer acts just like a chief surgeon in a surgical team and directs all the work activities. The team size should be about 7 to 10 people, composed of specialists such as designers, programmers, testers, documentation editors, and the chief programmer. This approach made sense and is a precursor to dividing a large problem into multiple components, then having the small chief-programming teams develop the components.

4.2.3 Incremental Model

The incremental model may be viewed as a modification to the waterfall model. As software projects increased in size, it was recognized that it is much easier, and sometimes necessary, to develop the software if the large projects are subdivided into smaller components, which may thus be developed incrementally and iteratively. In the early days, each component followed a waterfall process model, passing through each step iteratively. In the incremental model, the components were developed in an overlapping fashion, as shown in **Figure 4.3**. The components all had to be integrated and then tested as a whole in a final system test. The incremental model provided a certain amount of risk containment. If any one component ran into trouble, the other components were able to still continue to be developed independently. Unless the problem was a universal one, such as the underlying technology being faulty, one problem would not hold up the entire development process.

Another perspective in utilizing the incremental model is to first develop the core software that contains most of the required functionality. The first increment may be delivered to users and customers as Release 1. Additional functionality and supplemental features are then developed and delivered separately as they are completed, becoming Release 2, Release 3, and so on. Utilizing the incremental model in this fashion provides an approach that is more akin to an evolutionary software product development. When

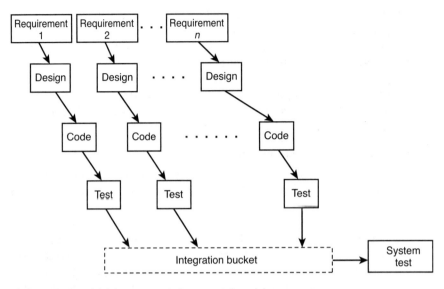

Figure 4.3 A multiple-components incremental model.

utilized in this development mode, the model in Figure 4.3 would not have the integration bucket.

The incremental model in Figure 4.3 would have individual releases. For example, Requirement 1 would be the core functionality release. Other requirements would each depict different deliveries. **Figure 4.4** depicts the incremental, multiple release scenario where the first release, Release 1, is the core function, followed by subsequent releases that may include fixes of bugs from previous releases along with new functional features. The multiple release incremental model also makes it possible to evolve the first release, which may have flaws, into an ideal solution through subsequent releases. Thus it facilitates evolutionary software development and management, a model that has been advocated by many, especially by Tom Gilb who has written about the "evo" process (Gilb and Gilb 2004). The number of releases for a software project will depend on the nature and goals of the project. Although each release is independently built, there is a link between releases because the existing design and code of the previous release is the basis upon which future releases are built.

Both incremental models utilize the "divide and conquer" methodology where a large, complex problem is decomposed into parts. The difficulty with this model is that

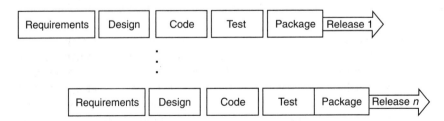

Figure 4.4 A multiple-release incremental model.

[handwritten: Iterative approach: time taken for each task]

such problems are also intertwined, making the decoupling of the parts into independently implementable components difficult. It will require a deep understanding of the problem, the solution, and the usage environment. Overlapping the different increments is another area of difficulty in that there may be some amount of sequential dependency of information among the components. How much overlapping can take place depends on how much prerequisite information is required.

4.2.4 Spiral Model

Another evolutionary approach to software development is the spiral model, proposed by Barry Boehm (1988) at a time when there were concerns with the waterfall model's document-driven approach. The early spiral model is based on experiences with various large government software projects at TRW. An important aspect of the spiral model is its emphasis in the reduction of risks in software development. The model is thus a risk-driven approach to software process. It provides a cyclic approach to incrementally develop the software system while reducing the project risk as the project goes through cycles of development, as illustrated in **Figure 4.5**.

The spiral model has four quadrants, and the software project traverses through the quadrants as it is incrementally developed. As shown in the figure, the spiral path may

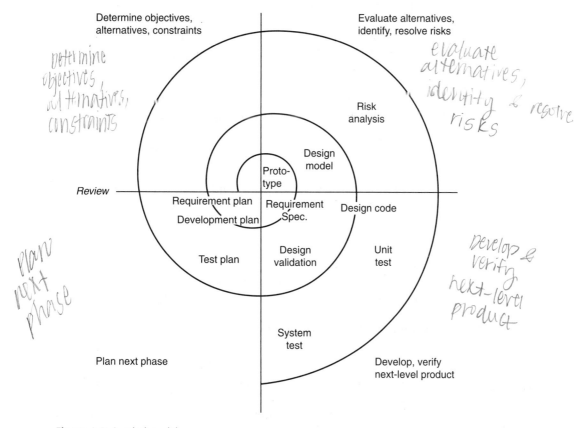

[handwritten annotations: determine objectives, alternatives, constraints; evaluate alternatives, identify & resolve risks; plan next phase; Develop & verify next-level product]

Figure 4.5 A spiral model.

not be very smooth. Each cycle involves the same sequence of steps for each of the concerns, components, or artifacts.

Equally applicable to software development and software enhancement projects, the spiral model is based on some objective. The spiral process then involves the continual testing or iterations of this objective or requirement until either the end result is achieved or shown to be unachievable. A typical traversal through the four quadrants is as follows:

1. Identify the objectives, alternatives, or constraints for each cycle of the spiral.
2. Evaluate the alternatives relative to the objectives and constraints. In performing this step, many of the risks are identified and evaluated.
3. Depending on the amount of and type of identified risks, develop a prototype, more detailed evaluation, an evolutionary development, or some other step to further reduce the risk of achieving the identified objective. On the other hand, if the risk is substantially reduced, the next step may just be a task such as requirements, design, or code.
4. Validate the achievement of the objective and plan for the next cycle.

An integral part of the cycle is the review of all the activities and products completed in the cycle by all the major stakeholders involved in the project. The review's major objective here is to ensure that all the parties are continuously committed to the project and concur with the approach for the next phase of the project.

Because the spiral model is based on risk reduction of the project through iterations, several convenient features are built into it.

- The model incorporates prototyping and modeling as an integral part of the process.
- It allows iterative and evolutionary approaches to all activities based on the amount of risks involved.
- The model does not preclude the rework of an earlier activity if a better alternative or a new risk is identified.

The ironic part of the spiral model is that one of its risks is the reliance on risk assessment expertise. Not all software engineers are trained or experienced in risk identification and risk analysis.

4.3   A More Modern Process

In recent years, many newer processes have been introduced. A popular process, which was initially developed by Rational Software Corporation, is described in this section.

4.3.1   General Foundations of Rational Unified Process Framework

The Rational Unified Process (RUP) is a software process framework, rather than a single process, developed by Rational Software Corporation, which was acquired by IBM. The origin of RUP is rooted in the original 1987 Objectory Process and the 1997 Rational Objectory Process as well as the **Unified Modeling Language** (**UML**). Fowler and Scott (1999) provide extensive coverage of UML in their book, *UML*

> **Unified Modeling Language (UML)**   An object-oriented modeling language that provides the elements and relationships to model software requirements and design.

Distilled. In many ways, RUP has incorporated earlier experiences from the incremental and iterative process model and the spiral model. This process framework is driven by three major concepts:

- Use-case and requirements driven
- Architecture centric
- Iterative and incremental

Use cases have been used mainly to capture requirements, but they may be used to describe any interaction between the software system and anything external such as a user of the system. This approach is different from the traditional functional specification approach where the functionality of the system is described but the complete interaction between the system and its users is not. The emphasis is on the users and the values to the users. Use-case driven means that the development process is initiated by the use case, that the designs are developed from the use cases, and that the test cases are derived from the use cases. Thus, use cases drive this software development process.

Architecture plays a significant role in RUP, describing the static and the dynamic aspects of the overall system, with the more important aspects highlighted and the less important details left out. In RUP, the architecture initially provides what Jacobson, Booch, and Rumbaugh (1999) call the "form" of the system, which is use-case independent. It describes the high-level design, such as the user-interface standard or error processing, which transcends all the use cases. From this baseline, the architecture is refined to accommodate the important major use cases. Each of the important use cases represents a key component of the software system, providing more details to the design. As more details of the use cases are considered, the architecture also evolves into a more mature and stable design. The use cases drive the architecture and the architecture influences the choices of use cases.

RUP is also iterative and incremental in that it promotes large software to be developed in smaller pieces or increments. In developing the chosen increment, RUP promotes the iterative approach. The first iteration would include all the use cases or requirements representing that increment or slice of the product. The second iteration would handle all the most important risks in the chosen increment. Successive iterations would then build upon the results of the previous iterations.

These three concepts of use case, architecture, and iterative and incremental form the basis of RUP. For more comprehensive studies on RUP, refer to the books in the Suggested Readings section at the end of this chapter.

4.3.2 The Phases of RUP

The phases in RUP are not named after the activities such as design, testing, or coding; an iteration may include many activities in varying degrees. There are four phases in RUP:

1. Inception
2. Elaboration
3. Construction
4. Transition

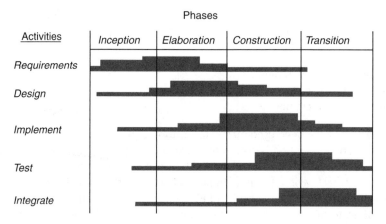

Figure 4.6 The Rational Unified Process (RUP).

As an increment of the product is developed, it may go through several iterations within each phase. The degree of the activities such as requirements specifications, testing, or coding that takes place within each phase is also different.

The inception phase may be viewed as the beginning stage when the product increment is still in an early stage of uncertainty. An initial idea is being developed during this phase. During the elaboration phase, the detailed use cases are being formulated, and the architecture and design are getting firmed up. The product increment is built, coded, and tested during the construction phase. Finally, the product increment is released to a small restricted group of users during the transition phase for further testing and correction. It is then released to the general public. **Figure 4.6** provides a view of the four phases of the Rational Unified Process and how the development activities relate to the phases. The software development activities on the left in the figure all flow through the four phases. Each activity will be in "peak mode" in different phases. The extent of each activity is represented by the thickness of the bar with relative approximations showing where the activities will peak. Although not explicitly shown in this figure, any activity such as design may also iterate several times within a phase. RUP not only provides incremental development but also includes iterative development. The four phases provide a mechanism to track project milestones.

Inception Phase   Inception is a planning phase that includes the following primary objectives:

- Establish the scope and clarify the goals of the software project.
- Establish the critical use cases and the major scenarios that will drive the architecture and design.
- Establish some architecture and early design alternatives.
- Estimate the schedule and required resources.
- Plan the implementation, testing, integration, and configuration methodologies.
- Estimate the potential risks.

In order to accomplish these primary objectives, the requirements activities must be building up to a full crescendo. The architecture of the software system is narrowed and various design alternatives must be considered during this phase. Implementation, testing, integration methodologies, tools, and so on. are being planned during the inception phase. The overall project schedule, needed resources, and potential risks are estimated based on the major requirements and early architecture. The project goals and measurement are established. The stakeholders should all concur with the estimates and the plan for the project.

Elaboration Phase   Elaboration may be the most critical phase of the Rational Unified Process. At the end of this phase, most of the unknowns should be resolved. The primary objectives of this phase include the following:

- Establish all the major and critical requirements for the system.
- Establish and demonstrate the baseline design.
- Establish the implementation, test, and integration platforms and methodologies.
- Establish the major test scenarios.
- Establish the measurement and metrics for the agreed-upon goals.
- Organize and set up all the needed resources for implementation, testing, and integration.

In order to achieve these objectives, all the requirements must be gathered, analyzed, understood, documented, and agreed to by all parties during the elaboration phase. Any prototyping of requirements must be completed, as well as the architecture and most of the design. Any design feasibility questions must be prototyped and answered. Major test scenarios are identified during this phase. Plans for implementation, testing, and integration are completed. Resources needed for implementation, testing, and integration are acquired and organized. Education for any new methodology or tools for implementation, testing, or integration is completed. A clear metric and measurement system is accepted and resources for measurement are acquired. That is, the project control for the rest of the phases is set in place. At the end of the elaboration phase, the software project is ready to go into full implementation and testing mode.

Construction Phase   The construction phase is equal to the production phase in manufacturing. At the end of this phase, the code for the software should be complete and all the major requirements tested. The following objectives are the key points of this phase:

- Complete the implementation in a timely manner within estimated cost.
- Achieve the version of the code that is releasable to a restricted set of Alpha test sites.
- Establish the remaining activities that need to be completed to achieve the goals of the project.

In order to meet these objectives, the coding of the design must be completed in the construction phase. All the planned test cases must be executed and most of the discovered problems are fixed in this phase. The software must meet most of the established goals of the project and the measurements taken must validate that. Assessment must be made of how much and what remaining activities are needed to achieve the planned goals. For example, an assessment of whether the software product quality goal is met needs to be performed. Any necessary activities to follow up on this goal, such as additional testing and fixes, must be set up.

Transition Phase   The transition phase is the last phase prior to the release of the software to general users. All the fixes and components are integrated. The noncode artifacts, such as manuals and educational materials, are also integrated into the complete product. The key objectives of this phase are the following:

- Establish the final software product for general release.
- Establish user readiness and acceptance of the software.
- Establish support readiness.
- Gain concurrence for release and deployment.

All Alpha and Beta tests with a restricted number of users must be completed and the fixes to the discovered problems are integrated into the final release during this phase. Users must be trained. All transitional activities, such as data migration and usage process modifications, are completed prior to the end of this phase. The software support group is trained and must stand ready to service users. If this is a software product for external sale, the sales organization must be educated, and the marketing material must be created and be available for distribution. A final assessment of the software, in terms of its goals, is performed and a decision on release is made.

4.4   Entry and Exit Criteria

The processes discussed so far have emphasized the sequencing and coordination of activities. The Rational Unified Process does, however, go further and provide some guidelines on what artifacts need to be developed by whom. Still, there are very few guidelines on how much of each activity must be performed. That is, what are the exit criteria for each activity and the entry criteria for the next follow-on activity?

Figure 4.7 shows that the entry criteria for an activity must be met before the activity can start. The exit criteria must be met before the activity can be considered complete and before the next activity may start. The difficulty comes in when the activities overlap

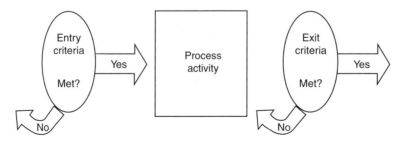

Figure 4.7 Entry and exit criteria.

in a concurrent manner. The entry and exit criteria must then be defined with much more granularity.

4.4.1   Entry Criteria

Prior to performing any of the activities portrayed in the process diagram, we must ask for the condition that allows the performer of that activity to start. The conditions for initiating the activity define the entry criteria. These include a listing and a description of the following resources:

- Required artifacts
- Required people
- Required tools
- Required definition of the activity to be performed

There must be a specified list of artifacts. Just listing them alone is not enough. These artifacts must be in a condition that they are usable by the activity. As an example, consider the design task that needs the requirement specifications. The state of each specification must be defined as *completed*, which means the following:

- All specifications have been reviewed by the customers and other stakeholders.
- All exceptions found during the review are changed.
- The modified specifications are accepted by all parties.

When the requirement specifications have attained these conditions, they are considered complete and have met the entry criteria for the design task. Note that if the desired process is incrementally driven, the completed state may apply to only the incremental requirement that is needed for the next activity of design.

The people required to perform the task must also be specified. They must be in a ready state, meaning that they are available and can be applied to the task prior to the commencement of the task.

Any tools that are required or that may be later used to perform a task are specified. Again, just listing the tools is not enough. The rationale and the expectations of using any tool for the task must be spelled out. The people who are pegged to use the tools have to be identified and trained prior to the beginning of performing the task.

The most obvious requirement, yet one that is often left out, is the definition and explanation of the task itself. If there is not a clear understanding of the task, different individuals may perform the task differently, which can cause erratic results.

The definition of the entry criteria for each of the steps or activities described in a process will bring the high-level definition of process down to an executable level. It also allows each part of the organization to tailor the process by specifying slightly different entry criteria for each of the tasks in a process.

4.4.2   Exit Criteria

Before an activity is declared complete, the exit criteria for such a declaration need to be specified ahead of time. Only when those criteria are met can the activity be considered complete. Again, in the case of incremental and overlapping activities, the exit criteria must then be declared at a much finer level.

The main purpose of the exit criteria is to describe the artifacts that must be available for the next activity. A clear description of what must be included in each completed artifact must be defined. Furthermore, it is important to clearly spell out any conditions such as the following:

- All the artifacts are reviewed.
- All or some prespecified percentage of the errors are corrected.
- People in the downstream activities have concurred and accepted the artifacts.

There are other conditions that we may include as part of the exit criteria—for example, that the person who is to participate in the next downstream activity is freed from the current activity. The important thing is that the exit criteria should be clearly specified ahead of time.

4.5   Process Assessment Models

Software engineering development and support processes continue to be modified, improved, and invented through countless studies, experiments, and implementations, some achieving great success and some utter failure (see Cusumano et al. 2003; MacCormack 2001). The software industry has embraced the importance of software development processes for years. One of the key organizations that has contributed to, advanced, and advocated the software development processes is the Software Engineering Institute (SEI), a research and development center funded by the U.S. Department of Defense and located on the Carnegie Mellon University campus. Its stated core purpose is to "help others make measured improvements on their software engineering capabilities." (See the Suggested Readings section for the SEI web address.)

Another organization that has contributed to software engineering is the International Standards Organization (ISO). Its ISO 9000 series of software quality standards includes the ISO/IEC 90003:2004 document, which provides guidance for organizations to apply ISO9001:2000 to the computer software activities. Specifically, there are four documents—ISO/IES 9126-1 through ISO/IES 9126-4—that address various aspects of software quality. Also, the ISO/IEC 12207 Standard for Information Technology document discusses and provides a framework for software life cycle processes. These documents can be purchased from the ISO website listed in the Suggested Readings section. Both the SEI and ISO contributed greatly to assessing the maturity of the organization in their software development and support.

4.5.1   SEI's Capability Maturity Model

The Capability Maturity Model (CMM), initially proposed by SEI, is a framework that is used to help a software organization define its level of maturity in software development. (See Paulk et al. 2003 for information on the original document on CMM.) The model presents five levels of maturity and is based on the concept of continual improvements. The level of maturity of a software organization is determined by its practice of different sets of key software development process activities. The levels are sequential and accumulative in that an organization assessed at a Level x is expected to have elevated from Level $(x - 1)$. There is a list of officially trained CMM assessors, which may be obtained from SEI,

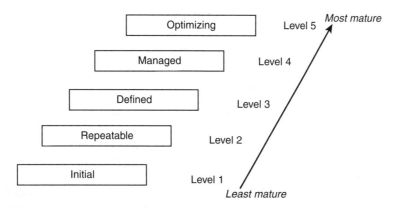

Figure 4.8 The five levels of the original Capability Maturity Model.

who perform the appraisal of an organization and provide the feedback on the strength and weakness of the organizations' key processes activities and commitments. The five levels of CMM are represented in **Figure 4.8**.

At the initial level (Level 1 in the figure) an organization has no process, and any success is probably attributed to a strong and experienced leader. The probability of repeating this success is low. As an organization defines, practices, and continually improves on the different processes, it moves up the scale of maturity.

At Level 2, there are six key processes that an organization must master:

- Requirements management
- Software project tracking and oversight
- Software quality assurance
- Software project planning
- Subcontract management
- Software configuration management

An organization at Level 2 (the repeatable level) has mastered these key project management-related processes and is expected to be able to repeat its success when given a similar project.

In order for an organization to elevate from Level 2 to Level 3 (the defined level), it must master seven more key processes:

- Organization process focus
- Training program
- Software product engineering
- Peer reviews
- Organization process definition
- Integrated software management
- Intergroup coordination

At Level 3, the organization has mastered the major processes related to construction of software along with additional project management-related processes.

An organization moves up to Level 4 (the managed level) when it focuses its effort on quantitative and quality management in addition to all the key processes of Levels 2 and 3. As such, two more key processes are added:

- Quantitative process management
- Software quality management

Metrics and measurements of the process and of the software artifacts are introduced. Quantitative management of attributes such as quality, productivity, or efficiency is part of the organization at this level. With the captured measurements, the feedback from prior activities becomes visible, which allows future improvements to both the processes and the product.

The highest level of CMM is Level 5 (the optimizing level). The emphasis here is on continuous improvement. In order to facilitate such improvement, three key processes must be included:

1. Defect prevention
2. Technology change management
3. Process change management

All the key processes at this ultimate level contribute to an organization poised for changes and improvements.

SEI's original CMM has been used by thousands of software organizations across multiple countries. Today, large and small companies around the world—from Wipro in India to Neusoft in China—have attained Level 5. Occasionally, several organizations within the same company may be assessed at different levels. For example, Lockheed Martin, the U.S. technological giant in the aerospace industry, is an example of a company that has several organizations within it that have attained CMM Level 5. The United States leads the world in the number of CMM-assessed organizations. Some organizations, however, just utilize the CMM framework for self-improvement and never request any formal assessment. Others have used the assessed CMM level as a marketing tool for their organizations. This is especially evident in the software service sector.

The time required for ascending from one level to the next higher level is usually on the order of one or two years, rarely in months or days.

4.5.2   SEI's Capability Maturity Model Integrated

In 2001, the CMM was upgraded to the Capability Maturity Model Integrated (CMMI). Again, the important factor to remember is that CMMI's purpose is to provide guidance for improving the processes of an organization and its ability to develop, manage, and support the software product and services. While there are multiple aspects of the CMMI (e.g., systems engineering, software engineering, integrated product and process development, and supplier sourcing), the one we are interested in and will be discussing here is the CMMI-SW, the software engineering model.

The CMMI-SW model has two representations:

- Continuous
- Staged

The continuous representation model is more applicable to the assessment and improvement of processes. The staged representation model is, like the CMM, better applied to assessing the maturity of an organization. In the next three sections we will first discuss the three key concepts common to both the continuous and the staged representations, and we will then delineate the differences between the two representations.

The Process Areas of CMMI   The first key concept related to both the continuous and staged representations in CMMI is that there are 25 major process areas covering four major categories of processes: (1) process management, (2) project management, (3) engineering, and (4) support.

The following five process areas fall under process management:

1. Organizational process focus
2. Organizational process definition
3. Organizational training
4. Organizational process performance
5. Organizational innovation and deployment

The following eight process areas fall under project management:

1. Project planning
2. Project monitoring and control
3. Supplier agreement management
4. Integrated project management
5. Risk management
6. Integrated teaming
7. Integrated supplier management
8. Quantitative project management

The following six process areas fall under engineering:

1. Requirements development
2. Requirements management
3. Technical solution
4. Product integration
5. Verification
6. Validation

The last six process areas fall under support:

1. Configuration management
2. Process and product quality assurance
3. Measurement and analysis
4. Organizational environment for integration
5. Decision analysis and resolution
6. Causal analysis and resolution

Level 5	Optimizing	Optimizing
Level 4	Quantitatively managed	Quantitatively managed
Level 3	Defined	Defined
Level 2	Managed	Managed
Level 1	Performed	Initial
Level 0	Incomplete	– – – – – –
	Continuous (Capability Levels)	Staged (Maturity Levels)

Figure 4.9 Different levels in CMMI.

These 25 process areas form the basis for process evaluation in CMMI.

Levels in CMMI   Both the continuous and staged representations utilize levels for assessment. In the case of continuous representation, there are 6 (0–5) capability levels for assessing the process areas. The staged representation has 5 (1–5) maturity levels for assessing the organization. **Figure 4.9** compares the capability and staged levels. The utilization of levels for designating assessment results is the second key concept in CMMI. Note that the names for Levels 2 through 5 are the same for both the continuous capability levels and the staged maturity levels. However, as will be explained in a later section of this chapter, these levels are different in their structures.

Goals and Practices in CMMI   A third key concept that is common to both the continuous and the staged representations in CMMI is the notion of goals and practices. Within each of the 25 process areas is a designated set of specific goals that uniquely describe the specific practices that must be implemented to satisfy that process area. Furthermore, the specific practices associated with each of the goals are also unique to each goal. Thus the specific practices are all different, as illustrated in **Figure 4.10**.

As an example, consider one of the 25 process areas, organizational process focus. For this process area, there are two specific goals with their respective specific practices. Specific goal 1 has three specific practices, and specific goal 2 has four specific practices.

- Specific goal 1: Strengths, weaknesses, and improvement opportunities for the organization's processes are identified periodically and as needed.
  - Specific practice 1.1: Establish organizational process needs.
  - Specific practice 1.2: Appraise the organization's processes.
  - Specific practice 1.3: Identify improvements to the processes.

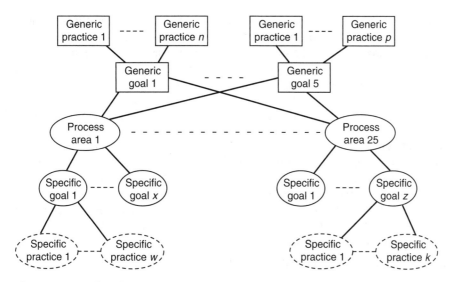

Figure 4.10 Goals and practices.

- Specific goal 2: Improvements are planned and implemented, organizational process assets are deployed, and process-related experiences are incorporated into the organization's process assets.
  - Specific practice 2.1: Establish and maintain process action plans.
  - Specific practice 2.2: Implement process action plans.
  - Specific practice 2.3: Deploy organizational process assets.
  - Specific practice 2.4: Incorporate process-related work products, measures, and improvement information into organizational process assets.

Consult the CMMI document, CMU/SEI–2002–TR–028, in the Suggested Readings section for a complete list of specific goals and their respective specific practices for each of the 25 process areas.

In contrast to the specific goals, which are different for each process area, there are five generic goals that are applicable to all the 25 process areas (see Figure 4.10). The five generic goals are as follows:

- Generic goal 1: Achieve specific goals of the process area.
- Generic goal 2: Institutionalize managed process.
- Generic goal 3: Institutionalize defined process.
- Generic goal 4: Institutionalize quantitatively managed process.
- Generic goal 5: Institutionalize optimizing process.

These generic goals also map into the continuous representation's capability levels 1 through 5, respectively. Capability level 0, which is the incomplete level, has no generic goal associated with it.

Associated with each of the five generic goals are sets of generic practices. Because the goals are applicable to all the process areas, the set of generic practices are also applicable to the 25 process areas. There is one generic practice associated with generic goal 1. There are 10 generic practices associated with generic goal 2. Generic goal 3 has two generic practices. Two generic practices are associated with generic goal 4, and generic goal 5 has two generic practices. Because the generic goals are applicable to all the process areas, their respective generic practices are also applicable to all the process areas.

Continuous Representation Model   The continuous representation model, in which each process area is appraised at its own capability level, uses both the specific goals and the generic goals for assessing the process areas. An example of a profile of an organization's capability level by process areas is depicted in **Figure 4.11**. This profile not only provides an assessment but also serves as guidance for an organization to improve on the process areas that need improvements. The continuous representation model has several functions in an organization:

- Allows an organization to select the order of improvements that best meets that organization's needs and structure.
- Allows comparisons across different organizations on a process area by process area basis.
- Allows easier migration from and comparison to Electronic Institute Alliance International Standard (EIA/IS) 731 and International Organization for Standardization and International Electro-technical Commission (ISO/IEC) 15504.

Each process area initially starts at capability level 0 (CL0), or the incomplete level. For any process area to move up from CL0 to the next level, either the performed level or CL1, two sets of activities must be completed.

- The specific goals for that process area must be achieved through completing all the associated specific practices for those specific goals.
- Generic goal 1 must be achieved through completion of its associated generic practices.

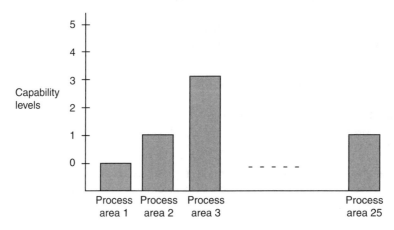

Figure 4.11 Capability level by process areas for continuous representation.

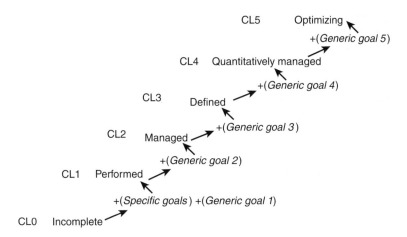

Figure 4.12 Achieving the capability levels by process area in the continuous representation model.

Once a process area reaches capability level 1, the performed level, subsequent levels are achieved by satisfying the subsequent generic goals and their respective generic practices (see **Figure 4.12**). The figure shows that in order for a process area to improve from CL*n* to CL*n*+1, generic goal *n*+1 must be satisfied.

Staged Representation Model   In a staged representation model, there are five maturity levels (MLs). The same 25 process areas are grouped into four of the five maturity levels. Maturity level 1, the initial level, has no process area associated with it. Essentially, ML1 is similar to CL0 of the continuous representation model. The organization achieves a maturity level by satisfying the set of process areas that are grouped under that maturity level. The groupings of process areas for the staged representation model's maturity levels are as follows:

ML5
- Organizational innovation and deployment
- Causal analysis and resolution

ML4
- Organizational process performance
- Quantitative project management

ML3
- Requirements development
- Technical solution
- Product integration
- Verification
- Validation
- Organizational process focus

- Organizational process definition
- Organizational training
- Integrated project management
- Risk management
- Integrated teaming
- Integrated supplier management
- Decision analysis and resolution
- Organizational environment for integration

ML2

- Requirements management
- Project planning
- Project monitoring and control
- Supplier agreement management
- Measurement and analysis
- Process and product quality assurance
- Configuration management

ML1

- None

The maturity levels are sequential, with any maturity level n being built upon maturity level $n - 1$. The staged representation model provides an organization a single maturity level appraisal based on the set of process areas satisfied. For example, an organization is assessed as maturity level 2 if all seven process areas grouped under ML2 are satisfied. The staged representation provides the following for an organization:

- A sequence of improvements of process areas by maturity levels
- The capacity to compare across organizations by maturity levels
- Easy migration from the earlier software CMM model

The rule for a process area to be considered satisfied in a staged representation model is similar to that of the continuous representation model. There are, however, some subtle differences. A process area that is grouped at ML2, managed level, would need to satisfy all its specific goals and associated specific practices along with generic goal 2 and its associated generic practices. For process areas that are grouped in ML3, defined level, those process areas need to satisfy all the specific goals and specific practices along with generic goal 2 and the associated generic practices. Each process area listed under ML4, quantitatively managed level, would need to satisfy all their specific goals and specific practices along with generic goal 3 and associated generic practices. Similar to ML4, each process area in ML5, optimizing level, would need to satisfy all its specific goals and specific practices along with generic goal 3 and generic practices. Note that in satisfying the staged maturity levels, generic goals 1, 4, and 5 do not play a part in the scheme.

4.6   Process Definition and Communication

We have discussed several traditional software development processes. While they serve as good models, it is very likely that they will need some modification to fit a specific organization. Depending on the goal(s) of the software project, a slightly different set of activities may be needed or emphasized. As Osterweil (1987) observed, the software development process is just a vehicle for carrying out those activities. Thus, specifying the process model is similar to constructing a software system itself. A process model or specification is an abstract representation of the actual process. It is important that this modified process be well defined and communicated to all participants so that the project can be carried out smoothly.

A software process specification is composed of two basic parts:

- The activities to be included in the software project
- The order in which these activities should be performed

These two main components are further expanded and refined to include the following set of items:

- Activities: Detailed descriptions of each of the activities included in the process
- Control: Necessary entry and exit criteria for each activity, in addition to the order in which each should be performed
- Artifacts: The resulting output from each of the activities
- Resources: The people who perform the activities
- Tools: The tools that may be used to enhance the performance of the activity

A software process definition for development and support projects needs to include all of the preceding information in differing degrees of detail. The modified process definition for a specific organization needs to describe the activities to be performed, specify the controlled conditions of the entry and exit criteria, and define the order in which these activities must be performed. It is necessary to identify and define the resulting artifacts, including null situations, from each of the activities. A software project is usually carried out by several people—each having different skills and experience. The number of people needed, their individual skill levels, and the experience level of each must be specified. Finally, any tools that can enhance the performance of the activities should be specified.

It is difficult and tedious to define all of the preceding activities and related items. Thus, a team may decide to place an emphasis on the parts that are most relevant to each project. On the other hand, in order to provide some flexibility for a very experienced team that has worked on similar projects before, they may choose to define all five parts at a high level for the purpose of management overview. Note that specifying the software process to the most detailed level would be nearly equivalent to performing the detailed design and programming of the software process itself.

4.7   Summary

In earlier chapters we alluded to the importance of having a process or a set of processes to guide the software developers in large development and support projects. In this chapter we traced through three traditional process models:

- Waterfall
- Incremental
- Spiral

A more modern process model, the Rational Unified Process (RUP), was introduced. The emphasis here is on the need to have well-defined criteria for both entrance to and exit from activities in a process model.

The Software Engineering Institute at Carnegie Mellon University has been a driving force in the process modeling and process assessment arena. Its first software process model, the Capability Maturity Model (CMM) is now well known among software industry practitioners. In recent years, the improved model, Capability Maturity Model Integrated (CMMI), is gaining momentum. CMMI's continuous representation model allows an organization to assess the capability level of its process areas separately while the staged model allows an organization to assess the maturity level of the complete organization, much like the CMM model. It is very likely that a standard process needs to be modified and refined before it can be utilized by a software project.

In the next chapter, we will introduce the more recent processes and methodologies such as Agile and Extreme Programming.

4.8　Review Questions

1. Discuss one advantage and one disadvantage of the waterfall process.

2. What is the goal of a software process model?

3. What are the four quadrants in a spiral model? Trace the requirements set of activities through each quadrant.

4. What are the entry and exit criteria to a process?

5. What motivated software engineers to move from the waterfall model to the incremental or spiral model?

6. What are the major concepts that drove the Rational Unified Process framework?

7. What are the four phases of the Rational Unified Process?

8. List all of the key processes addressed by SEI's CMM model. Which ones are required for maturity level 2?

9. How many process areas, in total, are included in SEI's Software CMMI? List those that fall into the engineering category and the support category.

4.9　Exercises

1. Look again at the simple process model in Figure 4.1. What development activity would you choose to add first to that process and why?

2. What is the difference between the multiple component incremental model and the multiple release incremental model?

3. Discuss the four phases of the Rational Unified Process and their relationship to the development activities such as requirements analysis, design, and testing.

4. Give two entry criteria examples and discuss their importance.

5. Give two exit criteria examples and discuss their importance.

6. Use the Internet to go to http://www.sei.cmu.edu and search for SEI's vision and mission. Do you believe we need such an organization and why or why not?

7. List the process areas that are required for staged maturity level 2 of CMMI. How do these differ from those of maturity level 2 in CMM?

8. Discuss the two representation models in CMMI. What do these two models assess?

9. In the continuous representation model, discuss how a process area moves up (or improves) from CL2 to CL3.

4.10 Suggested Readings

D. M. Ahern, A. Closure, and R. Turner, *CMMI Distilled—A Practical Introduction to Integrated Process Improvement*, 2nd ed. (Reading, MA: Addison-Wesley, 2004).

B. Boehm, "A Spiral Model for Software Development and Enhancement," *Computer* 21, no. 5 (May 1988): 61–72.

F. P. Brooks, *The Mythical Man Month* (Reading, MA: Addison-Wesley, 1975).

Capability Maturity Model Integration (CMMI) Version 1.1, CMMI for Software Engineering, CMU/SEI–2002–TR–028, August 2002.

M. Cusumano, A. MacCormack, C. F. Kemerer, and B. Crandall, "Software Development Worldwide: The State of the Practices," *IEEE Software* 20, no. 6 (November–December 2003): 28–34.

K. E. Emam and N. H. Madhavji, *Elements of Software Process Assessment and Improvement* (Los Alamitos, CA: IEEE Computer Society, 1999).

M. Fowler and K. Scott, *UML Distilled*, 2nd ed. (Reading, MA: Addison-Wesley, 1999).

T. Gilb, *Principles of Software Engineering Management* (Reading, MA: Addison-Wesley Longman, 1989).

——"Rule-Based Design Reviews," *Software Quality Professional* 7, no. 1 (December 2004): 4–13.

T. Gilb and K. Gilb, *Evolutionary Project Management and Product Development*. Unfinished book manuscript at http://www.result-planning.com, October 2004.

F. Guerrero and Y. Eterovic, "Adapting the SW-CMM in a Small IT Organization," *IEEE Software* (July/August 2004): 29–35.

W. S. Humphrey, *Managing the Software Process* (Reading, MA: Addison-Wesley, 1989).

——*A Discipline for Software Engineering* (Reading, MA: Addison-Wesley, 1995).

——*Introduction to the Personal Software Process* (Reading, MA: Addison-Wesley, 1997).

International Standards Organization (ISO), www.iso.org.

I. Jacobson, G. Booch, and J. Rumbaugh, *The Unified Software Development Process* (Reading, MA: Addison-Wesley Longman, 1999).

P. Kruchten, *The Rational Unified Process*, 3rd ed. (Reading, MA: Addison-Wesley, 2003).

A. MacCormack, "Product-Development Practices That Work: How Internet Companies Build Software," *MIT Sloan Management Review* (Winter 2001): 75–83.

L. Osterweil, "Software Processes Are Software Too," Proceedings of 9th International Conference on Software Engineering (April 1987): 2–13.

M. C. Paulk, C. V. Weber, B. Curtis, and M. B. Chrissis, "Capability Maturity Model for Software, Version 1 1," Software Engineering Institute, CMU/SEI–93-TR-24, DTIC Number ADA263404, February 1993.

R. S. Pressman, *Software Engineering: A Practitioner's Approach*, 6th ed. (New York: McGraw-Hill, 2005).

W. W. Royce, "Managing the Development of Large-Scale Software Systems," *Proceedings of IEEE WESCON*, August 1970.

J. Rumbaugh, I. Jacobson, and G. Booch, *The Unified Modeling Language Reference Manual* (Reading, MA: Addison-Wesley, 1998).

Software Engineering Institute (SEI), www.sei.cmu.edu.

J. Wood and D. Silver, *Joint Application Development*, 2nd ed. (New York: John Wiley, 1995).

CHAPTER 5

New and Emerging Process Methodologies

OBJECTIVES

- Understand the limitations of traditional process methodologies and the applicability of Agile processes.
- Understand the basic tenets of Agile software processes.
- Gain familiarity with several commonly used Agile processes.

5.1   What Are Agile Processes?

Agile processes are a family of software development methodologies that produce software in short iterations and allow for greater changes in design. It should be noted at the outset that not all the Agile process characteristics are new and revolutionary. Many are derived from years of experiences and are similar to the iterative and incremental process discussed in Chapter 4. Because software development is still very labor intensive, the Agile methodologies also focus upon the human and team aspects of software development.

A strong consensus among many proponents of Agile methodologies has been formed around the Agile Manifesto, presented in **Figure 5.1**. Additional information can be found at http://www.agilemanifesto.org.

Although there is no absolute definition about what constitutes an Agile method, there are several characteristics shared by most Agile methods. Unfortunately, a process is sometimes labeled Agile simply because the author states it to be so. The following is a list of characteristics and methods that depict Agile methods:

- *Short releases and iterations:* Divide the work into small pieces. Release the software to the customer as often as possible.
- *Incremental design:* Don't try to complete the design up front because not enough is known early about the system anyway. Delay design decisions as much as possible, and improve the existing design when more knowledge is acquired.
- *User involvement:* Rather than trying to produce formal, complete, immutable standards at the beginning, ask the users involved with the project to provide constant feedback. This usually leads to a better-suited system.
- *Minimal documentation:* Do only the necessary amount of documentation, which is just a means to an end. The source code is a big part of the actual documentation.
- *Informal communication:* Maintain constant communication, but not necessarily through formal documents. People communicate better informally. This approach works as long as understanding is achieved.
- *Change:* Assume that the requirements and environment will change, and try to find good ways to deal with this fact.

We are uncovering better ways of developing software by doing it and helping others do it. Through this work we have come to value

Individuals and interactions over processes and tools

Working software over comprehensive documentation

Customer collaboration over contract negotiation

Responding to change over following a plan

That is, while there is value in the items on the right, we value the items on the left more.

Figure 5.1 The Agile Manifesto.

When following this interesting and flexible approach, it is important to ensure that no one abuses the methodology, particularly the one associated with documentation. Clearly, enough documentation must be available if the released software needs to be maintained by a group different from the original developers.

5.2   Why Agile Processes?

Although traditional software processes have been applied with much success to some projects, they usually have some or more of the following problems:

- *Lengthy development times:* With traditional development methods, project lengths ranging from one to five years are not uncommon. For many companies, especially small- or medium-sized ones, this is definitely too long and not appropriate. A large number of small businesses may exist for only one year or less. In three years, many more companies will have changed their main focus or products. Even if the project is successful by traditional standards, it may be too late.
- *Inability to cope with changing requirements:* In most fields, the environment changes very rapidly, forcing the business to adapt and change. Most software development projects will have to deal with many requirement changes. Traditional software development methods do not handle changing requirements well. They assume that the later a change is made, the more expensive it will be.
- *Assumption that requirements are completely understood before the project begins:* This is an often unstated assumption for many traditional methods. Although for some projects it is realistic, for many more it is not. Most users are not capable of expressing their requirements in clear and unambiguous language. In many cases, they are not even sure of what they want. In spite of the valiant efforts of many systems analysts, the requirements will be incomplete, and many times incorrect.
- *Too much reliance on heroic developer effort:* Unfortunately, too many software projects depend on extra development effort to finish on time. Unless the team is extremely motivated, group members cannot sustain these efforts for too long. After a certain point, productivity declines, leading to even longer hours.
- *Complex methodology:* Most traditional methodologies provide detailed specifications of activities and work products. Such specifications can be daunting. For example, Rational Unified Process (RUP) contains more than 100 work products and 30 roles. Understanding the methodology is time consuming, and most practitioners cannot afford to become methodology experts.
- *Waste/duplication of effort:* Much documentation is mandated, including documentation that may or may not be needed. Much information is maintained in several forms, and much care is needed to keep it synchronized. For example, detailed design may be kept as Unified Modeling Language (UML) diagrams and as source code. Changes to the code may imply a need to also make changes to UML diagrams, which means the work has to be done twice. There is the risk of the information not being synchronized (e.g., the UML diagram having different classes than the code). Keeping all the artifacts synchronized requires a sophisticated configuration management system. Tool support can minimize this duplication, allowing you to keep and modify the information once, and generate the different views.

Agile development methods hold the potential promise to develop software in smaller iterations, guaranteeing there is a finished product at all times, and demanding only normal effort from their developers. Agile methods are extremely good at dealing with change, which means requirements do not need to be completely specified from the beginning. While most of the success stories come from small- to medium-sized software projects, we believe that many parts of the Agile methodologies and processes hold high potential for large projects as well.

5.3   Some Process Methodologies

This section will provide a better idea of what Agile process development methodologies look like. We believe no particular methodology will be applicable to all projects and all organizations, and thus the decision process needs to take into consideration the characteristics of the project as well as the organizational culture.

We do not endorse any particular methodology and believe there are many more Agile methodologies deserving study. Because space considerations restricted the number of methodologies we could focus on here, we chose a representative sample. From the traditional Agile methodologies we have chosen Extreme Programming (XP), which is the most popular, and the Crystal family of methodologies. The Unified Process is one of the most popular and important frameworks in software engineering today, and we discuss how it can be used within an Agile context. We also introduce the popular Scrum process. Finally, we briefly discuss open source software development and highlight the similarities with Agile development. Interested readers can obtain more information on these and other Agile development methods through the Suggested Readings section at the end of this chapter.

5.3.1   Extreme Programming (XP)

Extreme Programming, usually abbreviated as XP, is one of the first and better-known Agile development methodologies. It was first used by Kent Beck for the C3 project at (previously known) Chrysler Corporation. Using small teams working in the same room to encourage communication, XP proposes that only the strictly necessary documentation is created, with the code and unit tests serving as documentation. This section will use many of the terminologies from XP, some of which may appear a bit awkward at first. The core values of XP can be summarized as follows:

- Frequent communication between team members and with the customer.
- Simplicity in design and code.
- Feedback at many different levels. Unit tests and continuous integration provide feedback to the individual developer, or pair of developers. Also, small iterations provide customer feedback.
- Courage to implement hard but necessary decisions. One possible decision is to not use XP, if it does not seem appropriate for the project.

In addition, XP follows five fundamental principles that embody the core values:

1. *Rapid feedback:* Use pair programming, unit testing, integration, and short iterations and releases.

2. *Simplicity:* Try the simplest possible approach. Don't worry too much about considering cases that may or may not occur in the future.

3. *Incremental change:* Don't try to make big changes; try small changes that add up. This is applied to design via refactoring, planning, and team composition as well as the adoption of XP itself. Code refactoring is a form of code modification to improve the structure of the code.

4. *Embracing change:* Try to preserve options for the future while actually solving your most pressing problems. Delay decisions that commit you to a path until the latest possible moment.

5. *Quality work:* Try to create as good a product as possible. Do the best work all the time. This is assumed to be a natural tendency for most programmers, and it is encouraged by many of the practices.

XP also proposes several less-central principles: (1) ongoing learning; (2) small initial investment; (3) playing to win; (4) concrete experiments; (5) open, honest communication; (6) working with people's instincts, not against them; (7) accepting responsibility; (8) local adaptation; (9) traveling light; and (10) honest measurement.

Most of the time, the initial introduction to XP is through the 12 key practices of XP methodology. Each may be expanded into a lengthy discussion, but only one of the practices—planning—will be discussed in detail later in this section as an illustration. However, they can be briefly summarized as follows:

1. *Planning:* Quickly determine the features to be included in the next release, using a combination of business priorities and technical estimates. We discuss more about XP planning later in this section.

2. *Short releases:* Try to get a working system quickly, and then release new versions in a very short cycle. Typical release times for XP are two to four weeks. After a release, the customer runs its tests to see whether the new features actually work and provides immediate feedback to the team. New detailed plans are made for the next release.

3. *Metaphor:* Instead of a formal architecture, use a metaphor as a simple common vision of how the whole system works. It is simple, so everybody understands it and can use it to guide their design. However, this is easier said than done. Design styles and metaphors are difficult to come up with.

4. *Simple design:* Try to keep the design of the system as simple as possible. Eliminate unnecessary complexity as soon as you discover it. Do not complicate the design based on things that might be needed in the future, but choose the simplest solution that works now. The design may be changed in the future, if necessary.

5. *Test-driven development:* Ensure that testing is done continuously and is automated as much as possible. Write unit tests for all code. In certain situations, test-first development is actually performed. Write the tests before you write the actual code. Keep running the tests all the time. Ask customers to write functional acceptance tests to verify when the features are finished. Continue to keep these tests running after they run the first time.

6. *Design improvement (refactoring):* Practice refactoring, which involves a restructuring of the system without changing its behavior, aiming to remove duplication, improve communication, and simplify or add needed flexibility. Because developers have unit tests, and continuous integration is practiced, there can be relative confidence that the system behavior has not changed. The design is not completed all at once in the beginning, but it is modified when needed and improved over time.

7. *Pair programming:* Ensure that all production code is written with two programmers working at the same machine or facility. This is the revision step taken to the extreme. All code is always reviewed by at least one other person. Although pair programming does not always sound appealing at first (because two people are required to do the same job), the improvements in quality usually more than compensate for the small decrease in productivity. Imagine writing a program with another person. It is quite embarrassing to write "ugly" code, slack off, or avoid the tests, because a partner is always present. Also, the design and code has to be understandable, or the partner may not easily follow the design and the code and will complain.

8. *Collective ownership:* Establish ownership of the code by the whole team. Anyone can change any piece of code in the system at any time. Because unit test is emphasized along with continuous integration, you can be relatively confident that the changes do not destabilize other pieces of the system.

9. *Continuous integration:* Integrate the system and build it many times a day, every time a task is completed. This way, the development organization always has a working system and can detect integration errors immediately. The assumption is that the system builds are not like the large software projects that may take half a day to a whole day to complete.

10. *Sustainable pace:* Work only at a pace you can sustain; 40 hours a week is reasonable. As a rule, never work overtime 2 weeks in a row. If a developer constantly needs overtime, then the original estimate is not correct and the plan may need to be adjusted. Also, keep in mind that programming is a difficult intellectual activity. If a person constantly works overtime, his or her productivity decreases, resulting in accomplishing less work in more time. A fatigued mind also creates more mistakes.

11. *On-site customer:* Include a real customer on the team, always available to answer questions. This allows development to work without a completely prespecified set of requirements. The chance of project success increases dramatically for those fortunate projects that have full commitment from consumers.

12. *Coding standards:* Ask all programmers to write all code following the same set of rules, created to facilitate communication through the code. Developers are to work in pairs with other programmers in the team, and team members are going to be modifying other people's code. There needs to be a coding standard that is abided by all. The particular standard is not that important; most choices are about equally good. The important thing is for everybody to use the same rules.

These practices are not all equally easy to follow. For example, it is very difficult to have a full-time user or customer committed to be on-site for answering requirements-related questions. These customers or users usually have their own work responsibilities and may not always be available. Working no more than 40 hours a week is another difficult practice to follow without very enlightened management.

We will discuss planning, the first of the 12 practices, in some detail next as an example.

Planning   Planning is clearly important in any process. In XP, programmers plan only the immediate next iteration in detail, and changes to the plan can be made during the iteration if necessary. The basic assumption in XP is that there are four variables that can be adjusted in a project: (1) scope, (2) cost, (3) quality, and (4) time. Often, the easiest one to adjust is scope, and it is frequently the one that is changed.

During the planning period, many decisions must be made concerning the project. Trade-offs have to be weighed, and adjustments have to be made. XP methodology differentiates the decisions that should be made by business and by technical people. Business people and customers decide on the following:

- *Scope:* What needs to be done in order for the system to be useful?
- *Priorities:* What are the characteristics of certain features, and how should they be prioritized?
- *Release scope:* What needs to be included in each release?
- *Release dates:* What are the important dates to release the software or specific components of the software?

The technical staff must make decisions on the following:

- *Estimates:* How long will each feature take?
- *Consequences:* What are the best choices related to technology issues and programming language? Note that here the decisions may be made jointly with business people, after certain trade-offs are made and the cost consequence is understood.
- *Process:* How are the work activities performed? How is the team organized?

In XP, the traditional planning sessions are called the planning game. Within this process, release planning is a vital activity performed before each software release to decide what is to be included in that release. There is also an activity called iteration planning, which is performed within the iteration. There are typically several iterations per release.

Functionality requirements are defined through stories, which play a similar role as features or use cases in other methodologies. Stories are typically written on actual pieces of paper or story cards. XP proponents believe that using physical cards helps in several ways, although the stories may be put into a computer later. The actual cards can be passed around and rearranged as needed.

The goal of the planning game is to maximize the value of the software produced. The players include development personnel and customers, and the artifacts are story cards. The strategy is to invest as little as possible to get the most valuable functionality as quickly as possible. There are three phases in the planning game:

1. *Exploration:* Find out what the system can do with several so-called moves. The moves include writing a story, which is done by business personnel. Another move is to estimate a story, which is done by development personnel who come up with an ideal engineering time estimate. The estimate does not take into account many items and assumes no interruptions, meetings, vacations, and so on. A third move is to split a story if development cannot provide an estimate or if business decides a specific piece is more important than others.

2. *Commitment:* Business chooses the scope and date of the next release and development commits to delivering it. Here the moves include business sorting the stories by value into three categories: essential, important, and nice-to-have functional requirements or stories. Development performs the sorting of stories by risk, again into three categories: those that can be precisely estimated, those that can be estimated reasonably well, and those that cannot be estimated. Development also sets what is called the velocity, which is the ratio of ideal time to calendar time. Finally, the business chooses scope, which is the business requirements expressed on story cards. This is done through setting a release date and choosing only those story cards that would fit, or by choosing the story cards and recalculating the dates.

3. *Steering:* The plan is updated in the steering phase, which consists of several moves or activities. The first move is at the iteration level, in which business chooses an iteration's worth of story cards. The completion of the first iteration should result in a software system that performs some amount of functions. Recovery is another move. During this phase, if development realizes it has miscalculated the schedule velocity, it can ask business to reprioritize the requirements of story cards. A new story may be introduced if business realizes it needs a new story in the middle of a release. A new story may replace an existing story or stories with equivalent effort. Reestimate is a move, or an activity, in which development can reestimate all the remaining stories and set velocity again, if it feels that the plan needs to be modified.

Within each of the iterations, which are part of a release, the development team internally subdivides the stories into tasks and carries on a similar planning with the tasks. Planning is divided into the following tasks:

- *Exploration:* The moves are to write a task and to split/combine tasks.
- *Commitment:* The moves are to accept a task for which a developer accepts responsibility, to estimate a task and set a load factor in which each developer estimates his or her productivity compared with the ideal engineering time, and to balance the tasks for which programmers add up their tasks and make sure they are not overcommitted.
- *Steering:* This phase includes the following moves: (1) implement a task, (2) record progress status where every couple of days programmers are asked about their task status and remaining workload, (3) recovery where overcommitted programmers may ask for help, and (4) verify story, which is essentially executing the functional tests for the story. The steering phase of the iteration contains some moves that are more than planning. It actually includes performing the tasks and readjusting the plan for the iteration, if necessary.

The descriptions of XP methodology are certainly more granular at the programming level. It seems clear that some of the XP practices would take a very cooperative and mature set of team members and may also present some challenges to project management. For example, paired team programming poses a problem to many managers who have to give individual performance appraisals. The weighing of team effort versus individual accomplishments for an appraisal can be tricky.

5.3.2 The Crystal Family of Methodologies

The Crystal family of methodologies was developed by Alistair Cockburn, who proposed the idea that one methodology cannot be adequate for all projects, and that the methodology needs to be adapted to the project. He provided guidance as to what to adapt and what kinds of practices to use depending on the project.

Cockburn classifies projects according to three factors: (1) their size, which is measured in maximum number of developers; (2) their criticality, which is gauged by the losses that a malfunction would cause; and (3) their priority, which is measured by the time pressure on the project. Note that project size is not measured in lines of code or function points here. Projects with high pressure need methodologies optimized for productivity, whereas other projects may prefer to optimize for traceability at the expense of productivity. Furthermore, the following four levels of criticality as related to quality and complexity of projects are described: (1) life, which are malfunctions that can cause physical harm to a person, or possibly loss of life; (2) essential money, which are malfunctions that may cause loss of money essential for the organization's survival; (3) discretionary money, which are malfunctions that may cause loss of money but are not essential for the organization's survival; and (4) comfort, which are malfunctions that do not cause measurable monetary loss and yet still decrease comfort and pleasure to the users.

Cockburn defines some basic principles for software methodologies and describes how to adapt the methodology to the projects. There are three defined methodologies: Crystal Clear, Crystal Orange, and Crystal Orange Web. Basically the darker the color is, the heavier the methodology would be. But these do not cover the complete range of projects, stopping way short of life-critical or large-scale projects.

Crystal Clear is considered adequate for noncritical projects at the discretionary money level, and for projects that require teams of up to six or eight people. Crystal Orange is considered adequate for critical, but not life-critical, projects that require teams of up to 40 people.

In designing methodologies for the Crystal family, the following underlying methods should be part of the process:

- Use larger methodologies for larger teams.
- Use heavier methodologies for more critical projects.
- Give preference to lighter methodologies, because weight is costly.
- Give preference to interactive, face-to-face communication rather than formal, written documentation.
- Understand that people vary within a team and with time. People tend to be inconsistent. High-discipline processes are harder to adopt and more likely to be abandoned.
- Assume that people want to be good citizens; they can take initiative and communicate informally. Use these characteristics in your project.

In addition, there are seven properties that expand on these principles and provide further guidance, of which the first three are considered extremely important:

1. *Frequent delivery:* Deliver running and tested code to real users as frequently as possible, at least every few months. Here delivery can mean several things. At the highest end, the system is released to the full set of users. A middle ground is to release the software to a limited set of users who will only test the system. The lowest end is allowing only user viewing or a demonstration of the system. At this lowest level, the users may also use the software for a small period of time in a controlled environment.

   The functionality is usually delivered in iterations, which are usually time-boxed, meaning the release date is fixed with the scope features included and changing if necessary. This concept of iterations and frequent releases is very much like the concept proposed in XP.

2. *Reflective improvement:* Before, during, and after the project, stop to think about the process and about what can be improved. Improvements can be tried, even in the middle of a project. Although similar ideas are often mentioned, Crystal is one of the few methodologies to include this explicitly.

   Changing or modifying a process in the middle of the project must be performed with care. The project team must be informed and be ready to alter the process. The positive side is obviously that the current project, rather than future projects, will immediately benefit from the reflective movement.

3. *Close communication:* Encourage close communication among team members. This communication can be informal and, preferably, face-to-face. In Crystal Clear, this property is extended into osmotic communication, which means that information flows into the background hearing of members of the team. Thus they pick up relevant information without conscious effort, as if by osmosis. Hopefully, this also means questions are answered almost immediately without having to spend a lot of effort in seeking the answer. Osmotic communication basically requires that all team members are located in the same room, although it could work if small groups are in separate locations but still in very close proximity.

   The remaining four principles are not considered to be absolute requirements. However, in order to achieve even greater benefits, the following properties should be included.

4. *Personal safety:* Encourage team members to speak up without fear of reprisal. This includes voicing dissatisfaction with some practice or admitting one's ignorance, mistake, or even inability to complete an assignment. This provides psychological security for the team members and enables individuals to give honest feedback.

5. *Focus:* Addresses the issue of minimizing disruptions and being allowed to concentrate on the task at hand. This allows team members to know exactly what the task priorities are and to focus on the high priority ones. Sometimes a few team members may be unable to focus because they are constantly interrupted by other team members who want to take advantage of their special expertise on the methodology, domain, or technology. Usually teams self-adjust; they may deal with this problem by establishing a cone of silence—a special time that is set

aside to allow such experts to focus on their own tasks. Although this may sound elementary, it is often the best designer, coder, or debugger who is also the most approachable person on the team. They are often inundated with other people's problems and thus are unable to perform their own work.

6. *Easy access to expert users:* Make it possible for the team to get rapid feedback from expert users on the product, design, requirements, and any changes. Crystal Clear allows for a few days between the question and the answer. Note that there is a similar property in XP where users are co-located with the developers to provide easy and quick access to answers.

7. *Good technical environment:* Establish an environment that includes automated tests, configuration management, and frequent integration.

The fundamental items that characterize Crystal Clear and Crystal Orange are summarized in **Figure 5.2**.

	Crystal Clear	**Crystal Orange**
Teams	One team, same room.	Different teams for system planning, project monitoring, architecture, technology, functions, infrastructure, and external testing.
Roles/ separate people	At least four people, playing the roles of sponsor, senior designer, programmer, and user. Other roles may be filled by the same people, including project manager, business expert, or requirements gatherer.	Fourteen roles played by different people, including (besides those of Crystal Clear), project manager, sponsor, business expert, architect, design mentor, tester, and UI designer.
Work products	Nine items, including schedule, use cases, design sketches, test cases, and user manuals.	Thirteen items, including those in Crystal Clear plus requirements documents, status reports, UI design documents, and interteam specs. Work products are developed until they are understandable, precise, and stable enough for peer review.
Maximum release length	2 months.	From 2 to 4 months, two user viewings per release.

Figure 5.2 A comparison of Crystal Clear and Crystal Orange methodologies.

There are many characteristics that are common to both Crystal methodologies, and once again, there are multiple similarities with the XP methodology:

- Progress is tracked by software deliveries or by major decisions rather than by written documents.
- There is automated regression testing.
- There is direct user involvement.
- There are two user viewings per release.
- Methodology-tuning workshops are held at the start and middle of each release.
- Policy standards are mandatory but can be substituted by equivalent techniques.
- Coding style, templates, user-interface standards, and so on, are left as local standards to be maintained by the team.
- Techniques related to individual roles are left to the individual.

Crystal Clear and XP share many characteristics, with the main difference between the two being discipline. XP requires strict adherence to design and coding standards, pair programming, refactoring, and 100% running tests. It also relies as little as possible on written documentation. Crystal Clear is designed to tolerate variations among people, requiring a much smaller set of rules.

5.3.3   The Unified Process as Agile

Although the Unified Process is a framework that does not specify particular techniques for all the phases, it is usually considered a heavyweight methodology that often requires most, if not all, the requirements to be obtained at the beginning, during the inception phase. It also requires the architecture and the big design to be completely specified up front, and its popular instantiations, including the Rational Unified Process, mandate too many work products or artifacts.

On the other hand, it is an iterative and incremental process, which is one of the main points of Agile methodologies, and it is designed as a framework, allowing adaptation to local conditions. Also, the framework itself does not require all of the work products. RUP is the first and better-known instantiation of the Unified Process, requiring all the artifacts.

An obvious way to make RUP more in line with Agile methodologies is to restrict the required work products, eliminate or merge some of the roles, and add more customer involvement through the iterations. RUP can also be modified by adding one more level of iterations, repeating all the phases for each iteration. Of course, the devil is in the details. What exactly are we to eliminate from RUP to make it more Agile?

A number of people are actively working on how to combine the best characteristics of RUP and Agile projects, either by making RUP Agile or by adding RUP characteristics to Agile processes. IBM Rational has published several whitepapers and even a special RUP plug-in for XP.

5.3.4   Scrum

Scrum is another Agile development methodology that has demonstrated good results. It is lighter in prescriptions than XP, so it is usually associated with some of the XP practices.

This methodology was first introduced by Takeuchi and Nonaka (1986) based on its successful usage in the manufacturing industries. Many of the terminologies used in Scrum are adopted from the game of rugby. Ken Schwaber used this methodology and later coauthored with Mike Beedle a book titled *Agile Software Development with Scrum.*

The Scrum framework consists of team roles, events, artifacts, and rules. You must use all of these components, bbut might add other techniques or components, as well.

Scrum is an iterative method, and is based on short iterations called *sprints*. Sprints are basic units of development for units of functionalities of the total software product. They are short (one month or less) in duration and time-boxed (their duration is held constant, but scope may be adjusted if needed). Ideally, a potentially shippable product is produced at the end of each sprint.

A Scrum project defines three core roles (and may have other supporting roles) of parties who are vital to the success of the project:

- The *product owner*, who represents the voice of the customer and ensures that the team delivers value to the business
- The *development team*, usually 3 to 10 developers, who actually produce the software
- A *Scrum Master*, who keeps the team on track and ensures Scrum is followed, as a coach but not as a project leader

There are also two additional ancillary roles: the stakeholders and the managers.

Scrum is based on three "pillar" concepts for its success: (1) transparency (making the process visible), (2) inspection (of artifacts and progress), and (3) adaptation (whenever a significant deviation is detected, correct it). An important aspect of transparency is to have a common definition of when an item is completed so developers, the product owner, and the Scrum Master can agree on whether an item is finished.

Scrum Events   The Scrum process may be summarized as a set of sequential activities or events. Scrum defines four events (the sprint itself is not considered an event):

- The *sprint planning meeting*, in which the product owner and the team decide on what will be implemented during that sprint.
- The *daily Scrum*, a short meeting in which team members synchronize, make sure they are on-track, and ask for help if needed. A basic tenet is to keep these meetings very short (15 minutes or less). Oftentimes all participants are standing instead of sitting, to ensure meetings are short.
- The *sprint review*, held at the end of the sprint, to inspect its products and adapt the product backlog if needed. During this review the product owner identifies what has been done and discusses the product backlog. The development team demonstrates the work it has done answers questions, and discusses what went well, what problems they faced, and how they solved them. Finally the entire team collaborates on what to do next (which is input for the sprint planning for the next sprint).
- The *sprint retrospective* is held after the sprint review and on the last day of the sprint in which the team members discuss the sprint results, learn from them, and use those lessons as input for the next sprint planning.

Scrum Artifacts   In any software project, it is important to define the artifacts produced and used to manage that project. Scrum defines the following artifacts to be used for controlling the project:

- The *product backlog*, an ordered list of all the remaining requirements or user stories for a product. The product owner prioritizes and orders the requirements. Everybody can see what still needs to be done overall (although developers focus mostly on the sprint backlog).
- The *sprint backlog* is the ordered list of tasks need to be done for the current sprint. Tasks here are broken down to be small (4 to 16 hours usually), so developers know exactly what to do. Rather than tasks being assigned, developers choose their next task based on the sprint backlog and their particular skills.
- The *increment* is the current project; that is, the sum of all requirements implemented in this sprint and all previous sprints. This should be a shippable (albeit not feature-complete) project.
- The *burn down chart*, which is a frequently updated (daily or more often), publicly displayed chart showing the remaining log in the current sprint backlog.

Scrum is an Agile methodology that has demonstrated good results in many projects; there are currently many organizations using it, improving and adapting it, and combining it with other techniques, such as Kanban. Kanban is a lean and just-in-time methodology initially used in the automotive industry in Japan. Many organizations are now scaling Scrum to bigger projects, having several teams, and holding "Scrum of Scrums" meetings.

5.3.5   Open Source Software Development

In the past few years, open source software development has emerged as a successful model. Such software is made available, usually for free, in executable form, but access to the source is also provided. In addition to access to the source, permission to redistribute and to modify the source is granted. This leads to a situation in which many developers can modify and improve the program.

There are many successful open source programs, including the Apache web server, the most widely used web server program, the Linux and BSD operating systems, and Mozilla, a web browser integrated with other related programs. Mozilla includes a mail program and a page designer that are now also distributed as individual components, with Firefox, the popular web browser. Several popular database servers such as PostgreSQL and MySql, and many Internet infrastructure programs such as Bind, Sendmail, or Postfix are also open source programs.

There is a tremendous variation in open source programs and their development, with some of·them being essentially developed by one corporation such as the MySql product. Others, such as Linux, have strong corporate backing, and some are developed by individuals without any monetary compensation. Other variables include the team sizes, number of people involved, and the length of time the program has been open source. Many programs started as commercial ventures and turned into open source when the business cases presented themselves.

In spite of those differences there are some similarities within the development process of many open source programs and many similarities with Agile methods:

- *Small releases:* In the open source world, the phrase is "release early, release often." Most of the time releases are very frequent, ranging from a few weeks to a few months, and the source is available on the Internet even between releases.
- *Informal, written communication using Internet tools:* Communication is done informally, mostly through bulletin boards and mailing lists. Although it is not face-to-face communication, it is not formal documentation. One advantage of this is that communications are easily archived and disseminated.
- *Customer availability:* For most successful open source projects, the developers are the initial customers. Most programs start with somebody's need to "scratch an itch." That is why most successes are in areas of programming tools and systems infrastructure. A common cause of failure is lack of customer feedback.
- *Continuous integration:* Systems are integrated often, usually through Internet tools.
- *Shared vision:* Successful open source projects usually have strong leadership that promotes a shared vision. For example, Linus Torvalds, the creator of Linux and the closest entity to a maximum authority, has been described as a benevolent dictator who makes most of the architectural decisions. If this vision is not shared, developers abandon the project, or sometimes "fork" it, and start a new branch from the original source code.

Of course, there are many differences between open source projects and most Agile methodologies:

- *Larger teams:* Although the core team for most open source projects is quite small, ranging from one or two people to a few dozen, it is often larger than most Agile teams. Also, many more users and developers provide feedback, and add small changes and features.
- *Distributed teams:* In many cases the team members involved are from various countries or regions, which means that communications are often not synchronous. Most Agile methodologies put the team in the same room.
- *Scaling:* Some successful open source projects have achieved massive scale. The Linux kernel, for example, contains several million lines of C code. Most Agile projects are of a much smaller scale.

There are other factors affecting the success of open source projects, including the programmers' expertise. Most of these successful projects include exceptionally skilled and motivated programmers. Many of these programmers work for free, obtaining satisfaction from intangibles. Surprisingly, this actually increases their motivation.

There is still much to be learned about open source development methods, including a wide assessment of what would make them successful. We can see that the successful ones share certain characteristics, but we do not know how many other projects with the same characteristics have been unsuccessful. It appears that open source development

Table 5.1 Summary of the More Recent Methodologies and Processes

Method	Main Points	Agility	Discipline
XP	Most popular Agile process. Requires high discipline and adherence to principles and practices. Based on 4 core values (communication, simplicity, feedback, courage), 5 fundamental principles (rapid feedback, simplicity, incremental change, embracing change, quality work), and 12 practices.	High	High
Crystal Clear	Extremely light in methodologies. Does not require adherence to all principles. Based on 7 principles: frequent delivery, reflective improvement, close communication, personal safety, focus, easy access to expert users, and a good technical environment. Will only work for small projects and teams.	High	Low
Crystal Orange	A heavier methodology than Crystal Clear and suitable for larger projects. It has different teams for different functions. Still not suitable for large or life-critical projects.	Medium	Medium
Scrum	A disciplined methodology that can be adapted and combined with other techniques. It provides clear visibility to the project status and, in the long run, reduces the effort spent on project management.	High	High
RUP	Framework, usually instantiated as a very heavy process. Can be pared down to a relatively Agile process. Covered in depth in Chapter 4.	Low to medium	High

methods will become more important in the future, especially as many of their techniques become better understood and adapted into more mainstream methodologies.

5.3.6   Summary of Processes

This chapter has focused on several processes, most of them related to Agile methodologies. **Table 5.1** summarizes the processes covered in this chapter.

In the next section we will discuss how to choose a process for a project, and provide some direction in choosing methodologies and process.

Table 5.2 compares the main characteristics of each kind of process.

5.4   Choosing a Process

We firmly believe that there is no process that can fit all projects. The process needs to be adjusted to the project, to the organizational culture, and to the people participating in it. Both Agile and traditional processes can be used successfully for many projects.

A problem that frequently occurs when deciding which kind of process to use is that there are many variations within each class and even within methodologies. Both the Unified Process (UP) is actually a frameworks that can, and should, be adapted to better suit the project. The Rational Unified Process, described in Chapter 4, is an instantiation

Table 5.2 Characteristics of Agile Versus Traditional Processes

	Agile	Trad...
Requirements	Assumes they will change; requirements are collected informally at the beginning of the project, and then at the beginning of each iteration. Uses constant user interaction instead of formal requirements.	Assu... proj... me... ch... in...
Design	Informal and iterative.	
User involvement	Crucial, frequent, throughout the whole process.	(accept...
Documentation	Minimal, only what is necessary; relies on source code as the ultimate documentation.	Usually requires heavy, formal docu... of every phase of the project.
Communication	Done informally, throughout the project.	Relies mainly on documents and formal memos and meetings.
Process complexity	Relatively low; initial description contains less than 200 pages.	High. RUP (in 2002) describes more than 100 artifacts, 9 disciplines, 30 roles, and 4 phases.
Overhead	Low.	Relatively high, although it can be scaled down for smaller projects.

of the UP that also recognizes the need for adapting the project. XP, and most of the Agile methodologies, also recognize this need. Local adaptation is one of the XP tenets. When a success or failure is reported on projects using XP or other Agile methods, it is necessary to verify which pieces of the Agile methods were used.

5.4.1 Projects and Environments Better Suited for Each Kind of Process

Table 5.3 compares the kinds of projects and environments better suited for each kind of methodology, using XP as an example of an Agile process and RUP as an example of a traditional one. It is assumed here that the methodologies will be used unchanged rather than in piecemeal fashion.

5.4.2 Main Risks and Disadvantages of Agile Processes

Earlier in this chapter we discussed some of the problems with traditional development methodologies. We have described several Agile methodologies and how they address these shortcomings. The following disadvantages are related to Agile processes:

- *Possibly not scalable:* Agile processes have been utilized by relatively small teams, and are not able to scale without losing some, or a lot, of their agility. Many projects are too big or too critical to be developed with Agile methods; nevertheless, many of the Agile practices and ideas can be incorporated into traditional methodologies.

jects for Agile Versus Traditional Processes

	Agile (XP)	Traditional (RUP)
/size	Small; limited to 1 team of up to 10 people.	Better suited to larger projects; scales up to the largest projects; can be scaled down for smaller projects.
Criticality	Relatively low; not suitable for life-critical systems without adaptation.	Can be used for mission-critical systems (maybe with minimal modifications).
People	More suitable for team players, "good citizens" who can do design and programming adequately. XP requires strict adherence to certain practices.	Defines many roles, which can be appropriate for most kinds of people; doesn't require tight team playing; almost any personality will work, as long as the team member can follow rules.
Company culture	Better suited for small co-located companies with relaxed cultures.	Better suited for larger companies with possibly geographically remote sites and more formal cultures.
Stability	Copes easily with changes in requirements or environment.	Less suited to cope with changes. Assumes a relatively stable environment where requirements don't change much. Can be adapted.

- *Heavy reliance on teamwork:* Not all people are able to work well in teams. Often, one bad member can destroy the cohesiveness of the entire team. Agile methods rely on informal communication and team dynamics much more than traditional ones.
- *Reliance on frequent access to customer:* Agile methods need frequent feedback from the customer, the on-site customer in XP, and the small releases with feedback from customers. This level of constant customer feedback will simply not work when a team is set to develop a large enterprise application such as PeopleSoft or SAP. In these large industry-wide applications, multiple industry experts across a span of 10 to 20 companies are involved in the requirements process. Because these interactions with the customers are not free, they have to be well planned and coordinated ahead of time. Not all customers are willing or able to provide this level of cooperation and feedback. Without customer feedback, Agile methods are not able to validate requirements or adapt to change. Traditional methodologies concentrate the feedback at the beginning of the process during the requirements phase and at the end of the process during the acceptance tests phase.
- *Cultural clash:* Many XP practices clash with accepted software engineering wisdom, or with common management techniques. Performance evaluations, for example, are harder to perform in XP because the work is done in pairs, and the code is owned by the whole team.

5.4.3 Main Advantages of Agile Processes

There are some distinct advantages to adopting Agile processes. The most commonly mentioned ones are as follows:

- *Low process complexity:* The processes themselves are simple, which allows them to be easily understood and implemented.

- *Low cost and overhead:* The processes mandate very few activities that do not directly produce software.
- *Efficient handling of changes:* The processes are designed with the assumption that requirements will change, and the methodology is prepared for these changes.
- *Fast results:* Most Agile processes have fast iterations and produce a core system that can be used in a relatively short time. The system will then be improved and more functionality added as the project progresses. Given that the processes have low overhead, they also tend to produce final results faster. It is made for continuous integration.
- *Usable systems:* Because the customer is involved and the process deals well with changes, chances are the final product will be what the customers actually want when the project is completed rather than what was originally planned as requirements.

5.5 Summary

In this chapter we have covered some of the principles underlying Agile methodologies as well as several specific methodologies. We have also compared Agile methods with more traditional ones, specifically RUP.

We believe that processes and methodologies have to be adjusted for each project and have presented some of Cockburn's ideas about how to do so. A software engineer must know about many different methodologies to be able to adopt specific techniques that may be useful to his or her particular project.

5.6 Review Questions

1. List the four core values of XP.

2. List five XP practices.

3. What factors does the Crystal family consider when choosing a methodology?

4. Explain some of the characteristics of Agile methodologies.

5. Explain the main aspects that open source development shares with Agile methods.

6. Compare and contrast Agile and traditional methods.

7. Agile methods prefer working programs over comprehensive documentation. (True/False)

8. Agile methods prefer rigid processes over adapting to the people. (True/False)

9. What is test-driven programming, and which Agile process advocates it?

5.7 Exercises

1. As a class project or just for experience, try pair programming. Get in touch with a person you would like to work with, and agree to complete this project *only* as a

pair. After doing so, analyze your experience. Was the software better than if you had written it alone? Did it take more time than if you had done it alone?

2. As a class project or on your own, try test-driven programming. Try to write test cases before you write the code, and make sure all your cases run all the time. Chapter 10 provides more information about unit testing and test-driven development.

3. Consider a large, industry-specific product such as a hospital management system for a group of hospitals. Discuss the pros and cons of using Agile methodologies versus a traditional process where more rigid planning and documentation are required. Focus on issues such as project size, team size, continuing multiple releases over the years, expanding the product for an international market, and worldwide customer support.

5.8   Suggested Readings

P. Abrahamsson, O. Salo, J. Ronkainen, and J. Warsta, "Agile Software Development Methods: Review and Analysis," VTT Publication #478, http://www.vtt.fi/inf/pdf/publications/2002/P478.pdf, accessed January 2013.

K. Beck, *Extreme Programming Explained: Embrace Change* (Reading, MA: Addison-Wesley, 1999).

A. Cockburn, *Agile Software Development* (Reading, MA: Addison-Wesley, 2001).

——"Just in Time Methodology Construction," http://alistair.cockburn.us/just-in-time+methodology+construction, accessed September 2012.

L. Mathiassen, O. K. Ngwenyama, and I. Aean, "Managing Change in Software Process Improvement," *IEEE Software* (November/December 2005): 84–91.

G. Pollice, "Using the IBM Rational Unified Process for Small Projects: Expanding Upon Extreme Programming," http://ftp.software.ibm.com/software/rational/web/whitepapers/2003/tp.183.pdf, accessed September 2012.

E. S. Raymond, "The Cathedral and the Bazaar," http://www.catb.org/~esr/writings/cathedral-bazaar/, accessed February 2005.

K. Schwaber and M. Beedle, *Agile Software Development with Scrum* (Prentice Hall, 2002).

H. Takeuchi and I. Nonaka, "The New New Product Development Game," *Harvard Business Review* (January 1986): 137–146.

CHAPTER 6

Requirements Engineering

OBJECTIVES

- Define requirements engineering.
- Discuss the steps of requirements engineering.
- Describe the details of what to do and how to perform the tasks within each step in requirements engineering.
- Analyze several graphical languages that are used during requirements engineering such as data flow diagrams, use cases, and entity-relationship diagrams.

6.1   Requirements Processing

Requirements form a set of statements that describe the user's needs and desires. In developing a software system, these requirements must be clearly and fully understood by the software engineers who develop the software system. However, we often find requirements that encroach on the "how" part and enter into the realm of solution design. Although we should try to limit the requirements to the "what," it is not always that clear-cut.

> **Requirements**   The statements that describe what the software system should be but not how it is to be constructed.
>
> **Requirements engineering**   A set of activities related to the development and agreement of the final set of requirement specifications.

One of the top reasons for software project failures is incomplete requirement specifications, as discussed in Chapter 3. At the same time, one of the important reasons for project success may be attributed to clear requirements statements. The significance of user requirements is now well appreciated. Managing requirements and user involvement is emerging as a key task in software development, regardless of the software development process model.

The following **requirements engineering** activities are involved in a software project:

- Elicitation
- Documentation and definition
- Specification
- Prototyping
- Analysis
- Review and validation
- Agreement and acceptance

Not all of these activities involving requirements are needed to the same degree for all software projects. How much and when these activities are practiced and in what sequence is the central theme of this chapter.

6.1.1   Preparing for Requirements Processing

The first step to requirements gathering and requirements engineering is to ensure that all the preparations are made and that the requirements engineering activities are planned. The requirements solicitors and the providers must both understand and agree to a process whether the underlying structure follows an Agile and flexible approach or a more traditional and rigorous one. A set of preparations, such as those shown in **Figure 6.1**, must be performed.

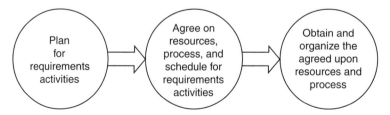

Figure 6.1 Preparation for requirements engineering.

One must first put together a plan for requirements engineering. The plan should include the following:

- Process (for requirements engineering) to be used
- Resources needed
- Schedule for completing the requirements activities

Depending on the size and complexity of the project, the plan itself may take several hours to several days or weeks to develop.

Once the plan is drawn, it must be reviewed and agreed upon by all parties involved. This agreement and commitment to the plan is extremely important because requirements are not just an imagination of the software designer or developer. The users and customers must be involved because requirements represent their needs and desires. Management must also be involved because resources are required to perform the activities. The management from both the users' side and the software development side must be willing to commit the resources. Finally, the schedule for the requirements engineering activities must be reviewed and agreed upon by all participants. There have been situations where prototype development, reviews, and changes to the user interface requirement alone have taken such a significant portion of the software development resources and schedule that the project was doomed for a later schedule crunch and cost over-run. It is sometimes advisable for requirements engineering to keep a fairly open and flexible schedule. Most of the large enterprises today are experienced enough to understand that complex projects need to have good requirements, and thus requirements engineering itself may be a costly and lengthy effort that should be addressed separately from the rest of the software project.

After the plan is agreed upon, the resources—from experienced analysts to the required prototyping tools—must be acquired and brought on board. Finding qualified requirements analysts may be a time-consuming effort, for a good requirements analyst must possess multiple talents such as communication skills, special industry skills, and technical skills. The people involved must also be properly trained on the tools and the process that will be used in the requirements engineering activities.

For most large software projects, the preparation effort, which may be viewed as satisfying the entrance criteria for requirements engineering activities, is important and vital to the success of the rest of the software project.

6.1.2   Requirements Engineering Process

Once the preparation for requirements engineering is completed, the actual requirements development may commence. There are many different steps within requirements engineering. It is essential to ensure that the planned and agreed-upon requirements engineering process is clear to all participants. **Figure 6.2** is an example of a common requirements engineering process.

The process begins with requirements analysts performing the elicitation and gathering of requirements from the users and customers. The gathered information is then analyzed. During the analysis step, the various requirements statements are checked for accuracy and conflict, categorized, and prioritized. Even though there is an arrow from

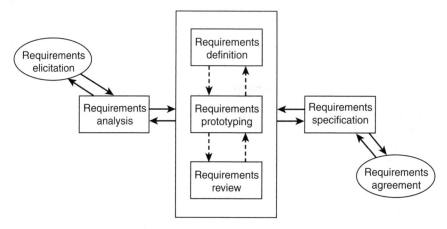

Figure 6.2 A requirements engineering process.

requirements analysis back to requirements elicitation, there is usually very little opportunity to continue going back because of the scarce availability of the users who provide
the requirements information. The analyzed material is then processed through three
potential subactivities.

1. Requirements definition and documentation
2. Requirements prototyping
3. Requirements review

Clearly, the analyzed requirements must be properly defined and documented. If necessary, some of the requirements, especially the user-interface aspects, need to be prototyped. In large systems, this effort itself may resemble a mini development project. The
defined and documented requirements statements and the prototyped user interfaces
must be reviewed by the users. The users must commit their time and people during the
requirements elicitation and review periods. These three substeps may iterate among
themselves and also with the analysis step. The iterations must be properly managed, or
it will turn into a vicious cycle of schedule and resource consumption.

The last two steps of the requirements engineering in Figure 6.2 involve the delivery
of a finalized requirements specification document. This document must be agreed
upon and will serve as the contract between the customer and the software development organization. Once the requirements specifications are agreed upon, they become
the baseline. Thereafter, any modification or change request needs to be controlled and
managed through a change control process to prevent the infamous project scope-
creeping problem, where the project slowly grows in size without anyone's detection.
Requirements scope-creep may happen any time during the software development
cycle and is one of the worst causes of schedule and cost overrun.

How many of the activities shown in Figure 6.2 need to be performed depend on
the specific software project. Recently, some of the Agile software developers have
mistakenly abandoned a large segment of requirements engineering. On the con-

trary, Agile processes actually recognize the difficulty with requirements changes and requirements gathering and advocate constant interactions with users to ensure that the requirements are interpreted correctly. The mistake of not taking the time and effort to gather and understand requirements can be costly, and it is not advisable for many good reasons. The following examples of negative consequences that occur if requirements engineering is not performed illustrate the positive reasons to perform requirements engineering:

- There are no documented requirements to base testing on.
- There are no agreed-upon requirements to control scope-creep.
- There are no documented requirements to base the customer training or customer support activities on.
- It is very difficult to manage project schedule and cost without clear and documented requirements.

It is thus clear that it is extremely unwise to base software development without any requirements engineering activities.

At the other end of the spectrum are the excessive costs of efforts devoted to prototypes, reviews, the creation of voluminous documents, and other bureaucratic and wasteful activities. There are, however, times when the requirements analyst is asked to develop a requirements specification for the purpose of producing a document called a request for proposal (RFP) for inviting software development bids from many different software suppliers. In the case of creating an RFP, requirements analysts are often found to err on the side of overengineering. Most of the time, we need to be performing somewhere between these two extreme ends of the spectrum.

6.2   Requirements Elicitation and Gathering

Many software engineers start their careers in coding, designing, or testing a software system. Only a few of them become requirements analysts after they have acquired some business and industry domain knowledge. The majority of requirements analysts come from the business side with good industry domain knowledge and good communication skills. Some experienced user/customer support personnel have also progressed to attain the position of requirements analyst. Both communication skills and industry domain knowledge are important in eliciting user requirements. Communication skills are needed because users/customers do not always know how to state their needs (Tsui 2004). The requirements analyst must be a good listener and interpreter. It is also essential that the analyst possesses industry domain knowledge because each industry often has its own unique terminology. For example, the medical and health industry has a vocabulary that is distinctively different from that of the aerospace industry or the financial industry. In order for requirements analysts to function successfully and be able to properly solicit requirements, they must be well experienced in the specific industry.

Users and customers are often intimately involved in the development of software and are continually clarifying the requirements, as we saw in Chapter 5, where Agile processes were discussed. This mode of operation has worked well for small software projects. However, it is impractical to expect the users and customers to be in constant communication with the developers for large, complex, and lengthy software projects. We will always need the experienced, subject matter expert requirements analysts for large projects because of the limited availability of the knowledgeable users.

There are two levels of requirements elicitation. At the high level, the requirements analyst must probe and understand the business rationale and justification for the software or the software project. At the low level, the requirements analyst must elicit and gather the details of the users' needs and desires. In either case the requirements analysts must be prepared to conduct the elicitation and gathering. They must have a set of organized questions to ask the users. The actual elicitation may be conducted in several modes:

- Verbal
- Written (preformatted form)
- Online form

Both written and online forms force the requirements analyst to have thought through the questions and enforce some discipline in the preparation. However, asking users to fill in preformatted forms can be too rigid. Thus a verbal follow-up is highly recommended. The personal and direct contact with the users will often trigger good follow-up questions and will also allow users to expand on their input. Throughout all the elicitation and gathering process, the requirements analyst must be patient, listen carefully, and ask for more information when needed—vital skills during this phase. Listening is especially difficult for some requirements analysts, who tend to be more outgoing and assertive.

The requirements analyst should also gather existing information that is available in the business process document, business and technical policy document, previous system manuals, and so on. The requirements for the new software or software project can often be clarified and explained by information gathered in the past. Reading and analyzing existing documentation is another necessary skill that requirements analysts should possess.

6.2.1   Eliciting High-Level Requirements

At the high level, the requirements analyst will need to seek out the management and executives who sponsored the software project to understand the business rationale behind it. The business rationale translates into requirements in the form of constraints on the software product and software project. The category of information that contributes to this high-level business profile includes the following:

- Opportunity/needs
- Justification
- Scope
- Major constraint
- Major functionality
- Success factor
- User characteristics

Opportunity and needs state what high-level problems the software suppliers have been brought in to address. This is usually a business-oriented problem rather than a purely technical problem. For example, the customer may have too high an inventory or may be losing 50% of customer orders due to poorly managed paper documents. To solve the problem, the customer needs a solution that may or may not include software but will usually involve a cost. In order to justify the solution and the cost, there must be some type of business payback. The requirements analyst in our inventory problem example needs to find out how high the inventory is. The customer may state that there is $2 million of extra inventory, and that is too high for them. The customer may also state that their customer orders need to increase by 30% above the current number. These all translate to justifications for the software project that is about to be commissioned by the customer.

The customer may have other issues and problems but states that the aforementioned inventory and customer orders are the two top problems that need to be solved as soon as possible. These statements establish the limits and scope of the software project. In this case, inventory control and order processing are the scope and become the areas for major requirements.

The requirements analyst must also understand any major constraints. One of the major ones is likely to be the allotted budget for the software project. The project budget is usually proportional to the business problem—in our example, the $2 million in excess inventory. Information on budget constraints is important when detailed requirements are being prioritized, and it contributes to the decision process of what is needed versus what is nice to have. Another major business constraint is the schedule. Although business executives understand that systems cannot be built overnight, their needs are always immediate. The implications of schedule constraints and the actual schedule must be clear to the requirements analyst.

It is vital to have a list of what the customer and the business executives perceive as the major functionality the new software will be delivering. In the inventory and order processing example, the major functionality to be delivered may be as follows:

- Improved inventory control via automating order and shipping processing
- Online customer order
- Online delivery/shipping control

Although more-detailed functional requirements must be elicited, these high-level statements put the proper customer expectations in place. They also facilitate high-level scoping of the software project and direct the requirements-gathering attention to the proper area of the business.

The success factor of the software project goes back to the opportunity and needs that were stated earlier. The software project, upon completion, must resolve the problems stated in the opportunity and needs. In this example, it must be able to reduce the inventory carried to less than before. It must also not lose customer orders. Furthermore, if these goals must be met within the next year, then the software system must be completed far before next year to allow time for training the users and for actual usage of the system by the customer, who must have time to utilize the system long enough to experience any of the benefits. The requirements analyst must be able to translate this into a schedule requirement that the system must be up and running by a certain date.

Oftentimes, the executives and paying customers are not necessarily the day-to-day users of the system. The success of the system depends heavily on how well these users are trained. Thus it is imperative to gather and analyze a user profile, which should include the person's job title and formal responsibilities, job activities, education and experience levels, and technical competence.

These high-level business-related requirements are essential to the overall success of the software project, and they can be used as a source for formulating the high-level project goals. The requirements analyst should turn these high-level requirements into high-level goals during the later analysis stage, and then have them reviewed and agreed upon by all constituents. Even when a few detailed requirements may be misplaced, the project is often deemed a success if the high-level business goals are met.

6.2.2   Eliciting Detailed Requirements

Once the high-level requirements are gathered, the detailed requirements must be elicited. During this activity, some of the more technically savvy requirements analysts should be brought in. While the requirements discussions should, in principle, stay above the actual implementation and only address what is needed, often the users will venture into a discussion of how to solve a particular problem. If a software system already exists, the users will often base their discussion of requirements on that currently existing system. Often during these requirements-gathering engagements, both the requirements analyst and the users may enter into imaginative and technical conversations.

Again, as in high-level requirements solicitation, there needs to be preplanned information that should be elicited. At the detailed level, it is so easy to engage in a lengthy discussion on a specific topic and lose control. There are six main categories of information that must be addressed, shown in **Figure 6.3**, as dimensions of requirements.

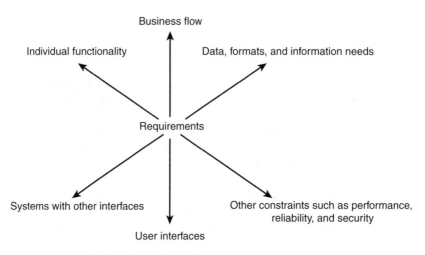

Figure 6.3 The six dimensions of requirements.

Individual functionality is the most obvious group and is usually the natural starting point of requirements elicitation. The requirements analyst is asking the users and customers what their problems are in terms of what functions need to be performed. For example, a functionality need for a payroll area may be initially stated as "there is a need to provide direct deposit payroll to the financial institution of the user's choice." In this case, direct deposit is a functionality requirement.

Functionality by itself is not enough; it must be explained in the context of the business flow or in the context of how the users' perform their tasks. For example, a functionality such as online purchasing needs to be described in the context of specific goods such as airline tickets. This same online purchasing functionality placed in the business flow context of purchasing corporate equities may require a slightly different set of steps. Thus business flow is an important category of information that must be gathered at the detail-requirements information level. This is similar to the notion of developing **use cases** in object-oriented methodology where the functionalities are performed by actors within some business context called a scenario; see Schneider and Winters (1998) for more details on use cases.

> **Use case**   A sequence of actions that a system should perform within the business flow context of the user or the actor.

Another category of requirements that must be collected at the detail level is the information pertaining to data and data formats. At the minimum, there must be some discussion of the application's input and output data. What is the information that needs to be entered into the system and for what purpose? If the entered data follow some business process flow, then that flow should also be described. If there are data that serve as input for some processing, those must also be described. For example, in payroll processing, the federal and state tax rules may be bought in a file form. These tax rules, as a purchased input file, still need to be described. The output data provide additional information and come in several forms. One is the result of a query. The format of the query response must be defined. The other is a report. Each report format needs to be clearly defined. In addition to these application data, there is the application system's information such as error messages or warning messages. Included in this last category of application system's information is the help text. There should be a statement of how much help text is needed. This description of data touches upon the next category, user interfaces.

How the input and output of a software system is presented falls in the domain of user interfaces. Today's software interfaces are mostly graphical in nature. Still, different users have their unique preferences. For example, both radio button and drop-down window may be used for logical "exclusive-or" types of choices, and the users' personal or business preferences may dictate one versus the other. Thus the requirements statements must be clear on the icons used for the interfaces. The flow of the software application is also a user interface, and it usually mimics that of the business flow. However, there are times the software needs to purposely differ from the existing business flow because the software system is meant to improve the current business process. The user interface requirements, both the look and the flow, are often captured by prototyping the interface. The users are then asked to review and comment on the prototyped interfaces.

Besides interfaces with users, there are other interfaces such as those with an existing application or to a network system. These interfaces must be clearly identified. In many situations, the existing system interface already has many clients tied to it. In such cases, the requirement statements should not only describe the interface but also indicate the likelihood of future changes. There are several dimensions to such an interface:

- Transfer of control (evocation of the interface)
- Transfer of data (directly or through a database)
- Receipt of responses (success or failure, error types and messages)
- Retry capabilities

The most often forgotten portion of the interface is the description of errors and error messages along with the respective recovery and retry methodologies.

The last group of requirements addresses issues such as reliability, performance, security, and adaptability. This category serves as a catchall group and acts as a prompter for all the nonfunctional requirements that are important to the software project. In large transaction-oriented applications, it is imperative that a performance requirement on transaction rate be specified. In life-threatening applications, the reliability and the availability parameters must be defined in the requirement statements. Availability addresses the system being up, and reliability addresses the issue of it functioning properly without defect and according to specification. In large financial applications or communications applications, the protection of the data and the protection of the transmission of the data are of paramount significance. For these applications, the requirement statements must address the issue of security. Each of these requirements or constraints on the software may be applied to a deeper and more specific level. For example, the requirements statement may specify an acceptable response time of a user query of product choices in a web-based retail application. There may be other constraints such as transportability or maintainability that should all be described in this category. In addition, there may be requirements related to the software project rather than to the product. The customer may request that the software be written in a certain programming language or with a certain tool because the customer is considering future modification of or support of the software product themselves.

6.3   Requirements Analysis

Even after the requirements are elicited and collected, they are still just an unorganized set of data. They must still be analyzed. The analysis of the requirements consists of two main tasks:

1. Categorizing or clustering the requirements
2. Prioritizing the requirements

There are many ways to categorize requirements. In clustering and grouping requirements, it is important to look for consistency and completeness. We will discuss several approaches to analysis and categorization of requirements. The methodologies all evolve around business and usage flow.

6.3.1   Requirements Analysis and Clustering by Business Flow

The requirements may be grouped in many ways. One of them is, in fact, categorizing them by priority, which will be discussed later. A natural clustering of requirements may follow the six dimensions of requirements that were discussed earlier:

1. Individual functionality
2. Business flow

3. Data, formats, and information needs
4. User interfaces
5. Interfaces with other systems
6. Constraints such as performance, reliability, and security

These categories are not always mutually exclusive. At times there may be some overlap. For example, under the category of constraints, there may be a requirement addressing reliability in the form of back-up recovery speed. In the individual functionality group there may be a requirement describing the need for back-up recovery function. During the analysis time, an overlap such as this example must be clarified so that there is no duplication. Each requirement must be labeled so that it is uniquely identifiable and traceable. A simple categorization scheme may be devised for the six-dimensionality by utilizing a prefix and a number as shown in **Table 6.1**.

The prefix identifies the category or the dimension of the requirements. When analyzing the requirements, it is best to start with the business flow category. Pick a business flow first. Assign it the first number, such as BF-1, then associate all the functionality requirements and number them IF-1.*x*. The additional *x* may be used if there is more than one functionality related to the workflow. In Table 6.1, there are three functionality requirements, IF-1.1, IF-1.2, and IF-1.3, related to the business flow, BF-1. The data and their respective data formats related to BF-1 are numbered the same way with DF-1.*x*. There are two data requirements related to BF-1 in the table, and there are two user-interface requirements related to BF-1. There is one system interface requirement and an additional constraint requirement related to BF-1. The numbering scheme of all categories is tied to business flow.

Given a business flow, BF-*n*, there may not be a requirement in the other five categories related to this business flow. For example, there may not be any further constraint. In that case there will not be an FC-*n*. A particular requirement in some nonbusiness flow category, such as a data requirement, may belong to more than one business flow requirement. That is, there may be a DF that is related to two business flows, BF-*x* and BF-*y*. The question is whether this DF should be labeled as DF-*x* or as DF-*y*. During the analysis of requirements, we have to determine which one of the two business flows uses the data for its primary purpose. The DF will take on the number of the BF that utilizes it for its primary purpose. In the event the DF is equally important to both business flows, then it will take on the number of the business flow that first utilizes it. The requirements analysis methodology here is based on clustering the five categories of requirements around the business

Table 6.1 Requirements Categorization Scheme

Requirement Area	Prefix	Requirement Statement Numbering
Individual functionality	IF	IF-1.1, IF-1.2, IF-1.3, IF-2.1
Business flow	BF	BF-1, BF-2
Data and data format	DF	DF-1.1, DF-1.2, DF-2.1
User interface	UI	UI-1.1, UI-1.2, UI-2.1
Interface to systems	IS	IS-1
Further constraints	FC	FC-1

flow requirements. The obvious question is what we should do if we have a requirement that does not easily fit any business flow. One way is to have a designated null business flow and have all the "misfit" requirements grouped with the null business flow. The numbering scheme is just a way to make the association of five categories of requirements to each business flow. Thus business flow must be included in the discussion during the requirements elicitation stage. Otherwise, these five categories of requirements will be grouped by some artificial or conjectured business flow. This methodology of keying on business flow as the principle requirement is similar to the object-oriented use case methodology.

6.3.2   Requirements Analysis and Clustering with Object-Oriented Use Cases

Object-oriented (OO) use cases are utilized to describe the requirements of a system. They are also used for the analysis of requirements and contribute to the design and testing of the system. A use case is fundamentally a depiction of the following requirement information:

- Basic functionality
- Any precondition for the functionality
- Flow of events, called a scenario, for the functionality
- Any postcondition for the functionality
- Any error condition and alternative flow

In developing OO use cases, the requirements elicitation and analysis are mingled together. Once the information is collected, the requirements analysis portion has several steps, starting with identification of system boundaries.

The term *system* here means the product that is to be developed may include both hardware and software. The identification of system boundaries starts with the delineation of what is included and excluded from the system but may still be needed for interfacing with the system.

OO utilizes the word *actors*—an unusual term that refers to all external interfaces with the system. **Figure 6.4** presents a graphical representation of an actor. The modeling language used by OO, as stated in Chapter 4, is Unified Modeling Language (UML). The actor

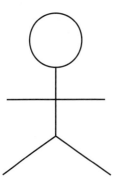

Figure 6.4 A graphical representation of an actor in Object Oriented terminology.

symbol of a human stick figure is just a part of the UML notation. A copy of UML may be obtained from the Object Management Group, which is a nonprofit computer industry consortium (see the Suggested Readings section at the end of this chapter).

Examples of actors include users of the system, other systems, hardware, network, and operators. Each actor takes on a certain role with regard to interfacing with the system. To identify these actors, which are external to the system but interface with it, the requirements analyst should ask the following questions:

- Who uses the system?
- Who operates and maintains the system?
- What other systems use this system?
- What other systems are used by this system?

Some examples of actors may be the user of an order shipping system and an external system that interfaces with it. They might be described as follows:

- *Shipping clerk:* A user of the system who packages the customer-ordered items, places ship-to address labels, ships the ordered items, and tracks the delivery of the ordered items.
- *Customer order system:* An external system that processes customer orders and provides customer order information to the order shipping system.

After identifying the external system, the next step in the use-case analysis is to identify all the activities related to each of the actors. These activities are the things that the actors want the system to perform and become the use cases. Thus each actor is related to a set of use cases. The listing of the use cases is the process of identifying what is inside the system. That is, the use cases will define the requirements of what the system must perform. An example from the order shipping system use case described at a high level would be as follows:

- *Shipping label processing:* Upon request from the shipping clerk, process the ship-to address from the customer order system database and print the delivery address on the special label.
- *Shipping item list processing:* Upon request of the shipping clerk, the ordered items list is processed from the customer order system database and printed out in duplicate copies, one to be included in the customer package and the other kept as a record.

We can group the order shipping system requirements with its use cases and actors using UML notation, as shown in **Figure 6.5**. Note that the two actors, shipping clerk and customer order system, are depicted by the human stick figures, and they are outside of the rectangular box. The two earlier described requirements as use case statements, shipping label processing, and shipping item list processing, are depicted as oval-shaped figures inside the rectangle. The rectangle represents the system. In this case, the rectangle represents the shipping system. The boundaries of the rectangle stand for the shipping system boundaries. While the use cases are depicted at a high-level form in Figure 6.5, the details of each use case may be further specified in a separate form with additional UML notations. We will not go into the details of the UML notations here. We

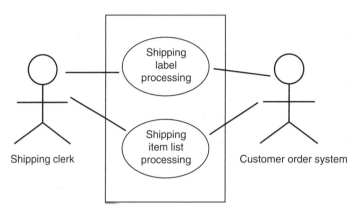

Figure 6.5 Use-case notation in UML.

have demonstrated how the requirements can be stated in use-case form, grouped, and related to the actors.

During the requirements analysis phase, we might ask further questions about the system boundary. For instance, in processing shipping labels, should the shipping clerk also worry about the weight and the resulting shipping cost? If so, is weighing the items a manual step to be handled by the shipping clerk outside of the order shipping system, or should the order shipping system include an automatic weight calculation and cost computation functionality? Performing system boundary analysis as a part of the requirements analysis can further improve and firm up the completeness of requirements.

In OO use-case methodology, the steps of identifying the following factors serve as a good requirements analysis methodology:

- Actors
- Related use cases
- Boundary conditions

Even though use cases are further expanded on later with details on preconditions, postconditions, activity flows, alternate paths, and error processing to help the design of the system, the use cases specified during the requirements phase describe only what the system needs.

6.3.3   Requirements Analysis and Clustering by Viewpoint-Oriented Requirements Definition

Viewpoint-oriented requirements definition (**VORD**) is a requirement analysis method based on the understanding that requirements are not viewed the same by all the different stakeholders. The customers who pay for the system often have a different perspective on requirements than those who interface with the system on a daily basis. For a large, complex system that has many subcomponents, the different users will articulate the requirements with varied emphasis and diverse

> **Viewpoint-Oriented Requirements Definition (VORD)**   Both a requirements elicitation and a requirements analysis methodology.

specifics. For example, with today's large enterprise resource planning (ERP) systems, there are several major components including financial, human resource, planning, and inventory. The financial person using the system will provide requirements with the financial lingo and an emphasis on finance. The human resource person will have another perspective, using the human resource terminology and having a bias toward human resources.

Sometimes the same requirement is stated in such different forms and context that they seem to be different requirements. Other times, the different requirements overlap so much that they should be reorganized and combined in a totally different way. The key is that there are many stakeholder viewpoints to the requirements. The disparate viewpoints often result in distinctly different perspectives of the same problem and they are used to help categorize and structure the requirements. The VORD methodology is divided into four steps:

1. Identify the stakeholders and the viewpoints.
2. Structure and categorize the view points, eliminating duplication and placing common ones together.
3. Refine the identified viewpoints.
4. Map the viewpoints to the system and the services that the system is to provide.

For more extensive descriptions and details on VORD, see Sommerville (2004) and Sommerville and Sawyer (1997).

6.3.4   Requirements Analysis and Prioritization

Categorizing and clustering requirements is only a part of an analysis that enables us to identify inconsistencies across groups of requirements and possible incompleteness in requirements. An additional problem is that many times all the identified requirements cannot be developed and delivered due to constraints such as the following:

- Limited resources
- Limited time
- Limited technical capabilities

As a part of the requirements analysis tasks, we need to prioritize the requirements so that the higher priority ones are developed and released to the customers first. Often a multirelease software product is planned out over several quarters or even years by prioritized requirements. Establishing the priority of the requirements may be based on many criteria, including the following:

- Current customer demands
- Competition and current market condition
- Future customer needs
- Immediate sales advantage
- Critical problems in the existing product

The requirements analysts usually perform the prioritization task with the help of many other people in the organization. Sometimes the customers and industry experts are also brought into the prioritization discussions. Much of the software requirements prioritization is performed with experienced people and customers using an informal

Requirement Number	Brief Requirement Description	Requirement Source	Requirement Priority*	Requirement Status
1	One-page query must respond in less than 1 second	A major account marketing representative	Priority 1	Accepted for this release
2	Help text must be field sensitive	Large account users	Priority 2	Postponed for next release

*Priority may be 1, 2, 3, or 4, with 1 being the highest.

Figure 6.6 Requirements prioritization list.

approach where the most persuasive or vocal people can bias the priorities of their favorite requirements. Although this approach is not perfect, it is far better than not prioritizing and trying to include everything. A typical requirements prioritization list is shown in **Figure 6.6**.

A requirements priority list is more like a table and includes multiple columns of information. It starts with a requirements number, then a brief description of the requirement itself is provided. The source of the requirement is important for the planners. The assessed requirement priority, along with the source of that requirement, contribute to the decision of whether a particular requirement is included in the current release, next release, or some future release. This informal approach is frequently used, but often produces suboptimal results.

A more methodical approach is to pair the requirements and compare their values in pairs, as proposed by Karlsson and Ryan (1997). This approach, called the analytical hierarchy process (AHP), places more rigor into the requirements prioritization process and is often bypassed by the more marketing-oriented people. Each requirement is compared with each of the other requirements in a pairwise fashion. An "intensity value" is assigned to this relationship. The requirement with the highest overall intensity values will essentially be the highest priority requirement. The requirement with the next highest overall relative intensity value will be the next highest priority requirement and so on. An example of AHP will clarify this approach.

Consider the situation where there are three requirements, R1, R2, and R3. The scale, or intensity value, for comparing the pairs of requirements is set from 1 through 9. Given a pair of requirements, (x, y), the intensity value is considered to be 1 if x is deemed to be of equal value to y. It is 2 if x is a little more valuable than y and so on until 9, where x is deemed to be extremely more valuable than y. For our example, consider the matrix shown in **Table 6.2** as the representation of the pairwise value.

In this example, requirement 1 is equal in value to itself; thus the intensity value is 1 for the (Req1, Req1) pair. Requirement 1 is deemed three times more valuable than requirement 2, and the intensity value for the (Req1, Req2) pair in row 1 column 2 is 3.

Table 6.2 A Pairwise Comparison Matrix

	Req1	Req2	Req3
Req1	1	3	5
Req2	1/3	1	1/2
Req3	1/5	2	1

Table 6.3 A Normalized Pairwise Comparison Matrix

	Req1	Req2	Req3
Req1	.65	.5	.77
Req2	.22	.17	.08
Req3	.13	.33	.15

Requirement 1 is valued at five times that of requirement 3 as the table shows. When we visit the pair (Req2, Req1), the value is just the reciprocal of that of the pair (Req1, Req2) as shown in row 2 column 1. The intensity value is 1/3, which is the reciprocal of 3.

We next calculate the sum of each column in Table 6.2 and then divide each element in the column in Table 6.2 by the sum of that column. The resulting normalized matrix is represented in **Table 6.3**.

We now sum up each of the rows. The sum of row 1, representing requirement 1, in the normalized table is 1.92. The sum of row 2 is 0.47 and the sum of row 3 is 0.61. Because there are three requirements in all, each of the row sums will be divided by 3. The results are 1.92/3 = 0.64 for requirement 1, 0.46/3 = 0.15 for requirement 2, and 0.61/3 = 0.20 for requirement 3. These three values for the three requirements now represent the relative values of the requirements. That is, requirement 1 carries 64% of the total requirements value, requirement 2 carries 15% of the total requirements value, and requirement 3 is worth 20% of the total requirements value. This provides us with a prioritization scheme of requirements with the following weights:

- Requirement 1: 64
- Requirement 3: 20
- Requirement 2: 15

Requirement 1 has the highest priority and the most weight, followed by requirement 3 and then requirement 2. The AHP-based pairwise value prioritization scheme forces us to look at the details of requirements by pairs and may not be practical when we are dealing with tens of thousands of requirements. It is, however, a reasonable scheme for prioritizing a small number of requirements.

The prioritization of requirements may sometimes be considered as a classification scheme, as well. It helps us to classify or prioritize which requirements will be implemented and released when.

6.3.5   Requirements Traceability

Although we have mentioned the need for requirements traceability, we have not elabo-rated on the reason. There are several reasons to ensure that requirements are traceable. The most significant is the ability to track back after development and verify that all requirements have been developed, tested, packaged, and delivered. It is also important to be able to account for anything extra that is not traceable back to the requirements. There should not be any functionalities or properties that are unaccountable. Kotonya and Sommerville (1998) have listed four types of traceability:

1. *Backward from traceability:* Links the requirement to the document source or the person who created it.
2. *Forward from traceability:* Links the requirement to design and implementation.
3. *Backward to traceability:* Links design and implementation back to the require-ments.
4. *Forward to traceability:* Links documents preceding the requirements to the requirements.

In addition, there may be a need to retain information that links related requirements. That is, some requirements may have corequirements or pre- or post-requirement rela-tionships. Requirements relationship matrices may be developed to keep track of the relationships between requirements or relationships to design, and so forth.

The earlier discussion on organizing and prioritizing requirements implied that each requirement must be uniquely identifiable. This unique identification of requirements is also important if the requirements are to be traceable.

6.4   Requirements Definition, Prototyping, and Reviews

Requirements definition, prototyping, and review are represented as three activities in Figure 6.2 that come after requirements analysis. In practice, these activities actually over-lap with requirements analysis and should be looked upon as a set of iterative activities within the broader context of analysis.

Requirements definition involves formally spelling out the requirements. The notation used is often English or English accompanied with other notations. One of the simplest notations for defining requirements in terms of English is the input–process–output approach shown in **Figure 6.7**.

At the writing of this material, the most popular notation in the industry is UML, which was introduced earlier. Another notation that has been popular in graphically depicting

Requirement Number	Input	Process	Output
12: Customer order	• Items by type and quantity • Submit request	• Accept the items and respective quantities	• Display acceptance message • Ask for confirma-tion message

Figure 6.7 An input–process–output diagram.

a system's data flow is the data flow diagram (DFD). This notation was introduced as part of the structured systems analysis techniques in the late 1970s by software engineering pioneers such as DeMarco, Gane, and Sarsen. The entity-relationship (ER) diagram is another popular notation used to show the relationship between entities. It was first introduced as part of the entity-relationship model by Peter Chen in 1976. All of these modeling notations or languages may be used for requirements definition and analysis as well as for design. In fact, the preferred approach is to use the same notation starting at requirements analysis and continuing through the design of the software.

As illustrated in **Figure 6.8**, a data flow diagram is composed of four elements: (1) source or destination of data, (2) flow of data, (3) processing, and (4) data store. A high-level example of using a data flow diagram to depict a customer order system is shown in **Figure 6.9**. In this example, both the source and the destination of the data is the customer. The shipping clerk only receives data. Orders are processed by order processing,

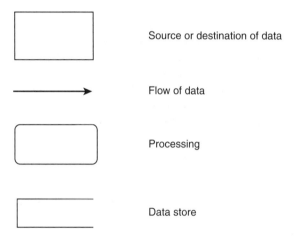

Source or destination of data

Flow of data

Processing

Data store

Figure 6.8 A data flow diagram.

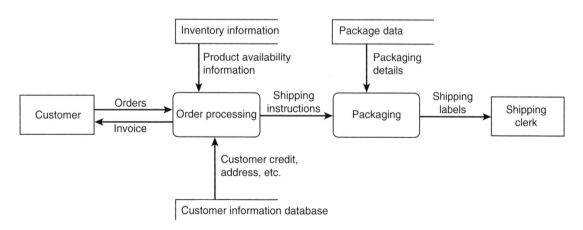

Figure 6.9 An example of a data flow diagram depicting a customer order system.

and shipping instructions are sent to packaging. There are three data stores, which may be currently in paper file form and later converted to databases during the design phase. The data flows are represented with arrows and accompanied by a description of the information that is flowing.

Although the ER diagram is not used to show the flow of information, it is used to depict the relationship among entities. It is also used to show the attributes of the entity. Again, as is the case with a DFD, it is initially used during the requirements analysis phase and kept on through the design phase. An example is shown in **Figure 6.10**, which illustrates the relationship between the objects or entities of author and book. The relationship is that the authors write books. That relationship is shown with a line connecting the two objects and with the word *writes* shown above the line. The relationship may have two constraints:

- Cardinality
- Modality

The cardinality specifies the number of participants. Note that in the requirement shown in this figure an author may write several books, but a book may not have multiple authors. Thus it is somewhat restrictive. An advantage of using well-defined language, such as the ER diagram, is that it is more precise. The restrictive relationship between the authors and the books, as stated in Figure 6.10, should trigger someone to ask if it is in fact correct at a requirements specification review time. The crow's foot represents multiple occurrences. There may be several forms of cardinality:

- One-to-one
- One-to-many
- Many-to-many

An example of a one-to-one relationship may be a diagram that shows people sitting on chairs. Each person sits on only one chair, and each chair may be occupied by only one person. The one-to-many example is already shown in Figure 6.10. A many-to-many relationship can be shown by changing the Figure 6.10 example so that it shows a relationship where an author may write several books and a book may be written by several coauthors.

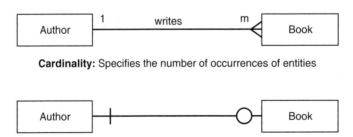

Cardinality: Specifies the number of occurrences of entities

Modality: Specifies the necessities of relationship to exist

Figure 6.10 An entity-relationship diagram.

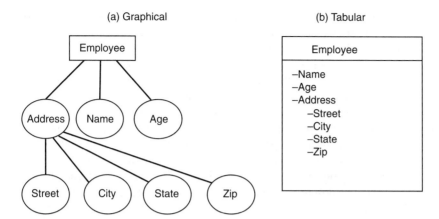

Figure 6.11 Example of an entity and its attributes.

The modality of the relationship specifies whether the existence of an entity depends on its being related to another entity via this relationship. In Figure 6.10, a circle shows that book is optional because there are authors who have not completed any book. However, the vertical bar indicates that author is mandatory in that there is no book without an author. Thus the requirement shown in Figure 6.10 states that books are optional and authors are mandatory in this relationship.

Each of the entities shown in the relationship may have several attributes. During the requirements phase, these attributes are also defined and analyzed. A pictorial example of an entity and its attributes is shown in **Figure 6.11**. The entity, employee, and its attributes are shown in both graphical and tabular forms. The tabular form may add further columns to record, as part of the requirements. As the project moves along into the design phase, the tabular form may be converted into a data dictionary.

Using various modeling languages such as UML, DFD, or ERD to define the requirements is a form of prototyping. In this case, we are prototyping the functional flow, the data flow, or the data attributes. As part of the requirements gathering and analysis, the user interface is a vital component that cannot be forgotten. Here we are not interested in the system internals and the algorithms. Instead, we focus on the users and their interaction with the system. We focus on the main use cases and their interfaces with the users. Two main aspects of user interface must be analyzed during requirements time:

- Visual looks and display
- Interaction with people and flow

In the early days, the user interfaces were modeled with paper boards and flip charts and were known as low-fidelity prototyping. Today, the user interface is prototyped with machine-executable code during requirements gathering and analysis time. These prototypes are sometimes kept and turned into the final release code. One of the earliest tools used for rapid prototyping of the user interface was HyperCard, which runs on Apple computers. Today, one of the most popular tools for quick user interface prototyping is Microsoft's Visual Basic. Also, with the growing popularity of Agile methods, the user-interface requirements are often prototyped with heavy user participation (see Ambler 2004). In addition to visual interfaces, there is a small but growing demand today for audio and video interfaces. For an introduction to Internet video, see Stolarz (2005) and for more details on developing and prototyping good user interfaces see Hix and Hartson (1993) and Shneiderman and Plaisant (2005).

Closely related to requirements analysis and user-interface prototyping is the review of requirements with the users and customers. These reviews may be conducted informally and very frequently as proposed by the Agile methods or they can be more formal in nature. Formal reviews and inspections methodology was first introduced by Michael Fagan of IBM in the early 1970s. Although the target of all those early formal inspections was to reduce design and programming errors, the same inspection process may be used for reviewing requirements in reducing errors and misunderstandings of requirements as early as possible. Most of the practitioners choose a hybrid between the formal inspections and informal reviews. Whichever review technique you choose, it is important to realize that reviewing requirements with users and customers is an essential part of the requirements analysis and prototyping. Catching requirements errors early is of extreme significance in that a single requirement error often expands into multiple design errors, each of which in turn may become a source of several programming errors. Preventing a requirement error from escaping is definitely an economically worthwhile activity.

After reviews are conducted, any modification and correction must be made to the requirements definitions. Sometimes a follow-up review over the modifications and changes is necessary if the extent of corrections is very large. Although it is better not to become overly bureaucratic, these changes must be documented clearly so that a requirement error, as mentioned earlier, does not escape through downstream activities such as design, coding, and testing and end up in the customer release.

6.5   Requirements Specification and Requirements Agreement

Once the requirements have been analyzed and reviewed, it is prudent to put them into a requirements specification document. The amount and extent of detail that must be included in this depends on several parameters:

- Size and complexity of the project
- Subsequent multiple follow-on releases that have been planned
- Estimated and expected number of customer support activities
- Knowledge and experience of the developers in the subject area

The more complex and large the number of requirements, the more there is a need to specify the requirements formally and completely. The more follow-on releases that are planned, the more clearly and orderly the requirements specifications must be to allow for such future activities. If the estimated number of customers is large, perhaps in the millions, then the requirements specification must be detailed and complete so that maintenance and support activities can be performed in an orderly fashion. If the testers, designers, and code developers have very little subject matter knowledge or experience in the application domain area for which the software is being developed, then it is imperative to have a detailed requirements specification document.

IEEE has a recommended standard, guideline 830, for the Software Requirements Specification document that complies with the IEEE/EIA Standard 12207.1-1997. Essentially, the guideline specifies that the following material should be included in a software requirements specification (SRS):

- *Introduction:* Provides an overview by describing the purpose, scope, references, and definitions of terms.
- *High-level description:* Provides a general description of the software product, its major functions, user characteristics, major constraints, and dependencies.
- *Detailed requirements:* The following is provided here: (1) detailed description of each functional requirement by input, process, and output; (2) descriptions of interfaces that include user interfaces, system interfaces, network interfaces, and hardware interfaces; (3) a detailed description of performance requirements; (4) a list of design constraints such as standards or hardware limitations; (5) additional descriptions of attributes such as security, availability, and recoverability; and (6) any additional unique requirements.

A copy of this IEEE guideline may be purchased at the IEEE website listed in the Suggested Readings section.

As the last step of requirements engineering, the requirements specifications document should be "signed off." This may be in a form of a formal document such as a contract, or an informal communication such as an email. Regardless of the final form of sign off, this activity closes the requirements phase and provides a formal baseline for the requirements specifications. Any future changes should be controlled or at least closely monitored to prevent uncontrolled growth and changes of requirements in the future. Uncontrolled requirements changes represent a major problem and are a critical cause for many software project failures, as discussed in Chapter 3.

6.6   Summary

This chapter covered the following major steps of requirements engineering:

- Elicitation
- Documentation and definition
- Specification
- Prototyping
- Analysis
- Review and validation
- Agreement and acceptance

For requirements elicitation, both high-level and detailed information gathering were discussed. More specifically, the following detailed information categories were identified as part of the elicitation process:

- Individual functionality
- Business flow

- Data, formats, and information needs
- User interfaces
- Interfaces with other systems
- Constraints such as performance, reliability, and security

The gathered requirements need to be analyzed through categorization and grouping. Several methodologies, including prioritization techniques, are introduced for grouping the requirements. Also, requirements need to be traceable.

Although English is still the predominant language for documenting the requirements, there are several modeling languages that are used today. These include UML, DFD, and ERD. As part of the requirements analysis cycle, requirements are also prototyped using these modeling languages. Executable prototypes are more popular today, especially with user interfaces. The user and quality reviews of these prototypes and categorized requirements are essential in preventing errors from escaping into later software engineering activities and into the customer release. Thus as many of the requirements as possible should be reviewed.

Finally, a software requirements specification document should be produced and signed off by the customer as a baseline for any future modification.

6.7   Review Questions

1. List and describe at a high level the steps involved in software requirements engineering process.

2. What are the three main items that must be planned prior to conducting requirements engineering?

3. What are the six main dimensions of requirements that you need to address when collecting requirements?

4. List four items that are included in the description of high-level business profile.

5. List and describe three items that you will need to consider when prioritizing requirements.

6. What is the viewpoint-oriented requirements definition method used for?

7. Consider the situation where you have the following four requirements for an employee information system:

    - Response time for short queries must be less then 1 second.

    - In defining employee record, user must be able to enter employee name and be prompted for all the remaining employee attributes that are needed for the employee record.

    - Employee information may be searched using either the employee number or employee's last name.

    - Only an authorized search (by the employee, by managers in his or her chain of command, or human resource department personnel) will show employee salary, benefits, and family information.

Perform an analytical hierarchy process and rank these based on your choices.

8. Explain in an ER diagram the relationship between programmers and modules where a programmer may write several modules and each module may also be written by several programmers.

9. What are the four types of requirements traceability?

6.8   Exercises

1. Discuss why it is important to document the requirements specified; list three reasons.

2. Based on your answer to Exercise 1, discuss how a novice Agile software developer involved in collecting and documenting requirements may misapply the Agile methodology.

3. During analysis of requirements, we often have to categorize and then prioritize items. Discuss why we would need to do these activities.

4. In collecting requirements for an employee information system, the employee is a major entity. What are some of the attributes of this entity that you would consider asking as part of the requirements? Express the entity and attribute in an entity-attribute table. Add an additional column to the table and express the data characteristics for each of the attributes.

5. Using one of the books on UML presented in the Suggested Readings section as a reference, discuss the similarity between use case in UML and business flow in the six dimensions of requirements.

6. What purpose does the final signing off of the requirements specifications document serve? What are the potential problems that may arise if there is no such process?

6.9   Suggested Readings

S. W. Ambler, *The Object Primer: Agile Model Driven Development with UML2*, 3rd ed. (New York: Cambridge University Press, 2004).

P. Chen, "The Entity-Relationship Model—Towards a Unified View of Data," *ACM Transactions on Database Systems* 1 (March 1976): 9–36.

T. DeMarco, *System Analysis and System Specification* (New York: Yourdan Press, 1978).

M. Fagan, "Design and Code Inspections to Reduce Errors in Program Development," *IBM Systems Journal* 15, no. 3 (1976): 182–211.

M. Fowler, *UML Distilled: A Brief Guide to the Standard Object Modeling Language*, 3rd ed. (Reading, MA: Addison-Wesley, 2003).

C. Gane and T. Sarsen, *Structured Systems Analysis: Tools and Techniques* (Upper Saddle River, NJ: Prentice Hall, 1979).

D. Hix and H. R. Hartson, *Developing User Interfaces: Ensuring Usability Through Product and Process* (New York: Wiley, 1993).

IEEE Computer Society, Software Requirements Specifications guideline, which complies with IEEE Recommended Practice for Software Requirements Specification, http://ieeexplore.ieee.org/ie14/5841/15571/00720574.pdf, accessed September 2012.

J. Karlsson and K. Ryan, "A Cost-Value Approach to Prioritizing Requirements," *IEEE Software* (September/October, 1997): 67–74.

G. Kotonya and I. Sommerville, "Requirements Engineering with Viewpoints," *BCS/IEE Software Engineering Journal* 11, no. 1 (January 1996): 5–18.

——*Requirements Engineering: Processes and Techniques* (New York: Wiley, 1998).

D. Leffingwell and D. Widrig, *Managing Software Requirements: A Unified Approach* (Reading, MA: Addison-Wesley, 2000).

M. Mannion et al., "Using Viewpoints to Determine Domain Requirements," In E. J. Braude, *Software Engineering Selected Readings* (Los Alamitos, CA: IEEE, 2000): 149–156.

Object Management Group, Unified Modeling Language, http://www. omg.org.

K. Orr, "Agile Requirements: Opportunity or Oxymoron?" *IEEE Software* 21, no. 3 (May/June 2004): 71–73.

B. Ramesh and M. Jake, "Towards Reference Model for Requirements Traceabiltiy," *IEEE Transactions on Software Engineering* (January 2002): 58–93.

K. Ryan and J. Karlsson, "Prioritizing Software Requirements in an Industrial Setting," *Proceedings of the 19th International Conference on Software Engineering* (1997): 564–565.

G. Schneider and J. P. Winters, *Applying Use Cases: A Practical Guide* (Reading, MA: Addison-Wesley, 1998).

B. Shneiderman and C. Plaisant, *Designing the User Interface: Strategies for Effective Human-Computer Interaction*, 4th ed. (Reading, MA: Addison-Wesley, 2005).

I. Sommerville, *Software Engineering*, 7th ed. (Reading, MA: Addison-Wesley, 2004).

I. Sommerville and P. Sawyer, *Requirements Engineering: A Good Practice Guide* (New York: Wiley, 1997).

D. Stolarz, *Mastering Internet Video: A Guide to Streaming and On-Demand Video* (Reading, MA: Addison-Wesley, 2005).

F. Tsui, *Managing Software Projects* (Sudbury, MA: Jones and Bartlett, 2004).

K. E. Wiegers, *Software Requirements*, 2nd ed. (Redmond, WA: Microsoft Press, 2003).

Design: Architecture and Methodology

7.1   Introduction to Design

Once the requirements of a project are understood, the transformation of requirements into a design begins. This is a difficult step that involves the transformation of a set of intangibles (the requirements) into another set of intangibles (the design). Software design deals with how the software is to be structured—that is, what its components are and how these components are related to each other. For large systems, it usually makes sense to divide the design phases into two parts:

- **Architectural design phase**: This is a high-level overview of the system. The main components are listed, as well as properties external to the components and relationships among components. The functional and nonfunctional requirements along with technical considerations provide most of the drive for the architecture.

- **Detailed design phase**: Components are decomposed to a much finer level of detail. The architecture and the functional requirements drive this phase. The architecture provides general guidance and all functional requirements have to be addressed by at least one module in the detailed design.

> **Architectural design phase**   The period during which the high-level overview of the system is developed.
>
> **Detailed design phase**   The phase in which the architectural components are decomposed to a much finer level of detail.

Figure 7.1 illustrates the relationships among requirements, architecture, and detailed design. Ideally there is a one-to-one mapping between each functional requirement and a module in the detailed design; the influence of the requirements on the architecture is illustrated with the wide arrow; notice in this case the most influential requirements may be nonfunctional requirements such as performance and maintainability. The architecture drives the detailed design, with the mapping being ideally from one architectural component to several detailed modules.

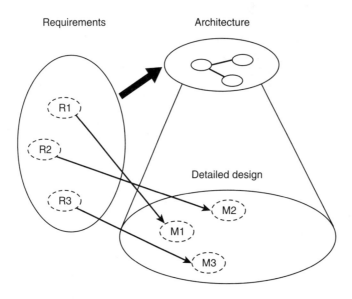

Figure 7.1 The relationships among requirements, architecture, and detailed design.

Smaller systems may get away with not having an explicit architecture, although it is useful in almost all cases. In traditional software processes, the ideal is for the design to be created and documented up to the lowest level of detail possible, with the programmers doing mainly translation of that design into actual code. Agile methodologies and the actual processes followed in many companies, especially for smaller systems, give the programmer a much more important role in the detailed design. In many Agile methodologies, the programmer ends up doing the actual detailed design.

There are many different ways of specifying a design. Given that for most people, pictorial representations of information are useful, it is desirable for a design notation to be graphical. Although many different notations have been proposed, in the last few years the Unified Modeling Language (UML) has gained widespread popularity and is the de facto standard, at least for **object-oriented (OO) design**. This chapter is not dedicated to OO design, but a brief discussion of OO and UML is presented in Section 7.3.3. Here, we will simply state that OO design is a technique that models a design with classes, their relationships, and the interactions among them.

> **Object-oriented design** A technique that models a design with classes, their relationships, and the interactions among them.

7.2 Architectural Design

7.2.1 What Is Software Architecture?

The software architecture of a system specifies its basic structure. In many ways, it is design created at a high level of abstraction. Bass, Clements, and Kazman (2003) define software architecture as follows:

> The software architecture of a program or computing system is the structure or structures of the system, which comprises software elements, the externally visible properties of those elements, and the relationships among them.

There are several important points to note about the architecture of a system:

- Every system has an architecture. Whether you make it explicit or not, whether you document it or not, the system has an architecture.
- There could be more than one structure. For large systems, and even many small ones, there is more than one important way the system is structured. We need to be aware of all those structures, and document them with several views.
- Architecture deals with properties external to each module. At the architecture level, we should think about the important modules and how they interact with other modules. The focus is on the interfaces among modules rather than details concerning the internals of each module.

7.2.2 Views and Viewpoints

An important concept in architectural design, and design in general, is the fact that a system has many different structures (that is, many different ways of being structured) and in order to get the complete picture you need to look at many of those structures.

A view is a representation of a system structure. Although in most situations we can use view and structure interchangeably, keep in mind the structure exists whether you represent it or not, and the view only depicts the structure. This is a distinction similar to the one for a photograph and its subject.

In a seminal paper that later became one of the foundations of the Rational Unified Process (RUP), Kruchten (1995) proposed having four architectural views to represent the requirements for a system and to unify it, plus use cases (which he called *scenarios* in his paper):

- *Logical view:* Represents the object-oriented decomposition of a system—that is, the classes and the relationships among them. In OO, a class is a conceptual element derived and conceived from the requirements. The interaction and the relationships among the classes are often also derived from the business or workflow expressed in the requirements. The notation used is basically that of a UML class diagram.
- *Process view:* Represents the run-time components (processes) and how they communicate with each other.
- *Subsystem decomposition view:* Represents the modules and subsystems, joined with export and import relationships.
- *Physical architecture view:* Represents the mapping of the software to the hardware. This assumes a system that runs on a network of computers and depicts which processes, tasks, and objects are mapped to which nodes.

Bass, Clements, and Kazman (2003) provide examples of more views, and classify them into three categories:

- *Module views:* Represent elements in static software modules and subsystems. Views of these types include the following:
  - Module decomposition views, which represent a part-of hierarchy of modules and submodules;
  - Uses view, which depicts how modules depend on each other; and
  - Class generalization views, representing the inheritance hierarchy of classes. Information represented by UML's class diagrams and Kruchten's logical view will also fall under this category.
- *Run-time views:* Represent the running structure of the program; also called component-and-connectors views. They indicate how executing modules or processes communicate with each other. Views here could be depicted with different graphical diagrams such as communicating process diagrams, client-server diagrams, and concurrency diagrams.
- *Allocation views:* Represent the mapping of software modules to other systems. Typical views of this type include deployment views, which represent the mapping of modules to hardware structures; implementation views, which map the modules to actual source files; and work assignment views, which show the person or team responsible for each module.

An important point to realize is that different views are useful to different stakeholders. For example, an implementation view, showing which modules are implemented on which files, is useful mostly to implementors, whereas a class diagram is useful for many more kinds of stakeholders.

When you are designing an architecture, it is important to keep in mind that there are many different views of it that may be useful; of course there is limited time, so you need to think hard about which views to produce.

7.2.3 Meta-Architectural Knowledge: Styles, Patterns, Tactics, and Reference Architectures

Although many systems have been developed with many different architectures, several architectures share common characteristics at many levels. Software engineers have been comparing system architectures and describing their similarities and differences for quite a long time. Much of this knowledge, sometimes called meta-architectural, has been codified in different ways to provide easier ways of comparing and choosing architectures, and to provide a starting point when creating an architecture.

The software architecture community has codified this kind of knowledge mainly in three different ways:

- Architectural styles or patterns
- Architectural tactics
- Reference architectures

Meta-architectural knowledge serves two main purposes. First, it can be used as a starting point for a particular system's architecture, saving some work and providing guidance for the final architecture. Second, it is an effective communication mechanism for providing a quick idea of the high-level structure of a system. When written in a format similar to design patterns, architectural styles are also called architectural patterns.

Architectural Styles or Patterns   Software architectural styles or patterns are akin to styles in physical building architecture. Just as many buildings share a common style that many people can recognize—from Gothic to Southern U.S. antebellum—many system architectures also have a recognizable style.

Among the most common architectural styles are the following:

- *Pipes-and-filters:* A style widely used for Unix scripts, and for signal processing applications. It consists of a series of processes connected by "pipes." The output of a process serves as the input of the next one; processes do not need to wait until the previous process finishes but can start processing input as soon as some of the input is available. Most of the time the topology is linear, but occasionally there could be forks. Although the most popular application of this style is in combining Unix commands, it is also the conceptual model for many audio and video processing applications. **Figure 7.2** shows a screenshot of gst-editor, an editor for the GStreamer multimedia framework.
- *Event-driven:* A style in which system components react to externally generated events and communicate with other components through events. Modern graphical user interface (GUI) libraries and the programs that use them are organized with this style at some level. Many distributed systems use this style as well, as it allows for decoupling of the components and easy reorganization of the system.

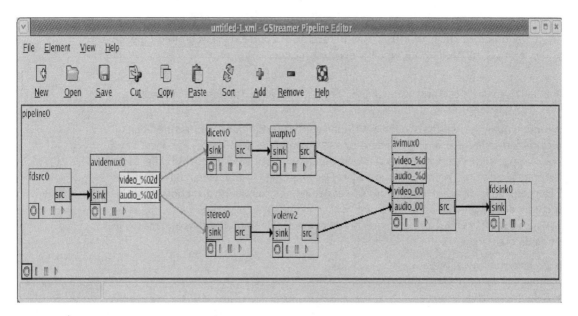

Figure 7.2 Screenshot of the GStreamer editor. A video file is read from a file, then demultiplexed into audio and video streams. Both streams are passed through two different filters, then combined again and saved to another file.

- *Client-server:* A style showing a clear demarcation between clients and servers, which reside on different nodes in a network. Components interact through basic networking protocols or through remote procedure calls (RPC). Usually there will be many clients accessing the same server. **Figure 7.3(a)** shows a client-server architecture, with several clients accessing the same server; Figure 7.3(b) shows a more complicated version, with several different kinds of servers.

  The client-server architecture was heavily influenced by various hardware changes and hardware cost. First, with less powerful terminals or client boxes, many of the processing resided on the server boxes. As the client machines improved in power and dropped in price, more functions were placed in the clients. An interesting side note on this development of placing more functions on the clients or personal desktops is that it created the need to support these clients. A whole profession called IT desktop support became a necessity as a result of the powerful client desktops.

- *Model-view-controller (MVC):* A popular way of organizing GUI programs that need to display several different views of data. The main idea is to separate the data from the display. In the original version a controller took care of translating user input, such as mouse movements and clicks or keystrokes, into appropriate messages for the view. Because modern GUI libraries usually do this, there is no need for a separate controller class. Modern variations of this pattern use just the model and view classes. The model is responsible for storing the data and for notifying the views whenever the data change. The views register with the model, can modify the model, and respond to changes in the model by redrawing themselves. **Figure 7.4** shows a simplified dia-

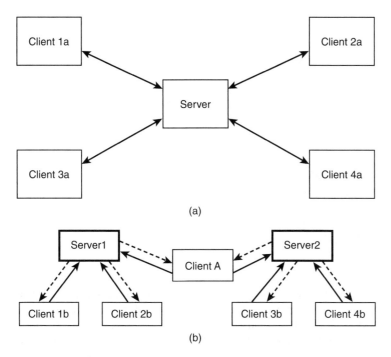

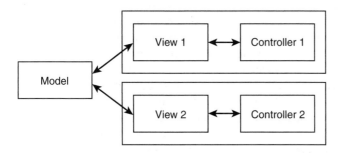

Figure 7.3 (a) Client-server style with one server and many clients. (b) Client-server style with several servers.

gram of an MVC architecture. MVC can be implemented with a client-server architecture with both the view and part of the controller residing on the client box while the model portion resides on the server.

■ *Layered:* A style in which components are grouped into layers, and the components communicate only with other components in the layers immediately above and below their own layer. When the layered architecture is combined with a client-server architecture and the layers may reside in different computers, they are usually called tiers rather than layers. **Figure 7.5** depicts a common layered system, with the Java API

Figure 7.4 Model-view-controller style.

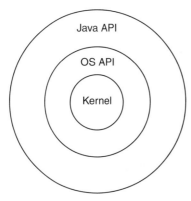

Figure 7.5 A common layered system, with the Java API implementation calling operation system functions, which in turn communicate with kernel functions.

implementation calling operating system functions, which in turn communicate with kernel functions. The Java API calls functions directly through the operating system API, not through the kernel. While layered architecture keeps the components themselves focused on specific tasks and facilitates the detection of problems, it sometimes presents a performance problem in terms of the number of layers a message may have to travel through before being processed.

- *Database-centric:* A style in which a central database and separate programs access the database. The programs communicate only through the database, not directly among themselves. A big advantage of this style is that it introduces a layer of abstraction for the database, which is usually called a database management system (DBMS). A modern DBMS can guarantee many user-defined constraints on any data entered in the database, which allows the programs to assume those constraints; this leads to a relatively coupled system of multiple programs to the database. Rather than building one huge system, you can build several smaller programs. By far the most popular DB technology is that of relational databases. In fact, in most cases, database centric really means relational database centric. Later in this chapter we discuss relational database technologies and database design in more depth.

  The database-centric style is commonly combined with the client-server style, as illustrated in **Figure 7.6**. There is a central database server, running a database management system (DBMS) that is accessible over the network. Programs running on client machines interact with the database server. In the traditional configuration, called two tier, the clients interact directly with the database.

- *Three-tier:* A variation on the database-centric and client-server approaches that adds a middle tier between the clients and servers, implementing much of the business logic. The clients cannot access the database directly and have to go through the middle tier. This way, the business logic gets implemented in one place, simplifying the system.

  For many systems, the business logic is very hard to express with just the kinds of constraints supported by relational DBMS. Although the basic technologies for relational databases are standardized, some more-advanced features, such as stored

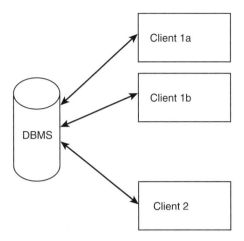

Figure 7.6 The database-centric style. Typically, the clients communicate directly with the database.

procedures and triggers, are not. These features would be needed to implement much of the business logic required for many systems, but implementing them inside the DBMS would mean that we have to keep using that specific DBMS or we would need to port all those triggers and stored procedures to a new DBMS.

The three-tier style is often used as a model for web-based applications. The client machines access an application server through a web browser; the application server implements the business logic and communicates with the database. This kind of architecture can also be viewed as a variation of the MVC architecture, with the database being the model, and the application server implementing the controller and generating the views that will be displayed by the clients with a web browser.

Three-tier architecture may be extended to *n*-tier with additional middle tier servers. **Figure 7.7** illustrates the three-tier architectural style. **Figure 7.8** illustrates a

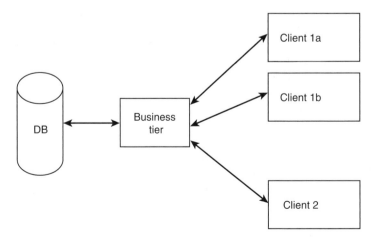

Figure 7.7 A three-tier style, in which clients do not connect directly to the database.

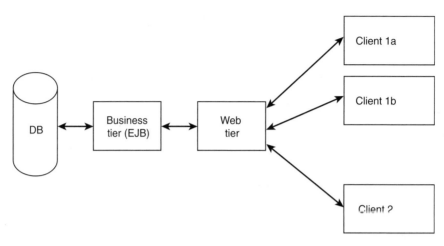

Figure 7.8 The J2EE reference architecture.

specific four-tier architecture, the J2EE reference architecture, which will be discussed later in this section.

Notice that for simplicity, these diagrams illustrate only one application. There may be several applications accessing the same database, in which case we can also view each application as a separate component within the database-centric architecture of the whole system.

Architectural Tactics   Different from styles and patterns, architectural tactics solve smaller problems and do not directly affect the overall structure of the system. They are designed to solve very specific problems for the various architectural styles.

For example, assume that we have a three-tier distributed system, and we want to increase its reliability. Specifically, we are worried about the possibility of some component failing without anybody noticing until something goes really wrong. Thus we try to improve on fault detection. We decide on two possible tactics; in both cases we have another component that is responsible for detecting failures.

The first tactic is to have each component send a message to the fault detector at prescribed intervals. The fault detector knows when it should receive those messages and produces a notification if it does not receive the message within the appropriate time. In distributed systems this is commonly known as a heartbeat.

The second tactic is to have the fault detector send a message to the other component and wait for a response. If it does not receive the response, it knows an error has occurred. This tactic is known as a ping/echo in Internet applications.

Although each specific tactic is applicable only to a limited number of problems, knowing the right tactics can save much time for the software architect. Bass, Clements, and Kazman (2003) provide a small catalog of tactics in their book *Software Architecture in Practice*.

Reference Architectures   A third category of meta-architectural knowledge is that of reference architectures—full-fledged architectures that serve as templates for a whole class of systems. Taylor, Medvidovic, and Dashofy (2009) define reference architecture as "the set of principal design decisions that are simultaneously applicable to multiple related systems, typically within an application domain, with explicitly defined points of variation." Design decisions include all aspects of design, including structure, functional behavior, component interactions, nonfunctional properties, and even some implementation decisions.

7.3   Detailed Design

The architectural design of a system, together with the requirements, need to be refined to produce a detailed design. The development process used determines the level of detail to which the design is decomposed and the level of formality of its documentation. If the design is carried out to the finest level of detail, the implementation task is an almost one-to-one mapping of that design to the implementation language; but often the design is not specified to its finest level, leaving some detailed design tasks to be done in the implementation phase.

7.3.1   Functional Decomposition

Functional decomposition is used mostly in structured programming, but some of the ideas can be used with other programming paradigms. The basic idea is to decompose a function or module into smaller modules, which will be composed together to form the bigger module. Traditionally the modules are other systems or procedures that are called from the main module.

When using object-oriented programming languages, this technique can be used to do the initial decomposition of a system into modules by functionality, or to decompose methods that are particularly hard to implement. Although object-oriented systems and languages receive most of the attention today, there are still many systems that are developed with procedural techniques. In fact, many small web-based applications can be modeled this way, with the system decomposed into functional modules and each module corresponding to one or a few related webpages.

We will illustrate this technique with an example. Suppose you are designing a system for managing course registration and enrollment. The requirements specify four tasks that need to be done: (1) modify and delete students from the database; (2) modify and delete courses from the database; (3) add, modify, and delete sections for a given course; and (4) register and drop students from a section.

Doing a functional decomposition of this system, you would decompose the main module into four submodules for dealing with students, courses, sections, and registration. The first three modules would be decomposed further into modules for adding, modifying, and deleting, while the fourth module would be decomposed into two modules for registering or dropping a student from a section.

The usual process is to produce module decomposition diagrams, where the modules are represented by rectangles, and there is some form of standardized numbering system, with numbers assigned to each module according to their level. The important characteristic of the numbering scheme is that each module gets assigned a unique number, and it is easy to see the level of the module and who its parent is.

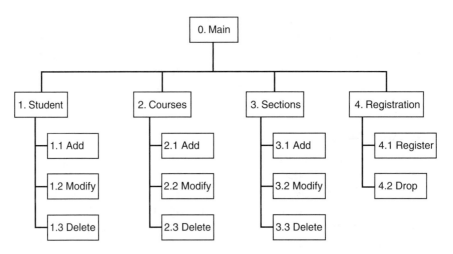

Figure 7.9 A module decomposition diagram for a student registration system.

A module decomposition diagram is presented in **Figure 7.9**. It depicts a simple system partitioning based on externally perceived functionality. Notice that there are usually several different ways to partition the system. For example, we could also partition the same system as shown in **Figure 7.10**, abstracting all the database operations into one specific database module.

In Figure 7.9, the Add, Modify, and Delete functions for the three entities—Students, Courses, and Sections—are uniquely tied to the three respective entities. In Figure 7.10, the design focuses on potential reuse of the three functions. The Add, Modify, and Delete functions are grouped under database common services for potential reuse and multiple

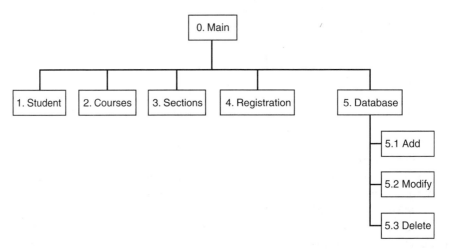

Figure 7.10 An alternative module decomposition with database operations in its own module.

usages. In design, we should not only be concerned with the actual structures but also ask which one is the preferred alternative. Note that in Figure 7.9, the individual entities and their functions serve a single purpose and individually appear very cohesive, while in Figure 7.10 the database common services serve multiple purposes and provide some reuse. However, with common services for reuse, there is a certain amount of coupling introduced among the entities. Which design is a better alternative is a complex topic. This issue of assessing "good" design will be discussed extensively in Chapter 8 where the notion of cohesion and coupling will be better defined and clarified.

7.3.2 Relational Database Design

All reasonably sized applications must handle a large amount of information. Today, we can assume the existence of a convenient database that can be incorporated into the design of any system for information storage and retrieval. We will include a database in our discussion of designing software systems, but not enter into extensive analysis of database technologies.

Most database and business applications use relational database technologies. First proposed by E. F. Codd of IBM in the late 1960s, relational databases are grounded on mathematical concepts of sets and relations and are relatively simple to use and understand. They are also relatively simple to implement and can be implemented efficiently, which has led to their popularity. See the Suggested Readings section for more information on relational databases.

In a relational database, information is stored in tables, also called *relations*. They are two-dimensional sets of data, with rows (also called *tuples*) and columns (also called *attributes*). In the simplest case, each row corresponds to an object or entity in the real world, and columns correspond to attributes of those entities. Relational database theory requires that a set of attributes is identified as the primary key of a table, but most implementations do not have this requirement.

Database design concentrates only on how to represent the data required for the program and how to store it efficiently on a relational database. It can be divided into four phases:

- *Data modeling:* This usually entails creating an entity-relationship (ER) model of the data. The ER model may have been created in the requirements analysis step, as discussed in Chapter 6, but it may still need to be extended and refined.
- *Logical database design:* Taking as input a detailed ER model, a normalized relational schema is produced. The relational schema is a set of tables together with foreign key relationships.
- *Physical database design:* In this step, the main decisions include what data type to use for each attribute and what indexes to create. Sometimes the logical schema is transformed for efficiency (but this should be done with extreme care). The output is a detailed set of structured query language (SQL) statements that implement the logical schema. Sometimes decisions may be made about more low-level issues, such as which relations are stored on which hard drives, although most of the time these decisions are made during deployment and maintenance.

- *Deployment and maintenance:* The final details are ironed out, including where the relations are stored. Not only do the details of the DBMS software used need to be known, but also the specific hardware the system is going to be deployed on needs to be specified. As the system is used, some of these decisions, along with issues dealing with physical design, such as index creation, may be modified to improve performance, reduce space, or reflect changes in hardware or system usage.

Data Modeling   During this phase, a detailed and complete ER model is created. Documentation for the ER model includes an ER diagram, along with annotations for information not reflected on the diagram. The best practices suggest the creation of a data dictionary containing all information pertaining to each attribute.

The requirements documentation may already include an ER diagram that would need to be refined, or a diagram would need to be created from scratch If one does not exist. An ER diagram contains three main types of objects: (1) entities (represented by rectangles), (2) attributes (represented by ovals), and (3) relationships (represented by diamonds). Entities represent objects or things in the real world (or, more precisely, in our mental model of the real world). They have attributes and are related to other entities by relationships. Relationships may also have attributes. In an ER diagram we usually represent entity and relationship types, rather than particular instances of entities or relationships.

Entity types represent the kinds of things we are modeling. Entities have attributes and one or more attributes are marked as the identifier, which will allow us to distinguish among entities of the same type. Weak entities do not have an identifier and are dependent on another entity for their identity.

Attributes are classified as simple or composite and as single-valued or multivalued. Simple attributes are those that do not need to be subdivided further (that is, those that your DBMS supports as primitives), while composite attributes are formed of several parts. For example, if we represent the full name of a person as a string, we consider it a simple attribute. If we divided into first, middle, and last names (as is commonly done in the United States), then it is a composite attribute. Each of the parts (first, middle, last) in this case would be strings, but in other cases they could be composed of several parts themselves.

Most attributes have at most one value. For example, you have one full name (you can divide it into pieces of course), one date of birth, and so on. However, for some other attributes, the same entity can have several values at the same time. Prime examples are email addresses and phone numbers; the same person can have many email addresses or many phone numbers. We call these kinds of attributes multivalued attributes and represent them with a double oval.

It is important to not confuse multivalued attributes with composite attributes. Composite attributes have different parts, while multivalued attributes have a set of values for one entity. It is also important to keep in mind that databases usually keep a snapshot in time of the values rather than full historical information. Basically, the fact that you could change your name does not make it a multivalued attribute; at any given time, you have only one official full name.

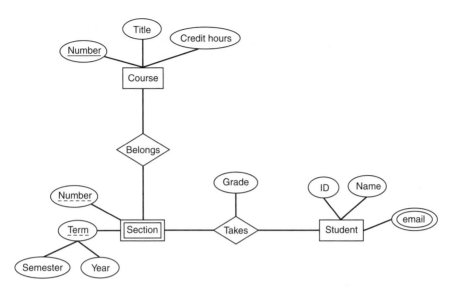

Figure 7.11 An entity-relationship diagram for courses, sections, and students in a course registration database.

Relationships specify associations among two or more entities. Relationships are classified by their cardinality (the number of entities that participate in a relationship), and modality. These concepts were also presented in some detail in Chapter 6.

Figure 7.11 shows an ER diagram for a portion of a course registration database. It represents courses, sections, and students. A section is a weak entity, because it needs the course number (which is an attribute of the course, not the section) to be uniquely identified. A student enrolls in a section, and, at the end of the term, is assigned a grade for the section. Notice that the grade is an attribute of the relationship, not of any of the entities. A student gets a grade for a particular section.

Logical Database Design   Logical database design implies transforming the detailed ER diagram into a set of tables, together with foreign key relationships. We can formalize the process as follows:

1. *Transform entities:* Create a table for the entity, with all its simple and single-valued attributes. For composite attributes, use only the simple parts, with an appropriate naming convention. Weak entities have a primary key formed with the primary key of the identifying relationship and their discriminator. For example, the course and section entities would be transformed as shown in **Figure 7.12**.

2. *Creation of new tables:* For each independent multivalued attribute, create a new table containing as attributes the primary key of the entity and the multivalued attribute. If the attribute is composite, then use the simple parts only. The primary key of this relation is formed with all attributes. For example, the student entity has a multivalued attribute, email. Because the same student can have more than

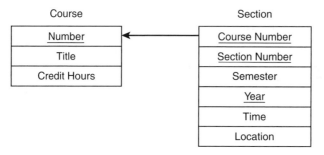

Figure 7.12 A relational schema diagram for course and section.

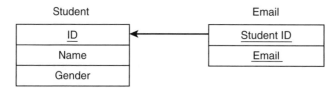

Figure 7.13 A relational schema diagram for students and email.

one email, we need to create one table for the student, and another one for those emails. The relational schema would resemble that of **Figure 7.13**.

3. *Transform relationships:* Notice that identifying relationships for weak entities have already been transformed in Step 1. The transformation to be done here depends on the kind of relationship.

   a. *One-to-many or many-to-one:* You do not need to create a new table, unless the relationship has attributes. Just add a foreign key reference on the table corresponding to the entity next to the "many" side—that is, the entity that can be related to just one entity. Note that this is what we did for Section in Figure 7.12, although that was for a weak entity.

   b. *One-to-one:* Follow the same process used with one-to-many, but you have a choice now. You can put the foreign key reference on either side. As a rule of thumb, choose the entity that always participates in the relationship to minimize nulls or the entity that you expect will have the fewest instances.

   c. *Many-to-many:* Create a new table, with foreign key references to the participating entities, plus any attributes of the relationship. The primary key is the union of the attributes in the primary keys of the participating entities. For example, the Takes relationship in **Figure 7.14** would need to be mapped to a new table. Figure 7.14 shows the mapping, along with the two tables it references, Section and Student.

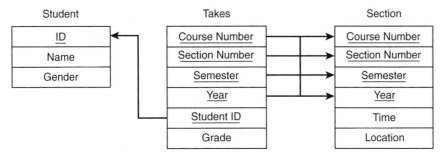

Figure 7.14 A relational schema diagram representing a many-to-many relationship.

Notice that in Figure 7.14 the arrows from Takes to Section are joined, denoting that the foreign key relationship is for the four attributes together rather than for each attribute individually. Also, many people would prefer to add a new identifier to the section table to avoid having composite foreign key references; in that case, the ER diagram would need to be updated.

   d. *Ternary relationships:* As with many-to-many relationships, you need to create a new table, containing foreign key references to the participating entities in addition to any attributes the relationship may have.

Following this process, and assuming your ER diagram was normalized, you will always achieve normalization—a situation where each row in a table represents just one simple fact rather than several. Alternatively, we can say that each table contains information pertaining to only one entity or relationship. Normalization helps ensure that information is stored only once, minimizing redundancy. There is a mathematical theory of normalization on relational databases that, for space reasons, we cannot cover in this text. See the Suggested Readings section at the end of the chapter or your favorite database textbook for additional coverage of this topic.

Physical Database Design   During physical database design, the following decisions are made:

   ■ *What data types to assign to each attribute:* Depending on which data types are supported by the DBMS, make sure that all possible data values are represented and that an eye is kept on performance. Most relational DBMS support fixed and varying size characters, fixed-precision numbers and dates, with possibly others such as IEEE floating point numbers, and integers stored in binary representation. A common issue is how to encode certain attributes; for example, you could store the gender of students in many different ways. It may be a string ("male" or "female"), a Boolean, or an integer. A common technique is to create a smaller encoding such as "M" or "F" and a new table that allows transforming that encoding to the label we want (e.g., male/female). Other issues such as encryption or compression of certain attributes may also arise.

- *What indexes to create:* Indexes consume space, but greatly increase search performance. By default, the primary key of each table is indexed to facilitate constraint checking and assuming the majority of joins would use the primary key. If you know that entities will be searched by specific fields, you may want to create other indexes.

- *Denormalization:* Sometimes, usually for performance reasons, tables will be denormalized; that is, information will be added to the table that does not really belong there or can be obtained from other tables, introducing redundancy. This should be done as a last resort, because it may confuse developers.

On very rare occasions, you may decide to combine the information on two tables. If the tables have a one-to-one relationship, this may make sense. We recommend checking the ER diagram. If the entities are conceptually different, keep them on separate tables.

Deployment and Maintenance   During deployment, the final decisions are made. Specifying the characteristics of the hardware the database will reside on and deciding which tables go on which files or hard drives are some of the decisions that will be made.

While you are using the system, the usage profile may change or some performance bottlenecks may become apparent. In many cases, performance can be improved by altering the data type of some attribute or, more commonly, by adding or deleting an index, without affecting the programs that access the database in any way. Of course, if the changes affect the programs, then you have to do program maintenance.

7.3.3   Object-Oriented Design and UML

Many modern software systems are developed using object-oriented techniques. The requirements are usually expressed mainly with use cases. Also, preliminary class diagrams may have been produced in the requirements analysis step.

Most documentation for object-oriented projects is presented in the form of UML diagrams. The UML is a graphic design notation, standardized by the Object Management Group (OMG), with wide industry and academic support. We will use UML in this section, but we will not try to cover UML in detail. For additional information on UML, see the Suggested Readings section at the end of the chapter.

During the design step, you will decide on exactly which classes to create, documenting each one with a class diagram. You may need to refine your use cases, and produce other diagrams to document the behavior of your objects.

Use Cases and Use-Case Diagrams   A use-case diagram is produced during the requirements phase, depicting the main use cases for the system, as we saw in Chapter 6 where use cases were introduced. Each individual use case is documented to some extent.

Figure 7.15 shows a use-case diagram for a course registration system. It depicts two actors, the Student and the Registrar. Students participate in two use cases, Register for section and Choose section. The registrar participates in four cases, Register for section, Add course, Add section, and Add student.

Each individual use case needs to be documented further. During the requirements phase, essential use cases are commonly developed. During the design phase, they will

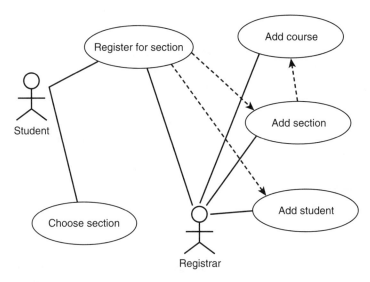

Figure 7.15 A use-case diagram for a course registration system.

need to be refined into system use cases. Essential use cases provide less detail and do not provide any details about the system; they mainly describe what the actor is supposed to do and what it tries to achieve. System use cases refine the essential case, adding detailed information about how the system achieves those goals. The details may be placed in a separate box as part of the use-case diagram. The content of the box may include the following:

Essential Use-Case Documentation

Name: Register for section
Preconditions: Student is registered, section exists
Postconditions: Student will be enrolled in section (if space is available, etc.)

Basic Course of Action

1. A student wants to enroll in a section (usually after having chosen the section).
2. Student logs on to system.
3. Student specifies which sections he/she wants to register for.
4. System verifies space is available in the section, that the student has the prerequisites, and that there is no scheduling conflict.
5. If there is no problem, the student is enrolled in all the requested sections. If there is any problem, the student is notified and given the chance to modify his or her choices.

A system use case will be defined at a much finer level of detail.

Class Design and Class Diagrams   One of the most important issues in detail design is designing classes as well as UML class diagrams to represent the design. In this section we will explain the basic concepts of class design and how to document them with UML. There are several basic concepts related to object orientation:

- Objects represent entities in the real world. This is similar to the concept of entity instances.
- Objects are organized into classes, which serve a similar purpose as "typing" an entity. Classes serve to group objects with similar structure and also as a template for creating new objects. Thus, a class is an abstraction of a set of similar objects. Classes are a central concept in most object-oriented languages. In our course registration example Student may be a Class, with Joe Smith as a specific student instance of that Class.
- Objects are associated with attributes, also called properties, similarly to the ER model. Each student object, such as Joe Smith, has a set of specific attribute values or data values associated with him or her. For instance, the values for address, gender, or age are associated with each specific object.
- In contrast with ER models, objects do not contain just data. They are also associated with methods, which are modules of executable code. The class, Student, may include functions or methods such as a set-birth-date method, which initializes a student's birth-date data attribute.

An important concept in class design is encapsulation. In an object, both data and methods are included. Expressing whether both, either, or neither data/methods can be publicly accessible is an important feature. In UML, publicly accessible methods and attributes are sometimes marked with a plus sign, and private methods, which are those that are only accessible to the class but not to other classes, with a minus sign.

In UML, classes are represented by rectangles divided into three areas: (1) name of the class, (2) the attributes, and (3) the methods. When you implement the class, it is common to never make an attribute public, but rather to create accessor methods (getX, setX); it is also common practice to not show those on the diagram but to have a convention about which ones get created.

In a UML diagram, a Student class with two attributes and two methods would be represented as shown in **Figure 7.16**.

Another important factor is that of an association between two objects, a concept similar to an ER relationship, with two important differences. Associations are always binary, and they cannot have attributes of their own. In UML, associations are shown by

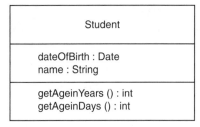

Figure 7.16 A UML class diagram for class Student.

Figure 7.17 A UML representation of association.

lines among classes and associations may or may not be available from both sides. We call this property *navigability*; if the association is navigable from both sides, we call it *bidirectional*; if it is not, we call it *unidirectional*.

Figure 7.17 is a simplified class diagram that shows a student being associated with a school with the IsEnrolled association. The association is bidirectional—that is, it can be navigated from both sides. We also show the allowed cardinalities. A student has to be enrolled in only one school. This would be the case with elementary schools, for example. A school can have zero or more students.

A special kind of association is that of aggregation, which corresponds with the "part-of" association. Notice this may be a real-world part-of (say an engine is part of a car) or one that only makes sense in the computer (an address is part of a student). A particularly strong version of aggregation is composition, in which the subordinate object cannot participate in any other association and is the sole responsibility of the containing class; basically, the contained class is just like an attribute of the containing class. In UML, aggregation is represented as an association with a diamond, and composition has the diamond drawn in black.

For example, assume we are modeling students and we want to represent their addresses as complex objects rather than just as one string. We can view the address as being part of the student object. If we know we will not share the address objects (that is, even if two real-world students live in the same place, in our program their corresponding objects will be assigned different address objects with the same attributes rather than the same address object), then we can represent this as composition, as in **Figure 7.18**.

Another central concept to OO design is class inheritance. When a class inherits from another class, it automatically gets all its attributes and methods. If class A inherits from class B, we call class A the superclass and class B the subclass. Although

Figure 7.18 UML representation of composition.

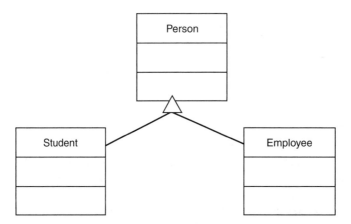

Figure 7.19 UML representation of inheritance.

the subclass can override any method it inherits from the superclass, changing its behavior, the intent is to mostly add additional methods. **Figure 7.19** shows a simplified UML class diagram illustrating inheritance. We have a Person class, with two subclasses, Student and Employee. Inheritance relationship is an "is-a" relationship between the subclass and the superclass. Thus, we would like to preserve as much of the superclass as possible during inheritance.

When preparing a design, note that in this example we can discover inheritance relationships through generalization or specialization. In generalization, we discover the Student and Employee classes, and later realize they share some characteristics and decide to create a common class, Person. In specialization, we first discover the Person class and later realize there are two special subtypes, Student and Employee. But in the diagrams only the inheritance relationship is shown. The diagram does not show how we came to discover this relationship. Generalization is a design technique closely related to abstraction where we simplify the design by keeping only the essentials and delaying the considerations of detail until a later time.

We should only create subclasses when there is a need to incorporate additional behavior or attributes. For example, although we may be tempted to create four additional subclasses for Student—namely Freshman, Sophomore, Junior, and Senior—it is probably unnecessary, as just adding a new property will allow us to discriminate among those, and there are no differences in the behavior or data that we model.

State Modeling   In many cases, objects can be in different states, and it is important to model those states and how they are allowed to change. This information is represented with **state transition diagrams**. For example, in our student domain, we start considering students when they are accepted into the university. After they enroll in their first class, they become active students. If they fail to enroll for a certain number of semesters, they become inactive students. Students may be expelled or graduate and become alumni. **Figure 7.20** shows a state transition diagram representing this situation.

> **State transition diagram**   A diagram representing information concerning the states of an object and the allowed state transitions.

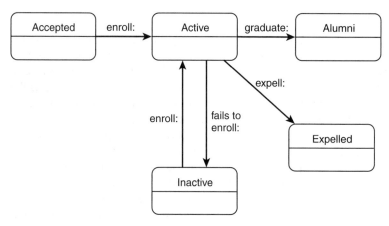

Figure 7.20 A state transition diagram.

The event-driven system mentioned earlier may be readily modeled with a state transition diagram. As external events occur, the system reacts to the events and changes states. Even though a state transition diagram is part of UML, it has been in use for modeling the system states by early computer scientists, automata theorists, and software engineers for many years.

Interactions Among Classes   Designing classes and their relationships provides only the static structure of the design. The interactions among the classes to collectively accomplish some task also need to be designed. In UML these interactions are usually illustrated through **UML sequence or communication diagrams**. Communication diagrams were called collaboration diagrams in UML 1, and are still called collaboration diagrams by many authors.

> **UML sequence diagrams**   Diagrams that illustrate the flow of messages from one object to another and the sequence in which those messages are processed.

The arrows in **Figure 7.21** illustrate the flow of messages, starting from the top and flowing from left to right. The returning messages are shown with dashed lines.

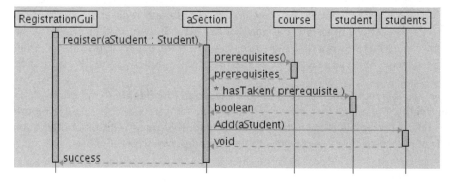

Figure 7.21 A UML sequence diagram.

7.3.4   User-Interface Design

The user interface (UI) is the part of the software most visible to the user and is one of the most important to get right. In many situations a prototype of the user interface is developed as part of the requirements analysis, as explained in Chapter 6. This prototype serves as a validation test. The client or user will confirm the prototype as the correct system or point out the defect(s). This activity also enables early testing. A big problem with user-interface design is that it is very different from programming and is very difficult for many software engineers. UI design is based on psychology, cognitive science, aesthetics, and art. Most software engineers are not well trained in any of these areas. Also, most software engineers are not typical users of software. Many software engineers tend to be very familiar with computing systems and tend to favor certain types of thinking that are not shared by the population at large. As assumed in the popular stereotype, many software engineers are "geeks" who use computers in different ways than do "ordinary" people. That makes designing good UI for the general population a difficult task.

It is better in most circumstances to leave UI design to specialists with training and skills more appropriate to this task. However, it is still important for software engineers to have a basic understanding of the issues. In many cases, it is not possible to have a separate person do the UI design, and it falls upon software developers or systems analysts to do the job. There are two main issues with user-interface design:

- The flow of interactions with the program
- The "look and feel" of the interface

The looks are not as important as the flow. We can easily design bad user interfaces and make them look pretty. Interaction design deals with the flow of interactions with the program.

Flow of Interactions in the Interface   The user of a system has specific goals to be achieved in the system. These goals are directly associated with the use cases and the sequence diagrams designed for the system. Chapter 6, "Requirements Engineering," shows a Shipping clerk needing to process a shipping item list and create the shipping labels in Figure 6.5 Use-case notation in UML. Figure 7.15 shows a use-case diagram for a course registration system. Consider the actor:Student needing to choose and register for the section. These are the goals of the actor:Student in their usage of the system. Figure 7.21 shows a UML sequence diagram for the detail design of registration for the system. We can see the inner design of the solution for register(aStudent: Student).

> **Low-fidelity prototype**   A simple mockup sketch of the target product.
> **High-fidelity prototype**   A detailed mockup resembling and behaving close to the final product.

The possible registration screens are prototyped in **low fidelity** (hand drawn) or in **high fidelity** (done with a variety of screen design software like Visual Basic). **Figure 7.22** shows an example of low-fidelity prototypes for the course registration. The "look and feel" of the interface is explored with these hand-drawn screens.

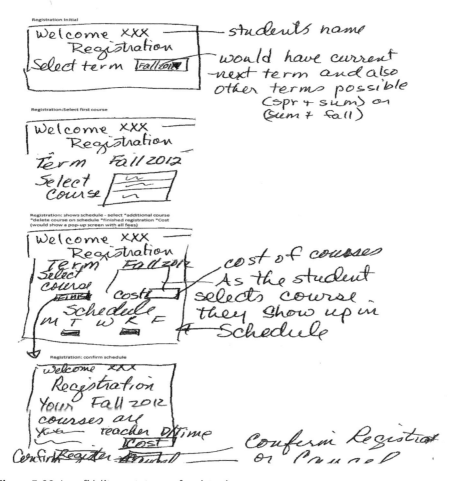

Figure 7.22 Low-fidelity prototypes of registration screens.

The low-fidelity prototype activity suggested the following four screens:

1. Registration: Initial—Select term
2. Registration: Term—Select first course
3. Registration: Desired schedule—Select additional course/delete course on schedule/finish registration/cost (would show a pop-up screen with all fees)
4. Registration: Confirm schedule

Figures 7.23 to **7.25** are the high-fidelity prototypes developed using Visual Basic. The look and feel of the interface continues to develop.

The possible registration screens developed are considered with each of the use cases for the system. The flows of interactions in the interface are shown to the client or user

Figure 7.23 High-fidelity prototype of registration: Initial screen.

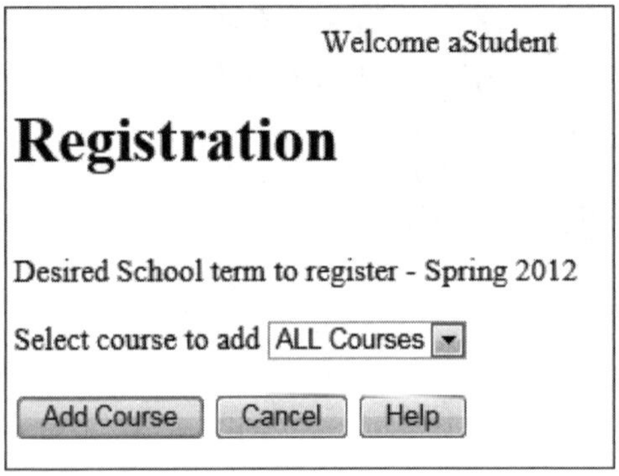

Figure 7.24 High-fidelity prototype of registration: Term—Select first course.

Figure 7.25 High-fidelity prototype of registration: Desired schedule.

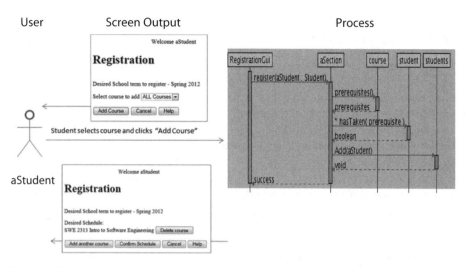

Figure 7.26 Flow of interaction.

for approval. **Figure 7.26** shows navigation of the possible screens for the Student user to select his or her initial course and then decide to add more courses, confirm schedule, and so on. Note the three columns in Figure 7.26—the User (student) on the left, screen outputs and user inputs in the center, and the inner system process (the sequence diagram for this use case) on the right.

The flow of all possible interactions—which include the user input, the screens, and the process—is considered and added as seen in **Figure 7.27** Considerations for all

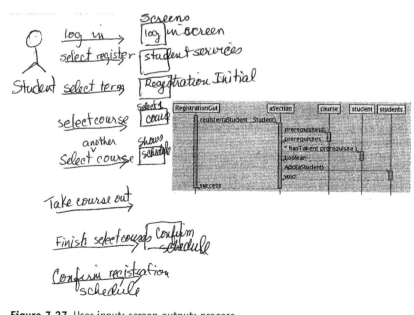

Figure 7.27 User input; screen output; process.

possible user expectations including the instructions, directions, feedback, confirmations, and help are taken into account in the development of the user-interface design.

Cognitive Models   Humans think in specific stages. Norman (1988) studied the psychology of everyday actions and developed a model with seven different stages. Users will (1) form a goal; (2) form an intention; (3)specify an action; and (4) execute the action. After the users execute the action, the feedback from the system is critical for their understanding of the system. Users will (5) perceive the system state (feedback); (6) interpret the feedback; and (7) evaluate. If, at the last stage, the users evaluate the mode as "intuitive," they will continue with the next cycle toward their goal.

The GOMS (goals, operators, methods, and selection) model is a classical model of user interaction that involves identifying, for a particular kind of users, their goals, the basic operators your program provides, the methods, that is the sequence of operations your user can use to achieve its goals, and Selection rules, which specify which Methods to apply for achieving a particular goal when several are available. See Card, Moran, and Newell in the Suggested Reading section for more on the GOMS model.

When designing a user-centered task-oriented system you need to know the goals of your users, study their expectations about the actions in the goal, and provide the appropriate operators and methods, making sure selection rules are clear. These goals should roughly map into the use cases or scenarios. Feedback to each of the actions within the user's goals is vital to successful usage of the system. For example, a system with a button that does not give any visibility change when pressing the button- will have a hesitation in the user's usage of the button.

In the interface, every button and menu option is an operator, and methods will roughly correspond to coarser-grained UI elements, such as dialogs or wizards. The designer needs to provide all the required operators and methods, because creating new ones is more difficult, and normal users will not be capable of combining them in meaningful ways even though there are macros and similar facilities.

Other Issues

- *Different kinds of users:* Often the interfaces that appeal to one kind of user are not appropriate for others. It is good practice to provide alternatives within the interface; for example, most GUI programs also provide for keyboard shortcuts. Many times features that make an interface easier to learn or use for the casual user will get in the way of expert users.
- *Heuristics for good user-interface design:* There are many good heuristics for user-interface design. The main heuristic is consistency throughout your program and with your platform and similar programs. Other heuristics include putting the user in control, reducing user's memory load, and making the system status visible.
- *User-interface guidelines:* Almost all GUI platforms, such as Apple's operating systems, Microsoft Windows, GNOME, and KDE, provide user-interface guidelines. These are much more detailed than the heuristics and provide information about which controls to use, what menu items have to exist, and many other detailed issues. Following the platform's user-interface guidelines will make all programs more consistent with each other.

- *Multicultural issues:* Creating a program that will be usable for people in many different countries and cultures is a great challenge. The creation of a program version for a specific group of users based on language or country is called *localization*. Colors and icons have different meanings for different cultures. Translating messages from one language to another is a difficult task. In many cases a localized version needs to be created not just for each language but also for each country that uses that language, as the words and expressions used change from one to another. There are many programming libraries available for dealing with some of the internationalization issues. Internationalization and localization issues will only become more relevant as world globalization continues. Designing a program that is usable by people of many cultures and countries will open up many markets and may be required for some systems.
- *Metaphors:* Many user interfaces are based on denotation to known objects. Most file management and operating system GUIs are based on the desktop metaphor. Most word processing programs try to utilize a paper document metaphor. An appropriate metaphor can facilitate program learning and transfer of real-world skills. However, in some situations, the real-world system is different from the metaphor and the users need to be made aware of those differences.
- *Multiplatform software:* Software engineers use different software platforms. Most users are very attached to their platform and will not change it just to run other programs. In many cases, the newly developed software needs to run in several different platforms and must integrate well with each one. The main problem with multiplatform software is consistency. A decision must be made about whether the software must be consistent across all platforms or whether, instead, it must integrate fully with each platform and follow that specific platform's guidelines.
- *Accessibility:* The software should be made as accessible as possible in order to be used by as many people as possible. Some people cannot see well or distinguish between certain colors, and some cannot operate a normal keyboard or mouse.
- *Multimedia interfaces:* Graphics and text are not the only ways to provide information. It is currently possible to use sound and, in some cases, tactile feedback to convey information. There is even a device to produce smells. How to take advantage of these output devices to make a better user interface will be a challenge in the years to come.

7.3.5 Some Further Design Concerns

Most commercial applications have three main components: user interface, application logic, and data. In the case of web applications, user interfaces are displayed via a browser, the data is usually stored in a relational database, and the application logic is written in either a programming or script language. This is the MVC architectural style. Earlier we mentioned that design decisions may even include implementation concerns. When object-oriented (OO) design is chosen, the entities in the graphical user interface must be mapped to the object defined in the OO programming language. Similarly, the object in the OO programming language needs to be mapped to the relational database table. The constructs in the user interface, in the programming objects, and in the relational database tables are different and do not necessarily match.

Here we will briefly discuss one mapping problem called *object-relational impedance mismatch*. Several issues arise when a relational database system is utilized by an OO programming style design. Difficulties are encountered when classes are mapped onto relational database tables and class attributes are mapped onto table columns.

One issue is that objects have an identity, and rows in a relational database are considered just values. While this is important, it can prove difficult at times. However, the issue can be ameliorated by adding a specific field—an object id—to each row in a relational database. One would still need to keep track of whether there is more than one copy of the same database object in memory.

Another issue is the difference in the support of data typing. The relational model prohibits the by-reference or pointer type, but an OO language supports the by-reference type. The way string data type and collations are supported also differ between relational database systems and OO programming languages.

Additional problems stem from the fact that relational databases deal with sets of rows, while objects reference each other in complex structures. When bringing an object from the database into main memory, it is not clear whether to bring the other related objects into memory as well. In extreme situations, one can conceptually require that the entire database be brought into memory.

While one may argue that these are implementation issues, they certainly need to be considered at detail design time. See Heinckiens (1998) in the Suggested Readings section for further discussions on database applications and impedance mismatch.

In the next chapter we will discuss some ways of evaluating different designs, the parameters and metrics used for evaluation, and some guidance for good design.

7.4   HTML-Script-SQL Design Example

In this section we will delve deeper into some details of designing a web application though a simple example utilizing HTML, PHP, and SQL. Note that this specific combination of tools may change, and one needs to make sure that the chosen tools will interact together.

A software project that follows the Model-View-Controller (MVC) architectural style (see Figure 7.4) can be done with three main parts for the detail design:

1. A HyperTextMarkup Language (HTML) interface design used for portraying the "view" and the information flow for the application

2. A scripting language as the engine of the system (we will use PHP) serving as the "controller" for the application

3. An SQL database that stores the information and acts as the "model" for the application

The web-based database application begins with an interactive interface composed of HTML pages. A study of the structure of an HTML document shows that it really has many parts. Formatting tags, hyperlinks, lists, tables, frames, and Cascading Style Sheets (CSS) are the essential materials needed to create the interactive interface. HTML forms

Sample HTML	Visual result (possible)
```<form method="GET" action="something.php"> <p> Username: <input type="text" name="username"> </p> <p> Password: <input type="password" name="password"> </p> <input type="submit" value="Login"> </form>```	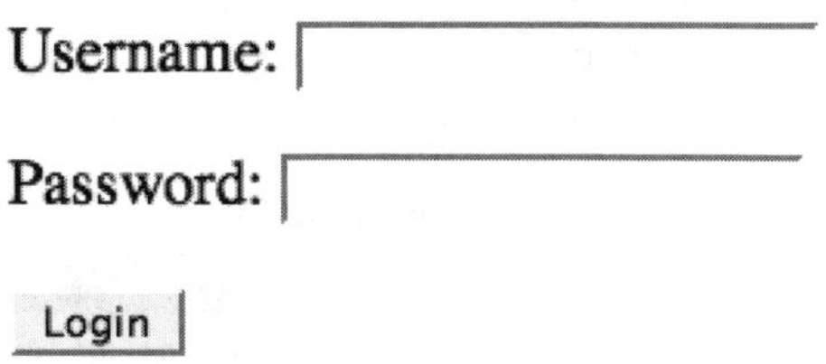 Username: [_____] Password: [_____] [Login]

Figure 7.28 Sample HTML with visual result displayed using Firefox browser on an Apple Mac Pro machine.

allow the webpages to have a wide variety of input fields for the user to input information, selections, and so on. A simple example using an HTML with PHP method is shown in **Figure 7.28**. The visual results shown used Firefox browser on an Apple Mac Pro machine.

Using the GET method of PHP, data in the HTML form is appended to the URL in the action field. Thus the data submitted is visible. We would note that this represents a security risk, but on the other hand it allows one to bookmark the page with the submitted data, or even write an external link to it. By copying the syntax, you can encode data to be sent to a server page in a link, with the data coming from a database, or some other program.

Besides the URL, data sent through a GET request has some size limitation, so when sending big amounts of data you need to use the POST method of PHP.

HTML pages are static documents, so we need a programming language that can generate HTML pages. For this example we use PHP as that programming language. PHP is a scripting and dynamically typed language designed for web development. A good source for information about PHP is www.php.net. A study of variables, printing, strings, arrays, control structures, loops, and functions is the first step if one is not familiar with the PHP scripting language. PHP code can be embedded inside an HTML file and is saved as a .php extension rather than an .html extension. The web server executes the PHP code and embeds its output in the HTML file that is sent to the browser.

The next step to consider in the application design is the database model and database access. For this example, the design and creation of the database would be established. PHP would be used to send SQL commands to the database management system (DBMS), specifically to PostgreSql. PHP provides an abstract layer for accessing many DBMSs through the same interface (called PEAR DB), but for simplicity we will cover only the functions that are PostgreSql specific (if you were to switch to another DBMS you'd probably need to change the first few characters of each function's name). Note that if you use something such as PEAR DB for general interface, there is probably a performance penalty.

The PHP functions we will use for accessing the database include those in **Table 7.1**.

Table 7.1 Sample PHP-DB Access Functionalities

Function	Purpose
pg_connect	Establishes a connection to the database and returns a handle to it.
pg_query, pg_query_params	Executes a query and returns a handle to the result set; notice the query can be an INSERT, UPDATE, or DELETE, in addition to a SELECT. pg_query_params is used for parametrized queries; that is, those for which the final form is obtained by interpolating strings or otherwise incorporating variables into a query string.
pg_numrows	Returns the number of rows in a result set.
pg_fetch object	Returns an object representing a row in a result set.

An example for retrieving all rows from the relational table named "student" in the database named "ok" would have the following lines of PHP code (explanations given here):

```
$conn = pg_connect("host=localhost user=namedbname=ok password=abc");
```

The above line establishes the connection and stores (a handle to) that connection in the $conn variable.

```
$query_str="Select * FROM student";
```

This line just initializes a string variable called $query_str. Notice that the value of that string variable is a SQL statement, which will be passed to the PostgreSql database.

```
$res=pg_query($conn, $query_str);
```

The above line actually sends the query to the DBMS (PostgreSql in this case). It uses the connection already established ($conn) and the query stored in $query_str, and stores (a handle to) the rows returned by the DBMS as a result of the query in $str.

The application will be conceptually organized into pages that serve as screens for the application. It is a good idea to keep each page in its own file. To implement a piece of functionality, one will usually need two components:

1. An HTML form.
2. A PHP page called from that form that uses the input provided by the form. The input is used to query, obtain, save, or pass along using one or more SQL statements.

These separate pages may be related through the usage of links. Many of the pages can include links to each other, and these links may even be generated using PHP. The number of links may be dependent on the information on the database; recall that we can actually encode information in a link by adding a question mark (?) at the end, and then name=value pairs. If we define a menu in a frame, that menu can link to several pages so that the user can keep track of the functionality, while the functionality being currently accessed is displayed in another frame.

Notice that each PHP page will be a separate page and that each request comes as a completely separate request. However, many times, we want to give the user the illusion that they are accessing an application and that the pages know which other pages that particular user has accessed recently. Within web applications, we call this idea of all the recent interactions of a user with a website a *session*. PHP supports keeping track of user sessions. Using session variables in PHP is very easy. For each page, we need to call the function `session_start()`, being careful that this call occurs before any output.

Common web application exercises that have request for accounts, login form, and then process orders can be created using this model. The detail design of each part of the MVC architectural style involve different strengths of a software engineering team. The database experts design the SQL database, the programming experts tackle the PHP code, and the usability experts on the team focus on the user interactions with the HTML pages.

7.5   Summary

In this chapter we have discussed most of the issues with design. We discussed high-level, or architectural, design. We then discussed detailed design, and techniques for functional decomposition, relational database design, object-oriented design, and user-interface design.

The design of your software is one of the most important issues of its development. Whether you do a formal, complete design or an informal one, it is always advantageous to think about how you are going to achieve your goals before doing much program ming.

In the next chapter we will discuss some ways of evaluating different designs, the parameters and metrics used for evaluation, and some guidance for good design.

7.6   Review Questions

1. Explain the role of requirements in architectural design. Explain the role of requirements in detail design.

2. What does aggregation mean in OO? Give an example.

3. When we employ the technique of generalization in design, what are we doing, and which part of OO design is closely related to this concept?

4. List two differences between the state transition diagram and the sequence diagram.

5. Describe three different views used in architectural design.

6. What is the difference between data modeling and logical database design?

7. Describe the difference between low-fidelity and high-fidelity prototyping in the design of the interface. Choose one and give the reasons why you would show the client this prototype.

8. Explain the three columns in Figure 7.26 labeled User, Screen Output, and Process with regard to design.

9. Choose one of the cognitive models and explain how the model impacts the design of the user interface.

10. Visit a website that is from a different country or culture. Give an example of a multicultural issue you found in the site. Explain how you would propose to re-design, taking into consideration the issue found.

7.7   Exercises

1. Write a command-line program for converting different units of measurement. Begin your program by converting kilograms and pounds and then yards and meters. Discuss your user interface with other students.

2. Write a GUI program for converting different units of measurement. Begin your program by converting kilograms and pounds and then yards and meters. Discuss your user interface with other students.

3. Find a person who speaks your language but comes from a different country or region, and discuss how the vocabulary and expressions you both use are different. On what kinds of words do you find the most differences?

4. For each one of the architectural styles mentioned in this chapter, find one example of a software system that uses it (not mentioned in the chapter).

5. Consider the case of a software system designed to keep track of team rosters and scheduled games for a sports league. Create a UML class diagram representing all the domain classes and a sequence diagram depicting one of the main interactions among those classes.

6. Consider the case of a software system designed to keep track of team rosters and scheduled games for a sports league. Create an ER diagram for this situation and convert the diagram into a relational schema.

7. Consider the case of a software system designed to keep track of team rosters and scheduled games for a sports league. Define the main functionality of the system and create a module decomposition diagram for it.

7.8   Suggested Readings

S. W. Ambler, *The Object Primer: The Application Developer's Guide to Object Orientation*, 2nd ed. (New York: Cambridge University Press, 2001).

L. Bass, P. Clements, and R. Kazman, *Software Architecture in Practice*, 2nd ed. (Reading, MA: Addison-Wesley, 2003).

G. Booch, *Object-Oriented Analysis and Design with Applications*, 2nd ed. (Reading, MA: Addison-Wesley, 1994).

S. K. Card, T. P. Moran, and A. Newell, *The Psychology of Human-Computer Interaction* (Mahwah, NJ: Lawrence Erlbaum, 1983).

P. Chen, "The Entity-Relationship Model—Towards a Unified View of Data," *ACM Transactions on Database Systems*, 1 (March 1976): 9–36.

E. F. Codd, "A Relational Model of Data for Large Shared Data Banks," *Communications of ACM* 13, no. 6 (June 1970): 377–387.

C. J. Date, *An Introduction to Database Systems*, 8th ed. (Reading, MA: Addison-Wesley, 2003).

M. Fowler and K. Scott, *UML Distilled*, 2nd ed. (Reading, MA: Addison-Wesley, 1999).

E. Gamma, R. Helm, R. Johnson, and J. Vlissides, *Design Patterns: Elements of Reusable Object-Oriented Software* (Reading, MA: Addison-Wesley, 1995).

P. M. Heinckiens, *Building Scalable Database Applications: Object Oriented Design, Architecture, and Implementation* (Reading, MA: Addison-Wesley, 1998).

D. Hix and H. R. Hartson, *Developing User Interfaces: Ensuring Usability Through Product and Process* (New York: Wiley, 1993).

P. Kruchten, "Architectural Blueprints—The 4+1 View Model of Software Architecture," *IEEE Software* (November 1995).

R. Malveau and T. Mowbray, *Software Architecture Bootcamp* (Upper Saddle River, NJ: Prentice Hall, 2000).

D. A. Norman, *The Design of Everyday Things* (New York: Doubleday, 1988).

M. Shaw and D. Garlan, *Software Architecture: Perspectives on an Emerging Discipline* (Upper Saddle River, NJ: Prentice Hall, 1996).

B. Shneiderman and C. Plaisant, *Designing the User Interface: Strategies for Effective Human-Computer Interaction*, 4th ed. (Reading, MA: Addison-Wesley, 2005).

A. Silberschatz, H. F. Korth, and S. Sudarshan, *Database System Concepts*, 4th ed. (New York: McGraw Hill, 2002).

C. Szyperski, D. Gruntz, and S. Murer, *Component Software—Beyond Object-Oriented Programming* (New York: Addison-Wesley/ACM Press, 2002).

R. N. Taylor, N. Medvidovic, and E. M. Dashofy, *Software Architecture: Foundations, Theory and Practice* (Hoboken, NJ: John Wiley & Sons, 2009).

Design Characteristics and Metrics

8.1   Characterizing Design

In Chapter 7 we discussed a number of designs and design techniques. Intuitively, we can talk about good designs and bad designs. We regularly use phrases such as "easy to understand," "easy to change," "low complexity," or "easy to code from." When pressed, however, we often find it quite difficult to define what a good design is, let alone attempt to measure the design-goodness attribute. In this chapter we will crystallize some of these thoughts and discuss ways to measure different designs. There is no one overriding definition of a good design. Much like quality, a good design is characterized by several attributes.

There are two often mentioned general characteristics that naturally carry over from the requirements:

- Consistency
- Completeness

Consistency across design is an important characteristic. It ensures that common terminology is used across the system's display screens, reports, database elements, and process logic. Similarly, a consistent design should ensure common handling of the help facility and a common approach to all the error, warning, and information messages that are displayed. The degree of error detection and diagnostics processing should be consistent across the functions. The navigational flow and depth of logic also needs to be designed in a consistent manner.

The completeness of a design is important from at least two perspectives. The first is that all the requirements are designed and that none are left out. This can be cross-checked by meticulously going over the requirements at a detailed level. The second is that the design must be carried out to completion. If the design is carried out to different levels of depth or detail, which is also a consistency problem, some of the required design for the code implementers may not be there. Unfortunately, when the needed design is not available, the implementers become very creative in filling the vacuum, often resulting in erroneous design. Consistency and completeness are thus major characteristics that design reviews or inspections must focus on.

8.2   Some Legacy Characterizations of Design Attributes

The characterizations of design attributes in the early days of software engineering dealt more with detail design and coding level attributes rather than the architectural design level. This is not surprising because programming and program modules were considered the most important artifacts for a long time. Thus the corresponding measurements were also targeted at the detail design and coding elements. We will describe some of the leading, early complexity measures for program modules and intermodular structures.

8.2.1   Halstead Complexity Metric

The Halstead metric, one of the earliest software metrics, was developed by the late Maurice Halstead in the 1970s, mostly to analyze program source code. It is included here for establishing a historical baseline.

The Halstead metric utilized four fundamental metric units when analyzing a source program.

- $n1$ = number of distinct operators
- $n2$ = number of distinct operands
- $N1$ = sum of all occurrences of $n1$
- $N2$ = sum of all occurrences of $n2$

In a program, there may be multiple occurrences of the same operator, such as the multiple occurrences of the "+" operator or the "IF" operator. The sum of all occurrences of all the operators in a program may be represented as $N1$. There may also be multiple occurrences of the same operand. The operand is either a program variable or a program constant. Again, there may be multiple occurrences of an operand. The total number of occurrences of all the operands in a program may be represented as $N2$. From the counting of operators and operands, Halstead defined two more measures:

- Program vocabulary or unique tokens, $n = n1 + n2$
- Program length, $N = N1 + N2$

All the unique tokens in the source program form the basic vocabulary for that program. Thus the sum of the unique tokens, $n = n1 + n2$, is a measure of the program vocabulary. The length of the program, $N = N1 + N2$, is the sum of all the multiple occurrences of the vocabulary of the program. This definition of program length is quite different from the more familiar metric such as the number of lines of code. Four more measurements are developed from these fundamental units:

- Volume, $V = N * (\text{Log2 } n)$
- Potential volume, $V^@ = (2 + n2^@) \log2(2 + n2^@)$
- Program implementation level, $L = V^@/V$
- Effort, $E = V/L$

Volume is a straightforward calculation from previously counted n and N. But potential volume is based on the concept of a "most succinct" program where there would be two operators composed of the function name and the grouping operator, such as $f(x_1, x_2, \ldots, x_t)$. The function name is f, and the grouping operator is the parentheses surrounding the variables, x_1 through x_t. The $n2^@$ is the number of operands used by the function, f. In this case, $n2^@ = t$ because there are t number of variables. Program implementation level is a measure of the closeness of the current implementation to the ideal implementation. The estimation for effort is given as V/L, and the unit for effort is the number of mental discriminations. This number of mental discriminations may be the effort needed to implement the program or the effort needed to understand someone else's program.

Halstead metrics have been criticized for a number of reasons. Among them is that the Halstead metrics really measure only the lexical complexity of the source program and not the structure or the logic. Therefore, they have a limited value in the analysis of program complexity, let alone design characteristics.

8.2.2 McCabe's Cyclomatic Complexity

Although cyclomatic number originated from graph theory, the cyclomatic complexity measure for software resulted from T. J. McCabe's observation that program quality is directly related to the complexity of the control flow or the number of branches in the detail design or in the source code. This is different from Halstead's approach of looking at complexity through the number of operators and operands in a source code program. The cyclomatic complexity of a program or a detailed design is calculated from a control flow diagram representation of that design or program. It is represented as follows:

Cyclomatic complexity $= E - N + 2p$,

where E = number of edges of the graph,

N = number of nodes of the graph, and

p = number of connected components (usually $p = 1$).

McCabe's cyclomatic complexity number can also be calculated two other ways:

- Cyclomatic complexity = number of binary decision + 1
- Cyclomatic complexity = number of closed regions + 1

Let's look at a simple example of the flow diagram shown in **Figure 8.1**. This diagram has seven edges (*e1* through *e7*) and six nodes (*n1* through *n6*). Thus McCabe's cyclomatic complexity equals 7 edges $-$ 6 nodes $+$ 2 $= 3$. Utilizing the closed region approach, we have two regions (Region 1 and Region 2) and the cyclomatic complexity equals 2 regions $+ 1 = 3$. The easiest approach may be to count the number of binary decisions or branches. In this case, there are two (*n2* and *n4*). The cyclomatic complexity number equals 2 branches $+ 1 = 3$.

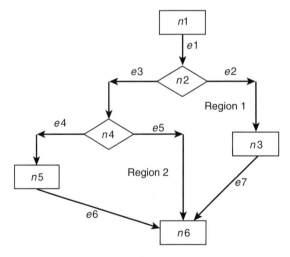

Figure 8.1 A simple flow diagram for cyclomatic complexity.

The cyclomatic complexity measures the structural design complexity within the program. It has been applied to design and code risk analysis during development as well as to test planning for assessing the number of test cases needed to test every decision point in the design or program. A large number of data has been accumulated, and we now know that the higher the cyclomatic complexity number, the more risk exists and that more testing is needed. An example of comparing the cyclomatic complexity numbers against a set of relative risk threshold may be obtained from the Software Engineering Institute (SEI) website. According to SEI, a cyclomatic complexity number in the range of 1 through 10 may be viewed as low risk and simple while the other extreme of very high risk is any cyclomatic number greater than 50. Thus, at the program design level, we should keep the control flow such that the cyclomatic complexity number is much smaller than 50.

A cyclomatic number is also the maximum number of linearly independent paths through the flow diagram. A path in the control flow is linearly independent from other paths only if it contains some edge, or path segment, that has not been covered before. Thus the cyclomatic complexity number is also often used to determine the number of test cases needed to drive through the linearly independent paths in the system.

8.2.3   Henry-Kafura Information Flow

The Henry-Kafura metric is another structural metric, but it measures intermodular flow. It is based on the flow of information in and out of a module. A count is made of all the information that comes in and goes out of every module. An information flow includes the following:

- Parameter passing
- Global variable access
- Inputs
- Outputs

Thus an information flow is a measure of interactions between modules or between a module and its environment. Based on information flow, Henry and Kafura developed a metric where fan-in and fan-out represent the following:

- Fan-in: Number of information flow into a program module
- Fan-out: Number of information flow out of a program module

The fan-in of a program module, mod-A, is often viewed as a count of number of modules that call mod-A. Fan-in also includes the number of global data variables accessed by mod-A. The fan-out of a program module, mod-A, is the number of program modules called by mod-A and the number of global data variables accessed by mod-A. Based on these definitions of fan-in and fan-out, the Henry-Kafura structural complexity for a program module p, C_p, is defined as the square of the product of fan-in and fan-out as follows:

$$C_p = (\text{fan-in} \times \text{fan-out})^2$$

Table 8.1 Fan-in and Fan-out by Program Module

Module	Mod-A	Mod-B	Mod-C	Mod-D
Fan-in	3	4	2	2
Fan-out	1	2	3	2

Consider an example where there are four program modules with the fan-in and fan-out numbers shown in **Table 8.1**.

The C_p for each of the four program modules, mod-A through mod-D, are computed as follows:

C_p for Mod-A = $(3 \times 1)^2 = 9$

C_p for Mod-B = $(4 \times 2)^2 = 64$

C_p for Mod-C = $(2 \times 3)^2 = 36$

C_p for Mod-D = $(2 \times 2)^2 = 16$

The total Henry-Kafura structural complexity for all four program modules would be the sum of these, which is 125.

The Henry-Kafura measure of design structural complexity was later modified by Henry and Selig to include the internal complexity of the program module as follows:

$$HC_p = C_{ip} \times (\text{fan-in} \times \text{fan-out})^2$$

The C_{ip} is the internal complexity of the program module p, which may be measured by any code metric such as the cyclomatic or the Halstead metrics. Clearly, we believe that a high Henry-Kafura number means a complex design structure. Whether this necessarily leads to a less understandable design and low-quality software is not yet conclusive.

8.2.4   A Higher-Level Complexity Measure

Card and Glass also utilized the concept of fan-in and fan-out to describe the complexity of a design, which also considers the data that are passed. This is a little higher-level measure in that it is a set of metrics that cover program level and interprogram level interactions. They define three design complexity measures:

- Structural complexity
- Data complexity
- System complexity

The *structural complexity*, S_x, of a module x is defined as follows:

$$S_x = (\text{fan-out}_x)^2$$

Again, fan-out is the number of modules that are directly invoked by module x. The data complexity, D_x, is also defined in terms of fan-out.

$$D_x = P_x / (\text{fan-out}_x + 1)$$

P_x is the number of variables that are passed to and from module x, and the system complexity, C_x, a higher-level measure, is defined as the sum of structural and data complexity:

$$C_x = S_x + D_x$$

Note that this measure of design, called *system complexity*, is based mostly on fan-out. Fan-in is not really included here except for the data that flow into the module.

8.3 "Good" Design Attributes

We all agree that design is an important activity and should be given ample time and attention so that we can develop a good design. But what are the characteristics of a good design? Immediately, we can hear ourselves throw out some of the following popular terms:

- Easy to understand
- Easy to change
- Easy to reuse
- Easy to test
- Easy to integrate
- Easy to code

In our discussions earlier in this chapter describing Halstead, McCabe, Henry-Kafura, and Card and Glass metrics, we alluded to intramodular and intermodular complexities as a factor that relates to software quality. Is there some more fundamental way to characterize a good design besides listing the different "easy to _____" items? They themselves may not be the characteristics of a good design and are in fact just the desirable results achieved with a good design. The common thread to all these "easy to" properties is the notion of simplicity. A large and complex problem may be simplified via separation and decomposition into smaller pieces that may be solved in an incremental fashion (as discussed in Chapter 2). Several design techniques also follow this principle of simplicity (see Chapter 7). According to Yourdon and Constantine (1979), the notion of simplicity may be measured by two characteristics: cohesion and coupling. G. J. Myers (1978) and, more recently, Lethbridge and Laganiere (2001) have also defined these concepts in their books. These two concepts are not far from the complexity measures mentioned earlier. Cohesion addresses the intramodule characteristics somewhat similar to Halstead and McCabe metrics, and coupling addresses the intermodule characteristics similar to the Henry-Kafura fan-in and fan-out information flow measurements and the system complexity measure of Card and Glass. In general, we are striving for strong cohesion and loose coupling in our design. Both concepts are explained in more detail in the following sections.

8.3.1 Cohesion

One of the key notions related to the issue of keeping the design simple so that it will have many of the desirable "easy to" attributes mentioned earlier is to ensure that each unit of the design, whether it is at the modular level or component level, is focused on

> **Cohesion**   An attribute of a unit of high- or detail-level design that identifies the degree to which the elements within that unit belong or are related together.

a single purpose. Terms such as *intramodular functional relatedness* or *modular strength* have been used to address the notion of design **cohesion**. This same notion will be later applied to the object-oriented (OO) paradigm in Section 8.4.

As we can see from our definition of the notion of cohesion, depending on the paradigm, the elements may be different. For example, in the structured paradigm, the elements may be I/O logic, control logic, or database access logic. In the OO paradigm, the elements may be the methods and the attributes. Whatever the paradigm, in a highly cohesive design unit the pieces of that design unit are all related in serving a single purpose or a single function. The term *degree* is used in the definition of cohesion. This suggests that there is some scaling of the attribute.

Generally, seven categories of cohesion can be shown to indicate their relative ranking from bad to good:

- Coincidental
- Logical
- Temporal
- Procedural
- Communicational
- Sequential
- Functional

Note that there is no numerical assignment provided to help the scaling. This is just a relative ordering of the categories of cohesion.

The lowest level is coincidental cohesion. At this level the unit of design or code is performing multiple unrelated tasks. This lowest level of cohesion does not usually happen in an initial design. However, when a design experiences multiple changes and modifications, whether through bug fixes or requirements changes, and is under schedule pressures, the original design can easily erode and become coincidental. For example, we might be facing a case where, instead of redesigning, a branch is taken around segments of design that are now not needed or partially needed and new elements are inserted due to convenience. This will easily result in multiple unrelated elements in a design unit.

The next level is logical cohesion. The design at this level performs a series of similar tasks. At first glance, logical cohesion seems to make sense in that the elements are related. However, the relationship is really quite weak. An example would be an I/O unit designed to perform all the different reads and writes to the different devices. Although these are logically related in that they all perform reads and writes, the read and write design is different for each device type. Thus at the logical cohesion level, the elements put together into a single unit are related but are still relatively independent of each other.

Design at the temporal cohesion level puts together a series of elements that are related by time. An example would be a design that combines all the data initialization into one unit and performs all the initialization at the same time even though the data may be defined and utilized in other design units.

The next highest level is procedural cohesion. This involves actions that are procedurally related, which means that they are related in terms of some control sequence. This is clearly a design that shows a tighter relationship than the previous one.

Communicational cohesion is a level at which the design is related by the sequence of activities, much like procedural cohesion, and the activities are targeted on the same data or the same sets of data. Thus, designs at the communicational cohesion level demonstrate even more internal closeness than those at the procedural cohesion level.

The last two levels, sequential and functional cohesion, are the top levels where the design unit performs one main activity or achieves one goal. The difference is that at the sequential cohesion level the delineation of a "single" activity is not as clear as the functional cohesion level. It is not totally clear that having a design unit at a functional cohesion level is always achievable. Clearly, a design unit at this level, being single-goal oriented, would require very few changes for reuse if there is a need for a design to achieve the same goal. The sequential cohesion level may still include some elements that are not single-goal oriented and would require some modifications for reuse.

These levels are not always clear cut. They may be viewed as a spectrum of levels that a designer should try to achieve as high a level as possible. In design, we would strive for strong cohesion. Although this approach to viewing cohesion is a good guideline, an example of a more tangible and quantitative measure of cohesion is introduced next.

Program Slice- and Data Slice-Based Cohesion Measure Bieman and Ott (1994) introduced several quantitative measures of cohesion at the program level based on program and data slices. We will briefly summarize their approach to measuring cohesion. First, several definitions will be given, and then an example will follow. Consider a source program that includes variable declarations and executable logic statements as the context. The following concepts should be kept in mind:

- A **data token** is any variable or constant.
- A **slice** within the program or procedure is all the statements that can affect the value of some specific variable of interest.
- A **data slice** is all the data tokens in a slice that will affect the value of a specific variable of interest.
- **Glue tokens** are the data tokens in the procedure or program that lie in more than one data slice.
- **Superglue tokens** are the data tokens in the procedure or program that lie in every data slice in the program.

> **Data token** Any variable or constant.
>
> **Program or procedure slice** All the statements that can affect the value of some specific variable of interest.
>
> **Data slice** All the data tokens in a slice that will affect the value of a specific variable of interest.
>
> **Glue tokens** The data tokens in the procedure or program that lie in more than one data slice.
>
> **Superglue tokens** The data tokens in the procedure or program that lie in every data slice in the program.

From these basic definitions, it is clear that glue tokens and superglue tokens are those that go across the slices and offer the binding force or strength of cohesion. Thus, when quantitatively evaluating the program cohesion, we would be counting the number of these glue and superglue tokens. More specifically, Bieman and Ott (1994) define the following two measures for measuring functional cohesion.

Weak functional cohesion = Number of glue tokens / Total number of data tokens

Strong functional cohesion = Number of superglue tokens / Total number of data tokens

Finding the maximum and
minimum values
procedure

```
MinMax (z, n)
integer end, min, max, i;
end = n;
max = z[0];
min = z[0];
For (i = 0, i = < end; i++){
    if z[i] > max then max = z[i];
    if z[i] > min then max = z[i];
        }
    return max, min;
```

Data Tokens:	Slice max:	Slice min:	Glue Tokens:	Superglue:
z1	z1	z1	z1	z1
n1	n1	n1	n1	n1
end1	end1	end1	end1	end1
min1	max1	min1	I1	I1
max1	I1	I1	end2	end2
I1	end2	end2	n2	n2
end2	n2	n2	I2	I2
n2	max2	min2	03	03
max2	z2	z3	I3	I3
z2	01	02	end3	end3
01	I2	I2	I4 (11)	I4 (11)
min2	03	03		
z3	I3	I3		
02	end3	end3		
I2	I4	I4		
03	z4	z6		
I3	I5	I7		
end3	max3	min3		
I4	max4	min4		
z4	z5	z7		
I5	I6	I8		
max3	max5	min5		
max4	(22)	(22)		
z5				
I6				
z6				
I7				
min3				
min4				
z7				
I8				
max5				
min5 (33)				

Figure 8.2 A pseudocode example of functional cohesion measures.

Both weak and strong functional cohesion use the total number of data tokens as the factor to normalize the measure. An example will clarify some of these concepts.

Figure 8.2 shows a pseudocode example for a procedure that computes both the maximum value, max, and the minimum value, min, from an array of integers in z. The labeling of the data tokens needs a little explanation. The first appearance of a variable, n, in the procedure is labeled n1. The next appearance of the same variable, n, is labeled n2. There are a total of 33 data tokens in this procedure. The data slice of code slice around the variable of interest, max, and the data slice of code slice around the variable of interest, min, are represented by data slice max and data slice min respectively in Figure 8.2. In this case, they have the same number—22—of data tokens because all the code, except for the initialization of min and max to z[0] and the if statements, are the same in contributing to the computation of the maximum or the minimum value. For this example, the glue tokens are also the same as the superglue tokens. The weak and strong cohesion measures are as follows.

Weak functional cohesion = 11/33

Strong functional cohesion = 11/33

This procedure computes both the maximum and the minimum value of an array, z, of numbers. Now, consider pulling out those instructions that contribute to computing minimum value and focus only on the maximum value. Then the data slice max, with 22 data tokens, becomes the whole set of data tokens. It would also be the set of glue tokens and the set of superglue tokens. The functional cohesion measures become as follows:

Weak functional cohesion = 22/22

Strong functional cohesion = 22/22

By focusing on only one function, maximum value, the cohesion measures have improved from 11/33 to 22/22. Although this example uses actual code, the concept of strong cohesion is well demonstrated.

8.3.2   Coupling

In the previous section we focused on cohesion within a software unit. Again, the term *software unit* may be a module or a class. Assuming that we are successful in designing highly cohesive software units in a system, it is most likely that these units would still need to interact through the process of **coupling**. The more complicated the interaction is, the less likely that we will achieve the "easy to" characteristics mentioned in the beginning of Section 8.3. A good example of

> **Coupling**   An attribute that addresses the degree of interaction and interdependence between two software units.

why analysis of coupling is important is provided by Gamma et al. (1995), who state that tightly coupled classes are hard to reuse in isolation. That is, a class or a module that is highly dependent on other modules or classes would be very difficult to understand by itself. Thus it would be difficult to reuse, modify, or fix that module or class without understanding all the dependent modules and classes. Also, if there is an error in a module or class that is highly interdependent and is tightly connected with other modules or classes, then the probability of an error in one affecting the others is greatly increased. Thus we can see that high coupling is not a desirable design attribute. Several research studies have shown the coupling attribute to be closely associated with factors such as proneness to error, maintainability, and testability of software; see Basili, Briand, and Melo (1996) and Wilkie and Kitchenham (2000) for more on these relationships.

Coupling is defined as an attribute that specifies the interdependence between two software units. The amount or degree of coupling is generally divided into five distinct levels, listed from the worst to the best:

- Content coupling
- Common coupling
- Control coupling
- Stamp coupling
- Data coupling

Content coupling is considered the worst coupling and data coupling is considered to be the best coupling. What is not listed is the ideal situation of no coupling. Of course, not many problems are so simple that the solutions do not require some coupling. The common terminology used to describe heavy interdependence and light interdependence is *tight coupling* and *loose coupling*, respectively.

Content coupling between two software units is the worst level. It is considered the tightest level of coupling because at this level two units access each other's internal data or procedural information. In this situation, almost any change to one unit will require a very careful review of the other, which means that the chance of creating an error in the other unit is very high. The two units would almost have to be considered as a pair for any type of reuse of software component.

Two software units are considered to be at the common-coupling level if they both refer to the same global variable. Such a variable may be used for various information exchanges, including controlling the logic of the other unit. It is not uncommon to see common coupling exhibited in large commercial applications where a record in the database may be used as a global variable. Common coupling is much better than content coupling. It still exhibits a fairly tight amount of coupling because of the permeating effects a change to the global variable or the shared database record would have on those that share this variable or record. In large application developments, the "where-used" matrix is generated during the system-build cycle to keep track of all the modules, global variables, and data records that are cross-referenced by the different software units. The where-used matrix is extensively used by both the integration team and the test team.

Control coupling is the next level where one software unit passes a control information and explicitly influences the logic of another software unit. The data that have been passed contain embedded control information that influences the behavior of the receiving software unit. The implicit semantics codified in the passed information between the sending and receiving modules force us to consider both modules as a pair. This level of coupling binds the two software units in such a manner that a single software unit reuse, separate from the others, is often hindered. Testing is also further complicated in that the number of test cases for interunit dependencies may increase dramatically when the embedded control information is deeply encoded.

In stamp coupling, a software unit passes a group of data to another software unit. Stamp coupling may be viewed as a lesser version of data coupling in that more than necessary data are passed between the two software units. An example would be passing a whole record or a whole data structure rather than only the needed, individual datum. Passing more information certainly increases the difficulty of comprehending what the precise interdependence between the two software units is.

The best level of coupling is data coupling, where only the needed data are passed between software units. At the data-coupling level, the interdependence is low and the two software units are considered loosely coupled.

These coupling levels do not include every possible interdependence situation. For example, a plain invocation of another software unit with only a passing of control and not even requiring a return of control is not mentioned. There is also no distinction made between data passed from one software unit to another, which may include the return of data where the returning information would be at a different coupling level. We should view the levels of coupling, like the levels of cohesion, as a guideline for good design. That is, we should strive for simplicity via strong cohesion and loose coupling in our design and coding.

Fenton and Melton (1990) provided a relatively simple example of measuring coupling between two software units, x and y, as follows:

1. Assign each level of coupling, from data coupling to content coupling, a numerical integer from 1 through 5, respectively.
2. Evaluate software units x and y by identifying the highest or the tightest level of coupling relationship between the x, y pair and assign it as i.
3. Identify all the coupling relationships between the pair x and y, and assign it as n.
4. Define the pairwise coupling between x and y as $C(x, y) = i + [n/(n + 1)]$.

For example, x passes y specific data that contain embedded control information that will influence the logic of y. Also x and y share a global variable. In this case, there are two coupling relationships between x and y. So $n = 2$. Of the two relationships, common coupling is worse, or tighter, than control coupling. So the highest coupling level between x and y is 4, which is common coupling. Thus $i = 4$, which then means that $C(x, y) = 4 + [2/(2 + 1)]$. With this definition, the smaller the values of i and n are, the looser the coupling will be. If all the software units in a system are pairwise analyzed as this, we can get a feel for the overall software system coupling. In fact, Fenton and Melton (1990) define the overall global coupling of a system to be the median value of all the pairs. Thus, if a software system, S, included $x_1, . . ., x_j$ units, then $C(S)$ = median of the set $\{C(x_n, x_m)$, for all the n, m from 1 through j $\}$. Thus, we would want to strive toward a lower $C(S)$ when designing a software system.

8.4 Object-Oriented Design Metrics

In this section we explore how the earlier notion of keeping the design simple through decomposition, strong cohesion, and loose coupling is affected, if any, by the object-oriented design and programming paradigm. Although there are several important concepts in OO, including class, inheritance, encapsulation, and polymorphism, there is really one central theme. That theme involves classes, how these classes are interrelated to each other, and how the classes interact with each other. A class is just a software entity that we want to, once again, keep simple through strong cohesion. The interrelationship and interaction among the classes should be kept simple through loose coupling. Thus the good, desirable design attributes have not changed. In OO, there are, however, some extensions to the way we would measure these attributes.

The desirable attributes of a good OO design may be measured by the six C-K metrics, which were identified by Chidamber and Kemerer (1994):

1. Weighted methods per class (WMC)
2. Depth of inheritance tree (DIT)
3. Number of children (NOC)
4. Coupling between object classes (CBO)
5. Response for a class (RFC)
6. Lack of cohesion in methods (LCOM)

Studies by Basili, Briand, and Melo (1996), Li and Henry (1993), and Briand et al. (2000) have shown that these (C-K) metrics correlate and serve well as indicators of error proneness, maintainability, and so on.

WMC is a weighted sum of all the methods in a class. Thus if there are n methods, m_1 through m_n, in a class, then WMC = SUM(w_i), where $i = 1, \ldots, n$. SUM is the arithmetic summation function, and w_i is the weight assigned to method m_i. A simple situation is to just count the number of methods by uniformly assigning 1 as the weight for all the methods. So a class with n methods will have its WMC equal to n. This metric is similar to counting the lines of code, where we find that the larger the size of the module, the more likely it will be prone to error. Larger classes, particularly those with larger WMCs, are associated with more error-proneness.

DIT is the maximum length of inheritance from a given class to its "root" class. It seems that the chance of error increases as we engage in inheritance and multiple inheritances. It is interesting to note that in the early days of OO, many organizations ignored inheritance features, designed their own unique classes, and never realized the desired productivity gain from reuse or inheritance. They thought it was simpler to design their own classes and not have to fully understand other, predefined classes. A class placed deep in the inheritance hierarchy was also difficult to even find, let alone fully comprehend. However, the various empirical tests have shown mixed results. Some have shown large DIT is associated with high defect rates, and others have found results inconclusive.

The NOC of a class is the number of children, or its immediate subclasses. This OO metric has also had mixed empirical results. When the NOC of all the classes are added together, it would seem that a large NOC of the software system could influence the complexity of the system. At the writing of this book, it is still uncertain how NOC influences the quality of the software.

CBO represents the number of object classes to which it is coupled. This is intuitively the same as the traditional coupling concept. Tighter or more coupling among classes where they share some common services or where one inherits methods and variables from other classes certainly introduces complexity, error-proneness, and difficulty of maintenance.

RFC is the set of methods that will be involved in a response to a message to an object of this class. RFC is also related to the notion of coupling. It has been shown that this metric is highly correlated to CBO and WMC. Because both large CBO and large WMC are known to affect defects and complexity of the software system, large RFC is also correlated with high defects.

LCOM is a count of the difference between the method pairs that are not similar and those that are similar within a given class. This metric characterizes the lack of cohesion of a class. It requires a bit more explanation and an example:

Consider a class with the following characteristics:

- It has $m_1, \ldots, m_n$ methods.
- The instance variables or attributes in each method are represented as $I_1, \ldots, I_n$, respectively.

Let P be the set of all the method pairs that have noncommon instance variables, and let Q be the set of all the method pairs that have common instance variables. Then LCOM = $\#P - \#Q$, where # represents cardinality of the set. Thus we can see that a class with a high

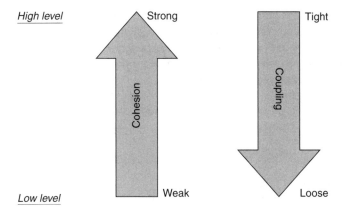

Figure 8.3 Cohesion and coupling.

LCOM value indicates that there is a high number of disparate methods. Therefore classes with high LCOM values are less cohesive and may be more complex and difficult to understand. High LCOM value equates with weak cohesion. To properly complete the definition of this metric, it must be stated that if #P is not > #Q, then LCOM = 0.

For example, a class, C, may contain three methods (m_1, m_2, m_3) whose respective instance variable sets are $I_1 = \{a, b, c, s\}$, $I_2 = \{a, b, z\}$, and $I_3 = \{f, h, w\}$. The I_1 and I_2 have $\{a, b\}$ in common. I_1 and I_3 have nothing in common, and I_2 and I_3 also have nothing in common. In this case, #P, the number of method pairs that are not similar or have nothing in common, is 2. The number of method pairs that are similar or have something in common, #Q, is 1. Thus LCOM for class C = 2 − 1 or 1.

All of these six C-K design metrics, are related either directly or indirectly to the concepts of cohesion and coupling. These metrics should assist software designers in better understanding the complexity of their design and help direct them to simplifying their work. As **Figure 8.3** shows, what the designers should strive for is strong cohesion and loose coupling.

8.4.1 Aspect-Oriented Programming

Aspect-oriented programming (AOP) is a new evolution of the concept for the separation of concerns, or aspects, of a system. This approach is meant to provide more modular, cohesive, and well-defined interfaces or coupling in the design of a system. Central to AOP is the notion of concerns that cross cut, which means that the methods related to the concerns intersect. It is believed that in OO programming these cross-cutting concerns are spread across the system. Aspect-oriented programming would modularize the implementation of these cross-cutting concerns into a cohesive single unit. Kiczales et al. (1997), Elrad, Filman and Bader (2001), and Colyer and Clement (2005) provide more information on aspect-oriented programming.

8.4.2 The Law of Demeter

Another good guideline for object-oriented design is the Law of Demeter, addressed by Lieberherr and Holland (1989). This guideline limits the span of control of an object by restricting the message-sending structure of methods in a class. The messaging restriction will reduce the coupling of objects and enhance the cohesion of an object. This is not a measurement but a guideline originating from the experience gained from the design and implementation of the Demeter System, an aspect-oriented programming project at Northeastern University, developed in the 1980s.

The Law of Demeter may be stated as follows. An object should send messages to the following kinds of objects:

- The object itself
- The object's attributes (instance variables)
- The parameters of methods in this object
- Any object created by the methods of this object
- Any object returned from a call to one of this object's methods
- Any object in any collection that is one of the preceding categories

The law essentially ensures that objects send messages only to objects that are directly known to them. It may be paraphrased as "only talk to your immediate neighbors" or "don't talk to strangers." A simple example, adapted from management control, may help. Consider the case of a software development vice president who wishes to enforce a design principle across the development organization. Rather than giving the command to his or her immediate subordinates and asking them, in turn, to relay the message to their subordinates, the vice president engages in direct conversation with every person in the organization. Clearly such an approach increases coupling and diffuses cohesion. This vice president has violated the Law of Demeter.

8.5   User-Interface Design

Up until now, we have focused on software units and the interactions among them. In this section we will concentrate on user-interface (UI) design—the interactions between a human user and the software. Instead of worrying about reducing software defects, we must now worry about reducing human errors. Although some designers may believe that having a graphical user interface solves many of the user anxiety problems with computing systems, it is still important to understand what is it that makes the interface easier to understand, navigate, and use. What is user-friendliness, and what characterizes a good user-interface design? The important characteristic here is that the interface has more to do with people rather than software systems.

8.5.1   Good UI Characteristics

In Section 8.1, we listed consistency and completeness as two general design characteristics. In UI design, consistency is especially important because it contributes to many of the desirable characteristics that a human requires. Imagine a user interface that has inconsistent headings or labels, inconsistent help texts, inconsistent messages, inconsistent response times, inconsistent usage of icons, or inconsistent navigation mechanisms. Imagine an even worse situation where some of the inconsistencies lead to an actual conflict that a user is pressed to resolve; see Nielson (2002) for additional discussion of UI consistency.

One of the main goals for UI design is to ensure that there is a consistent pattern across all the interfaces. Mandel (1997) has identified three "golden rules" for user-interface design:

- Place the user in control
- Reduce the user's memory load
- Design consistent user interface

These rules have further spawned another two principles for UI design: (1) user action should be interruptible and allowed to be redone, and (2) user defaults should be meaningful. These rules and principles all serve as good guidelines for UI design.

Shneiderman and Plaisant (2005) have identified the following eight rules of interface design:

1. Strive for consistency
2. Enable frequent users to use short cuts
3. Offer informative feedback
4. Design dialogues to yield closure
5. Offer error prevention and simple error handling
6. Permit easy reversal of actions
7. Support internal locus of control
8. Reduce short-term memory

Note that consistency, which we have already discussed, is the first on the list. The second rule, which involves short cuts to achieve an end goal, indicates that there may need to be different levels of user interface for novices and for experts. The feedback from the system to the user should be informative and understandable so that the user will know what follow-up action to perform, if any. The user activities should be grouped in such a manner that there is a start and an end; the user should experience a sense of accomplishment at the end of the series of activities. The fifth and sixth rules deal with human fallibility. The system should be designed to prevent the user from making mistakes. But if an error is made, there needs to be a mechanism that allows the user to reverse or handle the mistake. The seventh rule addresses the human need for control. That is, the users should not be made to respond to the software system; instead, the system should be made to respond to user-initiated actions. The eighth rule recognizes the limitations of human memory and that information should be kept simple. Wherever possible, information should be provided to the users in the form of defaults or in the form of preassigned lists of choices. This theory on short-term memory is often attributed to Miller (1956), who identified "seven, plus or minus two" limits on our ability to process information.

In addition to the preceding rules, there are also various UI guideline standards. Large corporations such as IBM, Microsoft, and Apple have their own UI guidelines. The International Standards Organization (ISO) has several standards related to user interfaces, including ISO 9241, which has multiple parts that can be acquired from the ISO website at www.iso.org.

8.5.2 Usability Evaluation and Testing

In the 1980s, with the advent of personal computers and graphical interface, UI designs received a lot of attention. Usability testing became a new task that was introduced into software development. In its early state, the UI design was of low fidelity in that the interfaces were mocked-up with paper boards and diagrams. As the technology and tools improved, UI design became high fidelity in that real screens were developed as design prototypes. Some of these prototypes were introduced during the requirements phase. With the high-fidelity UI design, more in-depth evaluation was performed. Elaborate usability "laboratories" with one-way mirrors and recording equipment were constructed, and statistical analysis of user performance was conducted. Users, or subjects, were carefully profiled and chosen for the usability tests.

Some of the key factors in analyzing application interfaces included the following:

- Number of subjects who completed the tasks without any help
- Length of time, on the average, required to complete each task
- Average number of times that help function was evoked
- Number of tasks completed within some predefined time interval
- Places where subjects had to redo a task, and the number of times this needed to be done
- Number of times short cuts were used

These and other types of information were recorded and analyzed. Sometimes there was also a questionnaire that would further ask for the subjects' comments on the general appearance, flow, or suggestions.

In the early days of usability testing, this activity was grouped as a type of postsystem testing and was conducted late in the development cycle. As a result of placing usability testing late in the testing cycle, only the most severe problems were fixed. The other, lesser problems were all delayed and assigned to the next release. Today, UI evaluation is moved up to the requirements and design phases. Many of the problems are resolved early, and the solutions are integrated into the software product in time for the current product release.

8.6   Summary

In this chapter, we first introduced two general characteristics of a good design:

- Consistency
- Completeness

A list of early concepts related to design complexity and metrics were then introduced.

- Halstead complexity measure
- McCabe's cyclomatic complexity
- Henry-Kafura flow complexity measure
- Card and Glass structural complexity measure

The two main criteria for a simple and good design that can provide us the various "easy to" attributes are discussed in detail. The goal is to attain the following:

- Strong cohesion
- Weak coupling

A specific example, using techniques from Bieman and Ott (1994), is also shown to clarify the notion of cohesion.

The six C-K metrics for OO design are shown to be also closely tied to the notion of cohesion and coupling:

- Weighted methods per class (WMC)
- Depth of the inheritance tree (DIT)
- Number of children (NOC)
- Coupling between object classes (CBO)
- Response for a class (RFC)
- Lack of cohesion in methods (LCOM)

Finally, with the advent of graphical interface and the Internet, the characteristics of good user-interface design are discussed. UI design should focus on the human rather than on the system side. In today's systems, much of the late usability testing is moved up into UI interface prototyping conducted during the early requirements phase.

8.7 Review Questions

1. What are the two general characteristics of a good design that naturally evolve from requirements?

2. What is the cyclomatic complexity of the design flow shown in **Figure 8.4** where the diamond shapes represent decision branches and the rectangles are statements?

3. What are glue tokens and superglue tokens? Which contributes more to cohesion and why?

4. What are the levels of cohesion?

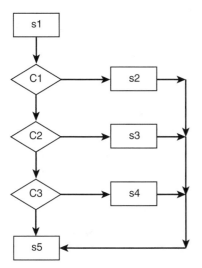

Figure 8.4 Case structure.

5. What are the levels of coupling?

6. What are the six C-K metric for OO design?

7. What is a depth of inheritance tree (DIT) in C-K metrics, and why may a large DIT be bad for design?

8. In contrast to general design, what is of the most interest in user-interface design?

9. List four of the eight rules of interface design presented by Shneiderman and Plaisant.

8.8 Exercises

1. Discuss the difference between a good design and what we are trying to achieve as a result of a good design.

2. In gauging design, one of the concepts involves fan-in and fan-out.

   a. Discuss the concept of fan-in and fan-out in a design.

   b. In Henry-Kafura's measure, complexity is defined as C_p, where C_p = (fan-in × fan-out)^2. Instead of multiplying fan-in and fan-out, discuss the effect if you change the operator to addition, especially for the situation when the number of fan-in or fan-out values increases.

3. Why do you suppose Card and Glass focused more on the fan-out value rather than on the number of fan-ins?

4. Define *cohesion* in your own words.

5. Define *coupling* in your own words.

6. The notion of an entity relationship (ER) diagram was evolved into a database design, as discussed in Chapter 7. If various components use the same database table to update records and query records, what type of coupling is involved? Explain.

7. Is there any conflict between strong cohesion and weak coupling? Discuss.

8. Does the cyclomatic measure have anything to do with the concept of cohesion or coupling? Explain how it does or does not.

9. Summarize one of Mandel's UI golden rules. Place user in control, subject to some of Shneiderman and Plaisant's UI golden rules, and discuss why you chose those.

10. Relate one of the UI golden rules, reduce user's memory load, to other design characteristics such as simplicity in design, strong cohesion, and weak coupling.

8.9 Suggested Readings

E. Arisholm, L. C. Briand, and A. Foyen, "Dynamic Coupling Measurement for Object-Oriented Software," *IEEE Transactions on Software Engineering* 30, no. 8 (August 2004): 491–506.

V. R. Basili, L. C. Briand, and W. L. Melo, "A Validation of Object-Oriented Design Metrics as Quality Indicators," *IEEE Transactions on Software Engineering* 22, no. 10 (October 1996): 751–761.

J. M. Bieman and L. M. Ott, "Measuring Functional Cohesion," *IEEE Transactions on Software Engineering* 20, no. 8 (August 1994): 644–657.

L. C. Briand, J. W. Daly, and J. Wust, "A Unified Framework for Cohesion Measurement in Object-Oriented Systems," *Proceedings of the Fourth International Software Metrics Symposium* (November 1997): pp. 43–53.

L. C. Briand, J. Wüst, J. W. Daly, and D. V. Porter, "Exploring the Relationship Between Design Measures and Software Quality in Object-Oriented Systems," *Journal of Systems and Software* 51, no. 3 (2000): 245–273.

D. N. Card and R. L. Glass, *Measuring Software Design Quality* (Upper Saddle River, NJ: Prentice Hall, 1990).

S. Chidamber, D. P. Darcy, and C. Kemerer, "Managerial Use of Metrics for Object-Oriented Software: An Exploratory Analysis," *IEEE Transactions on Software Engineering* 24, no. 8 (August 1998): 629–639.

S. Chidamber and C. Kemerer, "A Metrics Suite for Object-Oriented Design," *IEEE Transactions on Software Engineering* 20, no. 6 (June 1994): 476–493.

A. Colyer and A. Clement, Aspect-Oriented Programming with AspectJ," *IBM Systems Journal* 44, no. 2 (2005): 302–308.

T. Elrad, R. E. Filman, and A. Bader, "Aspect-Oriented Programming," *Communications of the ACM* (October 2001): 29–32.

K. E. Emam et al., "The Optimal Class Size for Object-Oriented Software," *IEEE Transactions on Software Engineering* 28, no. 5 (May 2002): 494–509.

N. Fenton and A. Melton, "Deriving Structurally Based Software Measure," *Journal of Systems and Software* 12, no. 3 (July 1990): 177–187.

E. Gamma, R. Helm, R. Johnson, and J. Vlissides, *Design Patterns: Elements of Reusable Object-Oriented Software* (Reading, MA: Addison-Wesley, 1995).

M. H. Halstead, *Elements of Software Science* (New York: Elsevier, 1977).

S. M. Henry and D. Kafura, "Software Structure Metrics Based on Information Flow," *IEEE Transactions on Software Engineering* 7, no. 5 (September 1981): 510–518.

S. Henry and C. Selig, "Predicting Source-Code Complexity at Design Stage," *IEEE Software* (March 1990): 36–44.

D. Hix and H. R. Hartson, *Developing User Interface: Ensuring Usability Through Product and Process* (New York: Wiley, 1993).

G. Kiczales et al., "Aspect Oriented Programming," *Proceedings of the 11th European Conference on Objected Oriented Computing* (June 1997): 220–242.

S. Lauesen, *User Interface Design: A Software Engineering Perspective* (Reading, MA: Addison-Wesley, 2004).

T. Lethbridge and R. Laganiere, *Object-Oriented Software Engineering: Practical Software Development Using UML and Java* (New York: McGraw-Hill, 2001).

W. Li and S. Henry, "Object-Oriented Metrics That Predict Maintainability," *Journal of Systems and Software* 23 (1993): 111–122.

K. J. Lieberherr and I. Holland, "Assuring good styles for object-oriented programs," *IEEE Software* (September 1989): 38–48.

M. Lorenz and J. Kidd, *Object-Oriented Software Metrics: A Practical Guide* (Upper Saddle River, NJ: Prentice Hall, 1994).

T. Mandel, *The Elements of User Interface Design* (New York: Wiley, 1997).

T. J. McCabe, "A Complexity Measure," *IEEE Transactions on Software Engineering* 2, no. 4 (December 1976): 308–320.

T. J. McCabe and B. W. Charles, "Design Complexity Measurement and Testing," *Communications of the ACM* 32, no. 12 (December 1989): 1415–1425.

G. Miller, "The Magical Number Seven, Plus or Minus Two: Some Limits on Our Capacity for Processing Information," *Psychology Review* 63 (1956): 81–97.

G. J. Myers, *Reliable Software Through Composite Design* (New York: Petrocelli/Charter, 1975).

——, *Composite/Structured Design* (New York: Nostrand Reinhold, 1978).

J. Nielson, *Coordinating User Interfaces for Consistency* (New York, NY: Academic Press, 1989; reprint by Morgan Kaufman Publishers, 2002).

——, *Designing Web Usability: The Practice of Simplicity* (Thousand Oaks, CA: New Riders Publishing, 2000).

——, http://www.useit.com, 2012.

A. J. Offutt, M. J. Harrold, and P. Kolte, "A Software Metric System for Module Coupling," *Journal of Systems and Software* 20, no. 3 (March 1993): 295–308.

B. Shneiderman and C. Plaisant, *Designing the User Interface: Strategies for Effective Human-Computer Interaction*, 4th ed. (Reading, MA: Addison-Wesley, 2005).

R. Subramanyam and M. S. Krishnan, "Empirical Analysis of CK Metrics for Object-Oriented Design Complexity: Implications for Software Defects," *IEEE Transactions on Software Engineering* 29, no. 4 (April 2003): 297–310.

F. Tsui, O. Karam, S. Duggins, and C. Bonja, "On Inter-Method and Intra-Method Object-Oriented Class Cohesion," *International Journal of Information Technologies and Systems Approach* 2(1), (June 2009): 15–32.

F. G. Wilkie and B. A. Kitchenham, "Coupling Measures and Change Ripples in C++ Application Software," *Journal of Systems and Software* 52 (2000): 157–164.

E. Yourdon and L. Constantine, *Structured Design: Fundamentals of a Discipline of Computer Program and Systems Design* (Upper Saddle River, NJ: Prentice Hall, 1979).

CHAPTER 9

Implementation

OBJECTIVES

- Describe some of the characteristics of good implementations and the best practices that help achieve them.
- Understand the role of comments in producing a good program and the characteristics of good comments.
- Learn some of the techniques for effectively debugging programs.
- Analyze the concept of refactoring and a few refactoring techniques.

9.1   Introduction to Implementation

The ultimate goal of most software engineering projects is to produce a working program. The act of transforming the detailed design into a valid program in some programming language, together with all its supporting activities is referred to as *implementation*. To simplify matters in this chapter, we assume a traditional software engineering life cycle, with an explicit, detailed design being produced. In many cases the detailed design is not done explicitly but is left as part of the implementation. Chapter 7 discussed techniques for software design, and Chapter 8 described how to evaluate good designs.

Doing the detailed design as part of the implementation is usually faster, but it may result in a less cohesive and less organized design, because the detailed design of each module will usually be done by a different person. In small projects, the detailed design is usually left as part of the implementation. In larger projects, or when the programmers are inexperienced, the detailed design will be done by a separate person. Of course, this decision does not have to be the same for all modules. The most important modules may be explicitly designed by the most experienced personnel, with the less important ones left to other programmers.

The implementation phase involves more than just writing code. Code also needs to be tested and debugged as well as compiled and built into a complete executable product. We usually need to utilize configuration management in order to keep track of different versions of the code.

In this chapter we cover all aspects of implementation except testing, which is covered in Chapter 10, and building and configuration management, which is covered in Chapter 11.

9.2   Characteristics of a Good Implementation

It is always a good idea to keep in mind the following characteristics that should be found in a good implementation:

- *Readability:* The code can be easily read and understood by other programmers.
- *Maintainability:* The code can be easily modified and maintained. Note that this is related to readability, but it is not exactly the same; for example, this involves the use of Hungarian notation, first put forward by Charles Simonyi of Microsoft (see Simonyi, 1976), in which variable names include abbreviations for the type of variable.
- *Performance:* All other things being equal, the implementation should produce code that performs as fast as possible.
- *Traceability:* All code elements should correspond to a design element. Code can be traced back to design (and design to requirements).
- *Correctness:* The implementation should do what it is intended to do (as defined in the requirements and detailed design).
- *Completeness:* All of the system requirements are met.

The first instinct of many programmers would be to concentrate on correctness, and then maybe on performance, without too much emphasis on readability and maintainability. For many software engineers engaged in large, multiple-release software projects, maintainability is as important as correctness (or even more important), and performance is of lesser importance in most cases.

It is important to realize that achieving these characteristics requires serious effort and that there are interactions and trade-offs between these desirable characteristics. Readability usually helps maintainability, and both of these usually help achieve correctness. Performance optimizations often reduce readability and maintainability, and sometimes even performance.

9.3 Programming Style and Coding Guidelines

Almost all software development organizations have some sort of coding guidelines. These guidelines usually specify issues such as naming, indentation, and commenting styles, issues that may be contentious for many programming teams. Notice that there are many tools that will automatically indent and reformat your code, so such issues do not need to be as contentious as might be expected.

The most important thing to realize is that most of those issues—especially those dealing more with syntax (such as capitalization and indentation guidelines)—are not terribly important, and basically are simply a matter of getting accustomed to a particular style. However, we strongly recommend that you be consistent in your notation to avoid confusion when others are debugging or maintaining your code later. In large software projects, there are usually some programming conventions. These conventions may seem to be of little value at first, but they may become extremely helpful in the build and integration cycle when, for example, all the parts with a prefix of a001 need to be compiled together, where the a001 prefix signifies a certain component.

A similar scheme is used for issuing error messages. For example, you want to write a message to users that is informative and clear, but along with that, you can prefix the message with some identifier that allows the programmers to identify, for debugging purposes, where the message was issued from.

Another point usually made in coding guidelines is the recommendation of banning certain language features and practices that have proved, for the organization, error-prone. For example, many organizations will ban the use of pointers or multiple inheritance in languages that support them, and of course, almost all organizations will require the code to compile without any warnings and without using any deprecated language features.

The most important issues for maintaining a good coding style are to be consistent and to try to highlight the meaning of your code. The following recommendations are related to the issues that affect coding style:

- *Naming:* This refers to choosing names for classes, methods, variables, and other programming entities. Naming is mainly a semantic issue about choosing good names. It is also one of the most important issues in improving readability and maintainability. A well-chosen name that conveys the intent of a module will make the code immediately understandable, while a badly chosen name will necessitate a comment, or even mislead the reader. We (and many others) have noticed a strong correlation between good names and understanding. In many cases, if you cannot think of a good name for a module, then you do not understand it well enough. We recommend choosing long names for global entities, and much shorter names for local entities that are used for a small section of code.

Another key issue with naming is consistency. Always use the same word (or abbreviation) for a given concept, and avoid using the same word for two different concepts, even in a different context. When choosing among available words for a concept, we recommend that you choose one that is consistent with external standards, following the convention of your particular programming language or platform.

Naming may become a more complex issue when dealing with multicultural and multilanguage teams. In this case, deciding in advance to take the names from one particular human language is a good idea.

- *Separating words and capitalization:* Many times a name will be composed of more than one word. In human languages, we use spaces to separate words, but most programming languages will not allow us to do so. Different programming languages have used different conventions for how to combine several words into one identifier. We strongly recommend using the standard conventions for your language, and making sure you follow it in every case.

  As a sample of conventions, the C language uses all lowercase identifiers, with underscores for separating words, as in do_something, while Java will use no separation but will capitalize the first letter of the second word, as in doSomething. Java also has some rules about when to start a name with an uppercase or lowercase letter. See the Suggested Readings section at the end of this chapter for more resources on this topic.

- *Indentation and spacing:* Indentation refers to adding horizontal spaces before some lines to better reflect the structure of the code. Spacing refers to both spaces and blank lines inserted in the code. A common beginner's mistake is to not indent properly. As an example, try to understand the following fragment, which is not indented:

```
public static int largest(int arr[]){
assert(arr.length>0);
int curLargest=arr[0];
for(int i=1; i<arr.length; ++i) {
if(arr[i]>curLargest)
curLargest=arr[i];
}
return curLargest;
}
```

Now look at a version that is indented incorrectly:

```
public static int largest(int arr[]){
    assert(arr.length>0);
    int curLargest=arr[0];
    for(int i=1; i<arr.length; ++i)
            if(arr[i]>curLargest)
                            curLargest=arr[i];
    return curLargest;
}
```

(Can you spot the error?) And finally look at this version, with correct indentation:

```
public static int largest(int arr[]){
    assert(arr.length>0);
    int curLargest=arr[0];
```

```
        for(int i=1; i<arr.length; ++i) {
            if(arr[i]>curLargest)
                curLargest=arr[i];
        }
        return curLargest;
    }
```

We consider indentation a very important issue affecting readability and maintainability. A common indentation style should be defined, and all programmers should follow it. The most important issue here is consistency, because programmers will rapidly grow accustomed to a given indentation style. Many times a de facto indentation standard style for a language exists, usually the one used in the primary language reference. We strongly suggest using it, as most programmers will be familiar with it.

- *Function/method size:* Many studies have shown that large functions or methods are statistically more error-prone than smaller ones. (Up to a certain point, actually, very small methods will have more errors on average; see Hatton [1997] for more details.) The size issue has been studied since the 1960s and the days of structured programming by the likes of Harlan Mills and Edsgar Dijkstra (see the two articles by Dijkstra in the Suggested Readings section). Practical considerations also affect method size; only a certain number of lines can fit in a string or on a printed page, and having the ability to look at the whole method is important in readability and maintainability. We recommend limiting the size of each method to around 50 lines whenever possible, which can comfortably fit on a screen or a page.

- *File-naming issues:* Having a standard for specifying how to name the files, which files to generate for each module, and how to locate a given file from a module is very advantageous. You could have a separate document specifying what modules go in which files, but having a file-naming convention can make things much easier.

- *Particular programming constructs:* Different programming languages support different features; although they usually have good reasons to include certain features, there are many that can be misused and need special precautions. Examples of features considered dangerous are the `GOTO` keyword and multiple inheritance. As an extreme case, C provides the functions `setjmp` and `longjmp`, which allow for a kind of global `GOTO`; see Dijkstra (2003), a transcription of a letter he wrote to the ACM editor in 1968.

    Most of these constructs were included in languages for a reason, and they have their applications. We recommend that dangerous constructs be banned by default, with the programmers being able to get authorization for particular uses if they can demonstrate that the benefits outweigh the dangers.

9.4 Comments

Comments are very important and can significantly aid or hurt readability and maintainability. There are two main problems with comments: (1) they may distract from the actual code and make the program more difficult to read and (2) they may be wrong.

Comments may become outdated as the code changes, or they may be wrong the first time they are written because they are not executable and cannot be tested.

We classify comments into six different types, of which the first five correspond to those defined by McConnell (2004):

1. *Repeat of the code:* These kinds of comments tend to be done by novice programmers and should be avoided. Misguided coding guidelines often require programmers to create these kinds of comments by mandating a comment block for each function, with a line for each parameter. For the most part, these comments will only be wasted effort and distract the reader. An extreme example would be the following comment:

   ```
   // increment i by one
   ++i;
   ```

2. *Explanation of the code:* Sometimes, when the code is complex, programmers are tempted to explain what the code does in human language. We strongly believe that in almost every case, if the code is so complex that it requires an explanation, then it should be rewritten.

3. *Marker in the code:* It is common practice to put markers in the code to indicate incomplete items, opportunities for improvement, and other similar information. We recommend using a consistent notation for these markers, and eliminating all of them before the code is in production. Sometimes programmers put markers in the code to keep track of changes and who made them. We believe that information is better tracked with version management software, and recommend doing so.

4. *Summary of the code:* Comments that summarize what the code does, rather than just repeating it, are very helpful in understanding the code, but they need to be kept up to date. It is important to ensure that these comments are really summarizing the code, not just repeating or explaining it. In many cases, the code that is being summarized can be abstracted into its own function, which, if named correctly, will eliminate the need for the comment.

5. *Description of the code intent:* These are the most useful kinds of comments; they describe what the code is supposed to do rather than what it does. These are the only kinds of comments that override the code. If the code does not fulfill its intent, then the code is wrong.

6. *External references:* These are comments that link the code to external entities, usually books or other programs. Many times these can be viewed as a kind of intent statement, as in, "This function implements the XYZ algorithm, as explained in …," but we believe such comments require special attention. There may also be external prerequisites and corequisites for the code, such as the existence of initializing data in the database tables.

The trade-off that comments imply should be recognized. Comments can help clarify code and relate it to other sources, but they also represent some level of duplication of the code. Effort is invested in their creation and, above all, in their maintenance. A comment that does not correspond to the actual code that it accompanies can cause errors that are very hard to find and correct.

Another danger comments present is that they can be used to justify bad coding practices. Many times programmers will be tempted to produce code that is too complicated or too hard to maintain, and add comments to it, rather than rewrite it to good standards. In fact, many experts recommend avoiding comments completely, and produce what is called "self-documented code"—that is, code that is so well written that it does not need any documentation. We believe that is an ideal that programmers should strive for, but that comments have their place, especially in the form of describing the programmer's intent.

We strongly encourage programmers to use good names and good programming practices and reserve comments mainly for external references and statements of intent. If the code cannot be abstracted and it is still complex, summary comments may be appropriate. Code explanations and markers should only be used as temporary measures, and repetitions of the code should be always avoided.

A problem with comments is that most programming books and tutorials, because they are geared for beginners (or at least for people who do not know a particular technique or library), tend to provide too many comments, usually repeating or explaining the code. Many programmers will either imitate this style, or go to the other extreme and avoid comments at all costs. McConnell (2004) and Kernighan and Pike (1999) provide examples of good commenting practices.

9.5   Debugging

Debugging is the act of locating and fixing errors in code. The errors are usually discovered through testing, but they can be found by other means, including code inspections and through normal use of the program. We can identify four phases in the debugging process (besides discovering the error, which we do not consider part of debugging). These phases will need to occur in almost every case. Keep in mind that debugging is a highly iterative process, in which you will be creating a hypothesis about what causes the errors, writing test cases to prove or disprove the hypothesis, and changing the code to try to fix the problem. If the hypothesis happens to be false, you will need to go back to generating and corroborating a new hypothesis. The four phases in the debugging process can be summarized as follows:

1. *Stabilization, sometimes called reproduction:* The purpose of this phase is to be able to reproduce the error on a particular configuration (in many cases the developer's machine), and to find out the conditions that led to the error by constructing a minimal test case. We do not need to look at the code at all in this phase; we just need to identify which input conditions, combined with which program states, produce the error.

   The output of the stabilization phase is a series of test cases that produce the error, and possibly some cases that perform correctly. Stabilization also involves minimization of the conditions that led to the error. After you write a test case that reproduces the error, try to write a simpler one that also fails. Although stabilization is a trivial task in many cases, it can be very difficult sometimes. Many errors will appear to occur at random, and testing the program twice with the same input will sometimes produce different results, depending on the state the program is in. Variables that are not initialized, dangling pointers, and the interaction of several threads tend to produce errors that appear to be random.

2. *Localization:* The process of localization involves finding the sections of the code that led to the error. This is usually the hardest part, although, if the stabilization phase produces a very simple test case, it may make the problem obvious.

3. *Correction:* The process of correction involves changing the code to fix the errors. Hopefully, if you understand what caused the error, you have a good chance of fixing the problem. A common mistake is to try to correct the problem without having really stabilized it or located it within the source code, which leads to random changes that do not fix the code and may introduce new errors.

4. *Verification:* The process of verification involves making sure the error is fixed, and no other errors were introduced with the changes in the code. Many times, a change in the code will not fix the error or may introduce new errors.

Errors in a program can be broadly categorized into syntax and logic errors. Syntax errors in compiled languages tend to be easy to find, as the compiler will detect them and can provide some information about its source. Although compiler error messages are not usually examples of clarity, programmers will quickly learn to use them to find and solve the problem.

Although debugging is a very complicated task, there are several rules of thumb that tell you where to find errors. It is important to realize that many routines will have a high number of errors, either because of complexity, bad design, or problems introduced by their creator. Some indications may be there from the design or code inspections. Routines with more than one error will tend to have even more errors. Newly created code tends to have more errors as it has not been exercised (and so tested) as much as the old code. You will also need to learn your own heuristics about which parts of your program, language features, or particular programs, are error-prone and in which ways.

The following tools can help with the debugging process:

- Source code comparators that can help you quickly find changes to the code.
- Extended checkers that find problems with your syntax, logic, or style. They can highlight error-prone code and many times find errors before they are detected by executing the program. The classic example of this kind of tool is lint, used to check C programs.
- Interactive debuggers that let you examine variables, step over certain points in your code, and establish breakpoints and interrupt the program at particular places. Interactive debuggers can help greatly, but they are commonly misused, especially by beginner programmers, who try to use them as a substitute for understanding the code.
- Specially constructed libraries that reimplement standard libraries but with extra safeguards, to detect and prevent errors.
- Tools such as profilers, which describe the pre- and postconditions (discussed in Section 9.6) and coverage tools that are primarily used for other purposes but can help in testing.

9.6   Assertions and Defensive Programming

A very useful technique is the use of assertions, which is related to the more formal concepts of preconditions and postconditions. A precondition is a condition that your module requires in order to produce correct results. A postcondition is a condition that should hold true after executing your code, if the preconditions were met. It is a good practice to make your preconditions explicit by the use of assertions—that is, statements that check a condition and produce an error if the condition is not met. Most modern programming languages have specific facilities for assertions. By making your assertions explicit and executable, you can catch many errors. Preconditions and postconditions can also be used with formal methods to prove that a code actually executes correctly.

9.7   Performance Optimization

Performance is an important aspect of almost any program, but we have to understand the trade-offs. Optimizing for performance usually (but not always) affects maintainability and readability for the worse. Keep in mind that correctness is obviously more important than performance, and maintainability is as well, because it helps future correctness. The only possible exception to this rule is in real-time systems, in which performing an action within certain time limits is a part of being correct.

One of the most common mistakes programmers make is to worry too early about performance. The first goal is to make a program that is correct and easy to maintain. After the program is finished, if the performance is unsatisfactory, then it is time to worry about it. In many cases, the performance will not be a problem, saving substantial effort. Another common mistake is to optimize all the code for performance, without measuring first. Most pieces of a program will be executed only a few times and will not impact performance significantly. There are only a few pieces of a program that will impact performance and that need to be optimized.

A profiler is a tool that runs a program and calculates how much time it spends on each part. It will help you find the performance bottlenecks and the modules that need to be optimized. Armed with this information, you can then review and optimize only those modules that will have a sizable impact on performance. After making the changes, measure and profile again to make sure the changes actually improve performance.

In a few cases, bad performance is a symptom of a bad design or bad coding, and making code simpler and clearer will also result in better performance. In most cases, it should be possible to modularize the code so that the performance optimizations are hidden in very specific places, and most of the code is clear. A good optimizing compiler can also take care of many performance optimizations without the programmer sacrificing any clarity.

As with most other activities, a cost-benefit analysis should be done before undergoing performance optimization. Given that a programmer's time is much more expensive than machine time, it may be cheaper to leave the program as is and just buy more capable hardware. Besides the programmer's cost, the decrease in maintainability and the possibility of introducing errors need to be weighed.

This warning about performance optimization should not be construed as a recommendation to produce bloated code. Good programming practices and judicious design choices can go a long way in producing code that is correct, maintainable, and fast. One of the best practices is to reuse as much existing high-quality code as possible. Most of the standard data structures and algorithms that can substantially increase performance of an application have already been implemented and are available, in many cases, as part of the standard library included with your language compiler. Know your library and which other high-quality code is available, and use such code rather than reimplement it in new code.

9.8   Refactoring

Even when using best practices and making a conscious effort to produce high-quality software, it is highly unlikely that you will consistently produce programs that cannot be improved. You will be learning more about programming and about the particular problem you are working on as you go.

Programming is, in many ways, similar to writing in a natural language; after all, a program communicates a process to the computer, and, more importantly, to other programmers. In the same way that written documents can be improved and polished after writing them, programs can also be improved for style. An important difference is that, in programming, we usually do not want to change the interface or observable behavior of the program or module, because this will impact other modules.

Martin Fowler (1999) popularized the term *refactoring* to refer to the activity of improving your code style without altering its behavior. He also uses this term for each of the individual changes you can do to improve the structure of your code. Fowler defines a catalog of symptoms indicating that your code needs refactoring, which he calls "bad smells," and provides a catalog of useful refactorings.

Recall that the concept of refactoring is also part of Beck's Extreme Programming methodology described in Chapter 5. Refactoring is one of the most powerful techniques for producing good code. Of course, you should use good programming practices and try to produce high-quality code the first time. However, you should also try to refactor it and improve it as you go.

The catalog of "bad smells" provided by Fowler includes the following:

- Duplicated code (clearly a waste).
- Long method (excessively large or long methods perhaps should be subdivided into more cohesive ones).
- Large class (same problem as long method).
- Switch statements (in object-oriented code, switch statements can in most cases be replaced with polymorphism, making the code clearer).
- Feature envy, in which a method tends to use more of an object from a class different to the one it belongs.
- Inappropriate intimacy, in which a class refers too much to private parts of other classes.

> **Refactoring**   A change made to the internal structure of software to make it easier to understand and cheaper to modify without changing its observable behavior.

Any of these symptoms, as well as the others that Fowler cites and the ones you will develop, will indicate that your code can be improved. You can use **refactorings** to help you deal with these problems.

According to Fowler (1999), refactoring is "a change made to the internal structure of software to make it easier to understand and cheaper to modify without changing its observable behavior." The following are a few of the refactorings that Fowler discusses:

- *Extract method:* A process that turns a code fragment into its own method, with an appropriate name, and calls the method.
- *Substitute algorithm:* A process that replaces the body of a method with a new algorithm that is clearer, and returns the same result.
- *Move method:* A process that moves an algorithm from one class to another where it makes more sense.
- *Extract class:* A process that divides into two.

9.9 Summary

In this chapter we reviewed the following characteristics of good implementation:

- Readability
- Maintainability
- Performance
- Traceability
- Correctness
- Completeness

We then discussed coding guidelines, naming conventions, commenting, and other items that contribute to the characteristics of good implementation. Debugging, performance considerations, and refactoring were also presented as additional activities that should be included as part of implementation.

9.10 Review Questions

1. List and explain in your own words three characteristics of a good software implementation.

2. Briefly discuss the issues associated with naming variables and procedures in a program.

3. List the four phases of the debugging process.

4. True or false: You should always optimize your code for performance. Why?

5. List three "bad smells" signaling that your code probably should be refactored.

6. List and briefly explain three of the refactorings mentioned in this chapter.

9.11 Exercises

1. Read a program that you wrote a long time ago (the older the better) and a recent program. Can you understand the older program? Do you notice any changes in your programming style?

2. Consider your favorite programming language (or one assigned by your professor). What is its most dangerous feature? Would you completely ban it if you were writing the coding guidelines for your programming team? Why or why not?

3. Find a program that you wrote (or one the professor assigns to you) and analyze it for style. Is it indented correctly? Are the names well chosen? Can it benefit from refactoring? Discuss the issues with your fellow students or with other software developers.

9.12   Suggested Readings

M. Bohl and M. Rynn, *Tools for Structured Design: An Introduction to Programming Logic*, 6th ed. (Upper Saddle River, NJ: Prentice Hall, 2003).

E. W. Dijkstra, "GOTO Statement Considered Harmful," letter to the editor, *Communications of ACM* (March 1968): 147–148.

——, "Structured Programming," transcribed by Ham Richards, http://www.cs.utexas.edu/users/EWD/transcritions/EWD02xx/EWD268.html, last revised July 2003.

M. Fowler, *Refactoring: Improving the Design of Existing Code* (Reading, MA: Addison-Wesley, 1999).

R. Green, "How to Write Unmaintainable Code," http://thc.org/root/phun/unmaintain.html, accessed September 2012.

Les Hatton, "Reexamining the Fault Density-Component Size Connection," *IEEE Software* 14, no. 2 (March 1997): 89–97.

"Hungarian Notation—The Good, the Bad and the Ugly," www.ootips. org/hungarian-notation.html, May 2005.

A. Hunt and D. Thomas, *The Pragmatic Programmer: from Journeyman to Master* (Reading, MA: Addison-Wesley, 1999).

B. W. Kernighan and R. Pike, *The Practice of Programming* (Reading, MA: Addison-Wesley, 1999).

S. McConnell, *Code Complete*, 2nd ed. (Redmond, WA: Microsoft Press, 2004).

C. Simonyi, "Meta-Programming: A Software Production Method," PhD diss., XEROX PARC report CSL-76-7, 1976.

R. Stallman et al., "GNU Coding Standards," http://www.gnu.org/prep/standards/standards.html, accessed May 9, 2005.

Sun Microsystems, "Code Conventions for the Java Programming Language," http://java.sun.com/docs/codeconv/html/CodeConvTOC.doc.html, accessed May 2005.

CHAPTER 10

Testing and Quality Assurance

OBJECTIVES

- Understand the basic techniques for software verification and validation and when to apply them.
- Analyze the basics of software testing along with a variety of software testing techniques.
- Discuss the basics of software inspections and how to perform them.

10.1   Introduction to Testing and Quality Assurance

One of the main goals of software development is to produce high-quality software, with quality usually defined as meeting the specifications and fit to use. To achieve that goal, there is a need for testing—maintaining a set of techniques for detecting and correcting errors in a software product.

Notice that the best way to obtain quality in a product is to put it there in the first place. If a well-defined process that is appropriate to the company and the project is followed, and all team members take pride in their work and use appropriate techniques, chances are that the final product will probably be of high quality. If a process is inappropriate or craftsmanship is careless, then the product will most likely be of low quality. Unfortunately, it is not often that all the ideal processes, people, tools, methodologies, and conditions are met. Thus testing of the artifacts, both along the way and at the end, becomes an ongoing process.

Quality assurance refers to all activities designed to measure and improve quality in a product, including the whole process, training, and preparation of the team. Quality control usually refers to activities designed to verify the quality of the product, detect faults or defects, and ensure that the defects are fixed prior to release.

Every software program has a static structure—the structure of the source code—and a dynamic behavior. Intermediate software products such as requirements, analysis, and design documents have only a static structure. There are several techniques for detecting errors in programs and in intermediate documentation:

- *Testing*, which is the process of designing test cases, executing the program in a controlled environment, and verifying that the output is correct. Testing is usually one of the most important activities in quality control. Section 10.2 provides more information on testing.

- *Inspections and reviews*, which can be applied to a program or to intermediate software artifacts. Inspections and reviews require the involvement of more than one person in addition to the original creator of the product. They are typically labor intensive but have been shown to be an extremely effective way of finding errors. Reviews and inspections have been found to be most cost effective when applied to requirements specifications. Section 10.5 provides more details on these techniques.

- *Formal methods*, which are mathematical techniques used to "prove" that a program is correct. These are rarely applied in business and commercial industries. Section 10.6 provides more information on these.

- *Static analysis*, which is the process of analyzing the static structure of a program or intermediate software product. This analysis is usually automated and can detect errors or error-prone conditions. Section 10.7 provides more information on static analysis.

All quality control activities need a definition of quality. What is a good program or a good design document or a good user interface? The quality of any product can be defined in two slightly different ways:

- It conforms to specifications.
- It serves its purpose.

Notice that these definitions are not equivalent, although they define similar notions. A product may conform perfectly to its specifications but serve no useful purpose whatsoever. In a less extreme case, a program may conform to its specification but not be as useful as planned because the environment changed. It is also possible that the specification did not contemplate all aspects.

Some of the pioneers in quality also wrestled with the definition of quality. Juran and Godfrey (1999) defined quality as fitness to use. Crosby (1979) posed quality as conformance to requirements and pushed the concept of prevention of error and of zero defects.

Corresponding to these two notions of quality, we have the following two activities:

- *Verification*, which is the act of checking that a software product conforms to its requirements and specifications. The requirements for a software product are traced through the development phases, and the transformation of software from one phase to another is "verified."
- *Validation*, which is the act of checking that a finished software product meets users' requirements and specifications. This can usually be done only at the end of a project, with a complete software system.

The three definitions of *fault*, *failure*, and *error* presented here will delineate the differences of a problem found by users from the source of the problem. We usually identify a **fault** as the cause of a **failure**, but it is not always possible to identify one specific fault as the cause of a failure. Oftentimes, faults may exist without being detected or observed in the form of failures. During testing, failures that reveal the presence of faults are observed.

Note that this distinction is important for all software documents, not just running programs. For example, a requirement that is hard to understand is a fault. It becomes a failure only if it leads to the misunderstanding of a requirement, which in turn causes an **error** in design and code that manifests itself in the form of software failure. A human error creates a fault, and fault may cause a failure. Not all defects turn into failures, especially those that stay dormant because the specific code logic was never executed.

> **Fault/defect**   A condition that may cause a failure in a system. It is caused by an error made by the software engineer. A fault is also called a bug.
>
> **Failure/problem**   The inability of a system to perform a function according to its specifications. It is a result of the defect in the system.
>
> **Error**   A mistake made by a software engineer or programmer.

When deciding how a program should behave, you need to be aware of all the explicit and implicit requirements and specifications. An explicit requirement needs to be mentioned in the requirement documents, and an explicit specification is recognized as authoritative by the software team. Notice that specifications are not always produced for all projects, but they can be generic and included by reference. For example, there may be a requirement such as "conforms to the Human Interface Guidelines of its platform," which makes those guidelines an explicit specification.

In many cases, there are also implicit specifications. These are not authoritative, but they are good references and should be followed whenever possible. When inspecting or reviewing a software product or planning test cases, these implicit specifications need to be made explicit, even if only as guidelines.

You must also distinguish between the severity of a fault, which is a measure of the impact or consequences it may have to the users or the organization, and the priority, which is a measure of its importance in the eyes of the developing organization. Software failures could have high severity and low priority and vice versa. For example, a bug causing a program crash under rare conditions will usually be given a lower priority than less severe bugs that occur under most common conditions. However, for the most part, high severity failures are also given a high priority.

10.2   Testing

In the *Guide to Software Engineering Body of Knowledge* (2004), testing is defined as follows:

> Testing is an activity performed for evaluating product quality, and for improving it, by identifying defects and problems.

Software testing consists of the dynamic verification of the behavior of a program based on a finite set of test cases, suitably selected from the usually infinite executions domain, against the expected behavior.

All testing requires the definition of test criteria, which are used to determine what a suitable set of test cases should be. Once the selected set of test cases is executed, the testing may be stopped. Thus, test criteria may also be viewed as a means to determine when testing may be stopped by observing that software product failures are not occurring when all the selected test cases are run. Additional information on test-stopping criteria can be found in Section 10.4.

Testing is a complex activity that involves many activities and thus must be planned. The goal of testing or the quality goal for the specific project must be determined, the test methodology and techniques that need to be utilized to achieve the goal have to be set, resources must be assigned, tools must be brought in, and a schedule must be agreed upon. A test plan that spells out all these details has to be developed. For large, complex software, establishing the test plan itself is a nontrivial endeavor.

10.2.1   The Purposes of Testing

Testing usually has two main purposes:

- To find defects in the software so that they can be corrected or mitigated.
- To provide general assessment of quality, which includes providing some assurance that the product works for many considered cases, and an estimate of possible remaining faults.

Myers (1979) established his position as a strong proponent of the first view. That is, the main purpose of testing is to find faults, the more the better, before the software product is released to the users. This view is a bit negative, and it often made testers uncomfortable. It stands in contrast with the more positive view of testing, which is to show that the software product works. It took a long cultural change for the testers themselves to feel that it is fine to report defects. The testers' contribution to software quality is the discovery of these defects and their help in having them corrected prior to product release.

It is important to realize that, outside of very simple programs, testing cannot prove that a product works. It can only find defects, and show that the product works for the cases that were tested, without guaranteeing anything for other cases that were not tested. If testing is done correctly, it can provide some reassurance that the software will work for situations similar to the test cases, but it is usually impossible to prove that the software will work for all cases.

For the most part, testers will concentrate on finding defects when testing; however, the testers need to keep in mind that they are also providing a quality assessment and contributing to the success and quality of the product. The test results are analyzed by the testers to determine if the specified quality and testing goals have been achieved. Based on the analysis and depending on the results of the analysis, more testing may be recommended.

10.3 Testing Techniques

There is a wide variety of testing techniques, applicable to different circumstances. In fact, there are so many techniques, and they are presented in so many ways, that any attempt to classify all of them will necessarily be incomplete.

The following questions will clarify thinking about testing activities. They can be used to classify different testing concepts, test case design techniques, test execution techniques, and testing organizations.

- *Who does the testing?* Basically, we have three options here:
  - *Programmers:* Programmers usually create test cases and run them as they write the code to convince themselves that the program works. This programmer activity related to testing is usually considered to be unit testing.
  - *Testers:* A tester is a technical person whose role for the particular item being tested is just to write test cases and ensure their execution. Although programming knowledge is extremely useful for testers, testing is a different activity with different intellectual requirements. Not all good programmers will be good testers. Some professional testers also statistically analyze the results from testing and assess the quality level of the product. They are often called to assist in making product release decisions.
  - *Users:* It is a good idea to involve users in testing, in order to detect usability problems and to expose the software to a broad range of inputs in real-world scenarios. Users are sometimes involved in software product acceptance decisions. The organization will usually ask some users to perform normal noncritical activities with the new software. Traditionally, if the users belong to the developing organization, we call this Alpha testing, and if the users are not from the organization we call it Beta testing. Many organizations publicly state that they will use preliminary versions of their own product as part of their normal operations. This is usually known by colorful names such as "eat your own dog food."
- *What is tested?* There are three main levels:
  - *Unit testing:* This involves testing the individual units of functionality—for example, a single procedure or method, or a single class.
  - *Functional testing:* This involves determining if the individual units, when put together, will work as a functional unit.
  - *Integration and system testing:* This involves testing the integrated functionality of the complete system. When dealing with very large software systems, functions

may be integrated into a component. Many components are then brought together to form a system. In that case, there is one more level, called component testing. Notice that, although these distinctions are important and useful in practice, we cannot always make a precise rule to distinguish among these levels. For example, when testing a unit that depends on many other modules, we are mixing unit and integration testing, and when we are developing components for use by others, the whole system may correspond to a traditional unit.

- *Why are we testing?* Which specific kinds of defects are we trying to detect or which risks are we trying to mitigate. There are different types of testing conducted for different purposes:

  - *Acceptance testing:* This is the explicit and formal testing conducted by the customers prior to officially accepting the software product and paying for it. The acceptance test criterion is usually set early at requirements time. The criteria for customer acceptance may include some specific test cases and the number of test cases that must pass.

  - *Conformance testing:* This involves the testing of the software product against a set of standards or policies. Test cases are usually generated from the standards and policies that the product must conform to.

  - *Configuration testing:* Some software products may allow several different configurations. For example, a software product may run with several databases or different networks. Each of these different combinations (or configurations) of databases and networks must be tested. The complexities and problems related to configuration management will be further discussed in Chapter 11.

  - *Performance testing:* This involves verification that the program behaves according to its performance specifications, such as some number of transactions per second or some number of simultaneous users.

  - *Stress testing:* This ensures that the program behaves correctly and degrades gracefully under stress conditions, such as a high load or low availability of resources. Stress testing will extend the testing of software beyond the performance specification to see where the breaking points are.

  - *User-interface testing:* This is testing that focuses only on the user interface.

- *How do we generate and choose test cases?* We can choose test cases based on the following:

  - *Intuition:* Here we do not provide any guidance as to how to generate cases, relying solely on intuition. Most of the time, alpha and beta testing relies solely on the user's intuition. Some of the intuitions are really based on past experiences that have left an indelible impression. Very experienced users and long-time product support personnel are often called to generate test cases from these intuitions.

  - *Specification:* Testing based solely on specifications, without looking at the code is commonly called **black-box testing**. The most common specification-based techniques are equivalence-class partitioning. The input for the software system is divided into several equivalence classes for which we believe the software should behave similarly, generating one test case for each class. Also, boundary-value analysis, which is an extension to equivalence class technique and where test cases are

Black-box testing   A testing methodology where the test cases are mostly derived from the requirements statements without consideration of the actual code content.

generated at the boundaries of the equivalence classes, is used. Both of these techniques are discussed further in the following sections.

- *Code:* Techniques based on knowledge of the actual code are commonly called **white-box testing**. These techniques are based on defining some measure of coverage for the code and then designing test cases to achieve that coverage. Path

> **White-box testing**   A testing methodology where the test cases are mostly derived from examining the code and the detailed design.

analysis is an example of a white-box testing technique, and it is discussed in Section 10.3.3.
- *Existing test case:* This refers to a technique called *regression testing*, which executes some (or all) test cases available for a previous version of the system on a new version. Any discrepancy in the test results indicates a problem with the new system or with the test case. The specific situation needs to be evaluated by the tester.
- *Faults:* There are two main techniques that create test cases based on faults. The first is error guessing, in which test cases are designed in an attempt to figure out the most plausible faults, usually based on the history of faults discovered on similar projects. The second technique is error-prone analysis, which identifies through reviews and inspections those areas of requirements and design that seem to continuously contain defects. These error-prone areas will often be the source of programming errors.

Another perspective to consider during testing is to examine the flow and amount of testing activities. For small projects, the amount of testing usually includes unit testing and functional testing. The large effort associated with system testing is usually not needed. However, in most large systems, the progression of testing can include four levels. The individual module is usually tested by its author, the programmer. Several modules may contribute to a specific function, and all the required modules need to be complete and available for the functional test. The functional test cases are often derived from the requirements specification. This type of testing is sometimes referred to as black-box testing. Unit testing, as mentioned before, is often performed with white-box techniques.

As the different functions of the software system complete the functional tests, the modules associated with those functions are gathered and locked in a repository in preparation for a component test. The components that have passed component testing are then gathered and locked into a repository. Finally, all the components must complete a system/regression test. Any changes to the software after the system test will require a retest of all components to ensure that the system did not regress. The progression of these test phases is illustrated in **Figure 10.1**.

Let's consider a payroll system as an example. We will test the check printing module in unit testing. Check printing is part of a function called check computation, deposit, and print. The check computation, deposit, and print function is tested during the functional testing phase. This functional area is part of a larger component that generates monthly payroll for full-time employees. The monthly full-time employee payroll is tested during the component test. Finally, all the components are merged into a system and the complete payroll system is tested during the system test phase.

10.3.1   Equivalence Class Partitioning

Equivalence class partitioning is a specification-based, black-box technique. It is based on dividing the input into several classes that are deemed equivalent for the purposes of finding errors. That is, if a program fails for one member of the class, then we expect

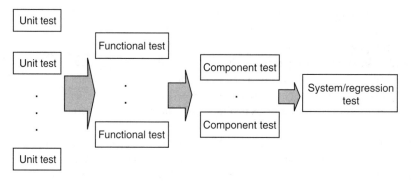

Figure 10.1 Progression of testing.

it to fail for all other members; conversely, if it is correct for one member of the class, we expect it to be correct for all members.

The equivalence classes are determined by looking at the requirements specification and by the tester's intuition, without looking at the implementation. The equivalence classes will cover the complete input domain. At no point does any class overlap with any other class.

For example, consider a marketing application that processes records for people. One important factor is age; the requirements call for dividing people into four groups based on age: children (0–12), teenagers (13–19), young adults (20–35), and adults (>35). Any age less than 0 or greater than 120 is considered an error.

It is a reasonable assumption, just by looking at the requirement, to partition our valid data into four equivalence classes, in this case corresponding to the four intervals that would produce output; we would then choose one test case for each equivalence class. We would also have two kinds of invalid data, negative numbers and really large numbers. These two additional groups provide a total of six equivalence classes. **Table 10.1** shows a possible choice of test cases for each of the six equivalence classes.

Note that the equivalence class partitioning technique does not specify which element to choose as representative for the class. It just asks that we choose one from the

Table 10.1 Equivalence Class Example

Class	Representative
Low	−5
0–12	6
13–19	15
20–35	30
36–120	60
High	160

Table 10.2 Equivalence Classes for `Largest` Function

Method
First > Second
Second > First
First = Second

class. Typical choices will be the one in the middle, if there is an interval, or just one of the common cases.

Also, it will not always be clear what to choose as the equivalence classes, and there may be differences of opinion. The bulk of the class analysis will be similar, but there may be small variations in the actual details.

For example, consider a function called `largest`, that takes two integers as parameters and returns the largest of them. We could define three equivalence classes as shown in **Table 10.2**. The third class in the table may be considered as the boundary between the first two classes, and it may be utilized only when doing boundary value analysis. It may also be folded into either of the other two classes, resulting in a class such as `First >= Second`.

Equivalence class partitioning is most useful when the requirements are expressed as a series of conditions. It is less useful when the requirements seem to call for loops. For example, if we are testing a function that sums all the elements in an array or vector, it would be hard to decide what the equivalence classes are, and there will be much difference of opinion; however, the basic idea would still be useful.

10.3.2 Boundary Value Analysis

Although equivalence class partitioning makes sense and is a useful technique, experience has shown that many errors are actually made at the boundaries rather than under normal conditions. If there is an error on age 6 in Table 10.1, it will probably mean the programmer forgot the whole range of ages, or the code is completely wrong. A more probable error is to have some confusion about the ranges where, for example, using < is confused with the boundary condition of <=.

Boundary value analysis uses the same classes as equivalence partitioning, testing at the boundaries rather than just an element from the class. A complete boundary value analysis calls for testing the boundary, the immediate case inside the boundary, and the immediate case outside of the boundary. Because the equivalence classes usually form a progression of intervals, there will be overlap in the test cases. We usually consider the test case as coming from the interval to which it belongs.

This technique may generate a high number of test cases. You can usually reduce test cases by considering the boundary as falling in between numbers and just test for above and below the boundaries. **Table 10.3** shows a boundary value analysis for the age-classification problem presented earlier. The equivalence classes are shown in the first column. The boundary value analysis is divided into three categories: (1) all cases (which include the boundary, one below the boundary, and one above the boundary) that the class generates, (2) the cases that would be considered belonging to the class, and (3) the reduced cases, considering the boundary as falling between numbers.

Table 10.3 Boundary Values and Reduced Test Cases

Class	All Cases	Belonging Cases	Reduced Cases
Low	−1, 0	−1	−1
0–12	−1, 0, 1 11, 12, 13	0, 1 11, 12	0 12
13–19	12, 13, 14 18, 19, 20	13, 14 18, 19	13 19
20–35	19, 20, 21 34, 35, 36	20, 21 34, 35	20 35
36–120	35, 36, 37 119, 120, 121	36, 37 119, 120	36 120
High	120, 121	121	121

Note that this technique produces a large number of test cases, even if only the reduced ones are considered. In many cases you might need to reduce them even further by considering which cases are most important. However, do not let the number of test cases become an excuse for not conducting a thorough test.

Also note that this technique is applicable only to ordinal variables—that is, those that can be sorted and organized in intervals. Without this organization there are no special values that can be recognized as boundaries. Fortunately, many programs deal mostly with this kind of data.

10.3.3   Path Analysis

Path analysis provides a test design technique that is reproducible, traceable, and countable. It is often used as a white-box testing technique, which means that you are looking at the actual code or the detailed design when developing the test cases. Two tasks are involved in path analysis:

- Analyze the number of paths that exist in the system or program.
- Determine how many paths should be included in the test.

First consider the example shown in **Figure 10.2**, where the rectangles and diamonds represent processing and decision functions, the arrows show the control flows, and the circles with numbers indicate the path segments. There are two independent paths, Path1 and Path2, shown in the figure. In order to cover all the statements indicated here, both

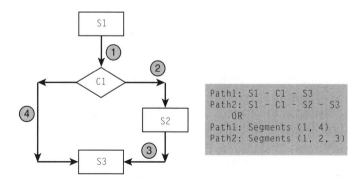

Figure 10.2 A simple logical structure.

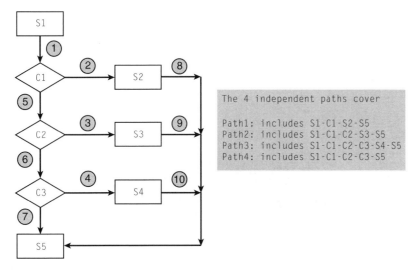

The 4 independent paths cover

Path1: includes S1-C1-S2-S5
Path2: includes S1-C1-C2-S3-S5
Path3: includes S1-C1-C2-C3-S4-S5
Path4: includes S1-C1-C2-C3-S5

Figure 10.3 A CASE structure.

paths are needed. Thus test cases must be generated to traverse through both Path1 and Path2. There is one binary decision processing in the figure. In order to cover both branches, again, both Path1 and Path2 must be traversed. In this case, two independent paths are needed to accomplish total statement coverage or to accomplish all branch coverage. We will show that this is not always the situation. Consider **Figure 10.3**, where the logic is similar to a CASE structure.

The rectangles and the diamonds, again, represent the statements and the decision processing, the arrows show the control flow, and the circles with numbers indicate the path segments. Note that there are four independent paths. However, we do not need to traverse all four paths to have all the statements covered. If Path1, Path2, and Path3 are executed, then all the statements (C1, C2, C3, S1, S2, S3, S4, and S5) are executed. Thus for full statement coverage we need only to have test cases to run Path1, Path2, and Path3. We can ignore Path4.

Now, let us consider branch coverage. In Figure 10.3, there are three decision conditionals, C1, C2, and C3. They each generate two branches as follows:

1. C1:
   - B1 composed of C1-S2.
   - B2 composed of C1-C2.

2. C2:
   - B3 composed of C2-S3.
   - B4 composed of C2-C3.

3. C3:
   - B5 composed of C3-S4.
   - B6 composed of C3-S5.

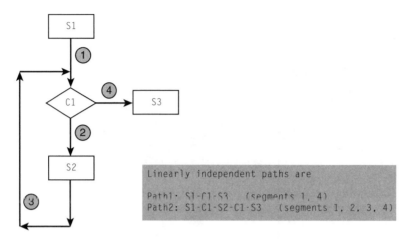

Figure 10.4 A simple loop structure.

In order to cover all branches, we will need to traverse Path1 to cover B1, Path2 to cover B2 and B3, Path3 to cover B4 and B5, and Path4 to cover B6. In this case, all four paths need to be executed to achieve total branch coverage. This example thus demonstrates that we would need more paths to cover all branches than to cover all statements. One may view all branches coverage testing to be a stronger test than all statements coverage testing.

Now, let us review the situation with a loop construct shown in **Figure 10.4**. All the symbols used are the same as before. The loop structure here depends on the condition C1. There are two independent paths. Path1 covers segments 1 and 4 through three statements (S1, C1, and S3). Path2 covers segments 1, 2, 3, 4 through all four statements (S1, C1, S2, S3). For this simple loop construct, only one path is needed to cover all the statements. Thus Path2, which includes all the statements, is the one path that we need to design the test case for all statement coverage. For Path2, we do have to design the test case such that S2 modifies the state so that the second encounter with C1 will direct the traversal to S3. While it is true that the statements C1 and S2 inside loop may be traversed multiple times, we do not need to design a test case for each potential iteration. For this simple loop structure Path2 provides all statement coverage. In terms of branch coverage, there are two branches that need to be considered:

- B1 composed of C1-S2
- B2 composed of C1-S3

Path2 covers both B1 and B2. For this simple loop, only one path, Path2, is needed to cover all statements and to achieve total branch coverage.

We casually used the term *independent paths* earlier. It was somewhat intuitive in the figures. Let us define this idea more precisely here.

A set of paths is said to be a linearly independent set if every path may be constructed as a "linear combination" of paths from this set.

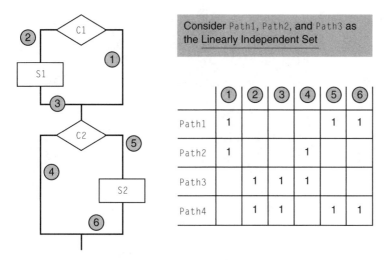

Figure 10.5 A linearly independent set of paths.

We will demonstrate this very powerful set with the simple example shown in **Figure 10.5**. There are two conditionals, C1 and C2, and two sets of statements, S1 and S2, and the path segments are represented with numbered circles. There are a total of four possible paths that are represented in a matrix form. For example, Path1 is shown as row 1 with path segments 1, 5, and 6 marked with a 1. The unmarked cells may be interpreted as zeroes. Thus Path1 may be represented with a vector (1, 0, 0, 0, 1, 1). Looking at the matrix in this figure, we can see that with Path1, Path2, and Path3, all the path segments are covered. In fact, Path4 can be constructed with a linear combination of Path1, Path2, and Path3 as follows:

```
Path4 = Path3 + Path1 - Path2
Path4 = (0,1,1,1,0,0) + (1,0,0,0,1,1) - (1,0,0,1,0,0)
Path4 = (1,1,1,1,1,1) - (1,0,0,1,0,0)
Path4 = (0,1,1,0,1,1)
```

Row 4 in the matrix shows that Path4 indeed traverses through path segments 2, 3, 5 and 6. Path1, Path2, and Path3 form a linearly independent set of paths.

There is a simple way to determine the number of paths that make up the linearly independent set. The McCabe cyclomatic complexity number introduced in Chapter 8 can be used as the number of paths in the linearly independent set. As indicated in Figure 10.5, we can compute the cyclomatic number as follows:

Number of binary decisions + 1 = 2 + 1 = 3

Thus for Figure 10.5, the cyclomatic number 3 states that there are three linearly independent paths for the construct in this figure.

One more example is provided in **Figure 10.6** to demonstrate path analysis in terms of the relative amount of test coverage provided. In this figure, there are three binary decision constructs placed in sequence. For each of the binary decisions, there are two separate logical paths. Because the binary decision constructs are in sequence, we

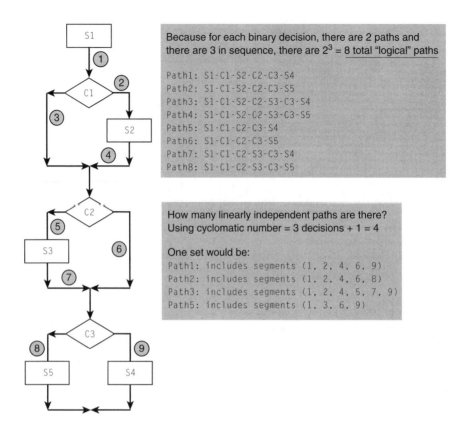

Because for each binary decision, there are 2 paths and there are 3 in sequence, there are $2^3 = 8$ total "logical" paths

```
Path1:  S1-C1-S2-C2-C3-S4
Path2:  S1-C1-S2-C2-C3-S5
Path3:  S1-C1-S2-C2-S3-C3-S4
Path4:  S1-C1-S2-C2-S3-C3-S5
Path5:  S1-C1-C2-C3-S4
Path6:  S1-C1-C2-C3-S5
Path7:  S1-C1-C2-S3-C3-S4
Path8:  S1-C1-C2-S3-C3-S5
```

How many linearly independent paths are there?
Using cyclomatic number = 3 decisions + 1 = 4

One set would be:
```
Path1: includes segments (1, 2, 4, 6, 9)
Path2: includes segments (1, 2, 4, 6, 8)
Path3: includes segments (1, 2, 4, 5, 7, 9)
Path5: includes segments (1, 3, 6, 9)
```

Figure 10.6 Total number of paths and linearly independent paths.

have $2 \times 2 \times 2 = 8$ total number of logical paths. Using the cyclomatic number, $3 + 1 = 4$, the number of linearly independent paths is four. One such set of four linearly independent paths is shown in Figure 10.6. A close examination shows that all the statements in the logic diagram are covered if Path1 and Path4 are executed. Path1 covers S1, C1, S2, C2, C3, and S4. Only S3 and S5 need to be covered. Either Path4 or Path8 will cover S3 and S5. Thus Path1 and Path4 provide full test coverage of the statements.

Now, let us examine the branches in Figure 10.6. Because there are three binary decisions, there are a total of six branches, two for each of the binary decisions. The branches are C1-S2, C1-C2, C2-C3, C2-S3, C3-S4, and C3-S5. Path1 traverses through C1-S2, C2-C3, and C3-S4. Path8 traverses though C1-C2, C2-S3, and C3-S5. Thus with Path1 and Path8, all of the branches are covered. Only two paths are needed, again.

Figure 10.6 provides us with a feel for the relative number of paths required to cover different types of testing:

- Eight total logical paths
- Four total linearly independent paths
- Two total paths to provide total branch coverage
- Two total paths to provide total statement coverage

Because every statement is "part" of some branch, total branch coverage would provide total statement coverage. The reverse, however, is not necessarily true. Now, imagine someone proudly proclaiming good quality because he or she performs 100% statement coverage testing! It turns out to be the lowest level of the test coverage hierarchy.

10.3.4 Combinations of Conditions

In many cases when we need to combine several variables, we get a very large number of combinations. Sometimes there is a need to reduce those combinations while trying to maximize coverage. A common technique is to generate only enough combinations to cover all pairs of values.

For example, consider a marketing module that classifies people depending on their age, income, and region of residency. Assume that we have the equivalence classes for the variables shown in **Table 10.4**.

Table 10.4 Equivalence Classes for Variable

Variable	Classes
Age	Young
	Adult
	Old
Income	High
	Medium
	Low
Region	North
	South

If all combinations are considered, then there will be 18 different classes ($3 \times 3 \times 2$), which is not a small number of test cases. Using boundary value analysis, we may generate 12 cases for the age variable, 12 for the income variable, and 9 for the region variable. This would generate combinations of $12 \times 12 \times 9$, or 1296, cases, which is definitely a large number of test cases. Having more variables or more equivalence classes per variable complicates the problem even more. It is clear that, for integration and system testing, the number of test cases can easily reach thousands or tens of thousands of test cases.

In some situations, the variables are not independent, which means that reducing the number of combinations that need to be tested would be very difficult. In most cases, testing all possible conditions is not practical, so we need to reduce the number of cases tested. This, of course, increases the risk of a defect being undetected. Techniques for reducing the number of cases while keeping risks manageable include coverage analysis, such as producing just enough test cases to achieve statement or path coverage rather than full condition coverage, assessment of the important cases, and producing combinations in order to test all possible pairs of values but not all combinations.

10.3.5 Automated Unit Testing and Test-Driven Development

Unit testing refers to testing the most basic units of functionality, like individual methods or classes. Most programmers will need to do unit testing while programming to gain confidence that their code works. After the whole component is completed, then the code will go to the testers, who will independently do unit testing again.

Inexperienced programmers tend to perform limited unit testing, rather writing big chunks of code and testing only the high-level pieces; this practice makes it hard to locate errors when they arise. If the individual pieces are tested as they are being written, then the chance of catching the errors increases considerably.

Another common mistake is to write the test cases as part of the main function and to discard them after they run. A much better practice is to use an automated unit testing tool such as JUnit for Java. There are equivalent libraries written for many other programming languages. This makes it possible to keep the tests and do regression testing at the program version level as we change the program.

Having the unit tests would allow us to refactor the program. Refactoring changes the program structure without changing its behavior, as described in Chapter 5. If we refactor constantly we will usually end up with good code. The presence of unit regression testing at the program unit level helps ensure that no error is introduced while conducting refactoring.

Another advantage of keeping the tests is that they serve as an executable detailed specification and they document the assumptions made during the writing of the program.

A good practice would then be to write unit tests immediately after writing a piece of code. The smaller the units that are tested, the better. Some of the techniques described earlier may be used to create good test cases.

An even better practice may be to write the unit tests before writing the code, and then using them to make sure the code works. This allows you to first state the requirements as a test case, and then implement them. It also helps guide you to write only small pieces of code without testing. This technique is known as test-driven development, which assumes you will proceed in the following fashion:

1. Write a test case.
2. Verify that the test case fails.
3. Modify the code so that the test case succeeds. (The goal is to write the simplest code you can, without worrying about future tests or requirements.)
4. Run the test case to verify it now works and run the previous test cases to verify that the code has not regressed with any newly introduced defect.
5. Refactor the code to make it pretty.

In the following section we provide an example of how test-driven development would proceed for a simple problem.

10.3.6 An Example of Test-Driven Development

Let's look at the triangle problem, a popular exercise in introductory programming and software engineering. The problem asks us to decide, given the length of the three sides of a triangle, if it is isosceles, equilateral, or scalene. We also have to determine whether the lengths of the sides form a valid triangle.

We have modified the problem to adapt it to object-oriented programming, and simplified it to just check whether the triangle is valid. The requirements ask that we write Java code for a class called `Triangle` that represents a triangle. The class will store information about the three sides of a triangle and define several methods. For convenience, we will use a, b, and c for the three sides rather than `side1`, `side2`, and `side3` or an array.

The following public methods are to be defined:

1. A constructor, taking three integers, representing the first, second, and third sides.

2. Method `getA`, which takes no parameters and returns the length of the first side, and corresponding `getB`, `getC` methods.

3. A method `isValid`, which takes no parameters and returns a Boolean true if the triangle is valid, false otherwise. A valid triangle is one for which all sides have positive length (strictly, greater than 0) and all satisfy the triangle inequality; for all sides, the sum of two sides is greater than the third.

Test-driven development (TDD) calls for writing test cases *before* any code. It also advocates that the tests be automated so that they can be run as many times as necessary. In the following paragraphs, the TDD example is illustrated in a somewhat personal and conversational manner.

We first create the `JUnit` test class, an easy process; we just need to create a class extending `junit.framework.TestCase`. After that, any public method whose name starts with `test` will be automatically run by `JUnit`. For convenience, we define a main method that runs all the tests. The skeleton for the class is as follows:

```
import junit.framework.TestCase;
public class TestTriangle extends TestCase {

public static void main(String args[]) {
junit.swingui.TestRunner.run(TestTriangle.class);
  }
}
```

We now define the first test case. Note that it is usually hard to test the first few methods in isolation; you need at least a `get` and a `set` method to be able to verify that something worked. We decided to create a test case for verifying the constructor and the three `get` methods. Purists of test-driven development could argue that we should have done just the constructor and one of the `get` methods, but we thought the code was simple enough.

The test case goes as follows:

```
        public void testConstructor() {
        Triangle t=new Triangle(3,5,7);

        assertTrue(t.getA()==3);
        assertTrue(t.getB()==5);
        assertTrue(t.getC()==7);
    }
```

In this case we are testing the following:

- There is a class and a public constructor, taking three integer parameters.
- There are three methods, getA, getB, and getC.
- The value returned by getA is the first parameter passed to the constructor, getB is the second, and getC is the third.

We then try to compile, and it does not work, just as we expected. So we create the code for the following class:

```
class Triangle {
   private int a, b, c;

   // constructs a triangle based on parameters
   public Triangle(int a, int b, int c)
   {
   this.a=a;
   this.b=b;
   this.c=c;
   }

   public int getA() { return a;}
   public int getB() { return a;}
   public int getC() { return a;}
   }
```

We run the tests again, and see that the code does not work. We go and check the code again. Can you see the error? (We cut-and-pasted from getA to create getB and getC but forgot to change the value returned.) So we correct the errors and try the test again. This time, it works.

We now create a test case for the isValid method. Given that we feel this method is not that simple, we will do TDD in smaller steps. We will write very simple test cases, and then very simple code, making the test cases drive the code.

We can write a very simple test case such as the following:

```
public void testIsValid() {
Triangle t=new Triangle(-5,3,7);
assertFalse(t.isValid());
```

We run it, and it fails (with a compilation error). Now we try to write the code.

A good practice for complicated code is to write the simplest code you can think of that will make your test succeed. It does not matter if the code is wrong, as long as your test case succeeds. This will force you to write more test cases, therefore ensuring you test better.

In this case, we'll follow that practice. The test case just calls for a triangle that is not valid; we can simply write the code like this:

```
        public boolean isValid() {
return false;
}
```

Now the test case succeeds, and we need to write more test cases. We rewrite our test case as follows:

```
        public void testIsValid() {
Triangle t=null;

t=new Triangle(-5,3,7);
assertFalse(t.isValid());

t=new Triangle(3,5,7);
assertTrue(t.isValid());
}
```

We make sure it fails, and then continue to write more code. We could write code just to see whether a is less than 0, but we decide to test for all three conditions. The code looks like this:

```
   public boolean isValid() {
return a>0 && b>0 && c>0;
}
```

We test the case and it succeeds. Now, because we know our code will get more complicated, we decide to refactor. The isValid method needs to decide on two different conditions: (1) whether all sides are positive, and (2) whether the sides satisfy the triangle inequality. We thus decide to write two tests: (1) allPositive, to see whether all sides are positive, and (2) allSatisfyInequality, to see whether all sides satisfy the inequality. We change isValid and write the allPositive method as follows:

```
boolean allPositive() {
    return a>0 && b>0 && c>0;
}

public boolean isValid() {
return allPositive();
}
```

Note that we are not making allPositive public, because it is not called for in the specification. We make it a package method rather than a private one so that the test class can access it and test it.

We now need to test the allPositive method. We write a few test cases, covering the three main cases (a<0, b<0, c<0), one more for one boundary (a=0), and then one more to verify that the function works for a triangle with sides all positive. We run the tests, and they pass. We believe this is enough testing for this function. Would you feel comfortable now? If not, what test cases would you add?

We now go to work on the allSatisfyInequality method. We create a simple test case such as the following:

```
        public void testAllSatisfyInequality() {
Triangle t=null;

t=new Triangle(10,5,2);
assertFalse(t.allSatisfyInequality());
t=new Triangle(5,6,3);
assertTrue(t.allSatisfyInequality());
}
```

The test fails to compile, so we write the following code:

```
// returns true if all sides satisfy the triangle
// inequality false otherwise
  boolean allSatisfyInequality() {
  return (a<(b+c)) && (b<(a+c)) && (c<(a+b));
}
```

Now the test passes. To gain confidence that the code works, we decide to extend the test case to cover at least each side breaking the inequality and one boundary condition. So we extend it as follows:

```
        public void testAllSatisfyInequality() {
    Triangle t=null;

    t=new Triangle(10,5,2);
    assertFalse(t.allSatisfyInequality());

    t=new Triangle(5,15,2);
    assertFalse(t.allSatisfyInequality());

    t=new Triangle(3,4,7);
    assertFalse(t.allSatisfyInequality());

    t=new Triangle(5,6,3);
    assertTrue(t.allSatisfyInequality());
}
```

We run the test case, and it works. As developers, we feel quite confident that the code is correct. We can now pass it on to later stages in the process, which may include inspection, formal unit testing by the testing organization, and functional and integration testing.

A few more observations about test-driven development can be made at this point:

- Test-driven development is an effective technique that helps programmers quickly build reliable code; however, it is not a substitute for other quality control activities.
- Test-driven development should be combined with formal unit and integration testing, code inspections, and other quality control techniques to ensure a high-quality implementation of the requirements.
- Test-driven development usually leads to writing more tests, and simpler code. In fact, TDD usually achieves at least statement coverage.
- Test cases in TDD are produced based on the developer's intuitions and experience, although other techniques may be used.

10.4   When to Stop Testing

A key question often asked by novice testers and students of testing is when one should stop testing. A simple answer is to stop testing when all the planned test cases are executed and all the problems found are fixed. In reality, it may not be that simple. We are often pressured by schedule to release software product. Two techniques will be discussed here. The first is based on keeping track of the test results and observing the

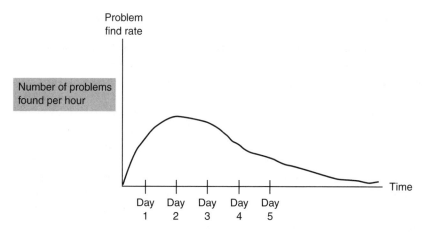

Figure 10.7 Decreasing problem find rate.

statistics. If the number of problems discovered stabilizes to near zero, we would usually consider stopping the testing. Consider **Figure 10.7**, which illustrates a problem find rate through time.

The number of problems found per hour will eventually be so small that the value received from testing starts to diminish. In Figure 10.7, the curve hits a peak on day 2 and starts to decline on day 3. The testers could have set a goal in the plan stating that testing will stop when the problem find rate reaches some prespecified level, such as 0.01/hour or 1/100 hours. They could also create a graph depicting the accumulative number of problems found. Such a curve will usually look like a stretched S figure and is often called an S-curve. They might then specify that when the observed length of time (for example, 12 hours, 1 day, 1 week) of accumulative problems found achieves some point of stability, further testing will be terminated.

Another technique is to pepper the existing code with defects and observe how many of the seeded defects are discovered. This technique requires the seeding of the defects to be done by some person other than the actual tester. For example, consider seeding a program with 10 defects. As failures are observed, the defects are then sorted between seeded defects and real defects. Assume that after executing many of the test cases, 7 of the seeded defects and 45 nonseeded defects are detected. The following approach can then be used to estimate the number of remaining unseeded defects:

```
7/10 = 45/RD, where RD = Real Defects
```

RD is estimated as approximately 64. You can thus assume that there still are approximately 19 more unseeded defects remaining in the software product. This is equivalent to saying that there is a good chance that 19/64, or 30%, of the estimated real defects still remain in the product. If discovering 70% of the real defects was the target, then the testers could proclaim victory and stop testing. On the other hand, if the target is to discover 90% of the estimated real defects, then the testers would need to find 9 of the 10 seeded defects before they stop testing. One caution is that the testers must ensure that the seeded defects are all pulled out of the software product prior to releasing to the users.

Note that this technique assumes that defects naturally occurring in the code are similar to the ones we have seeded. Although this is a reasonable assumption, it is not always true, which would lead us to produce bad estimates about remaining defects.

If we want to produce quality software, we must strive to stop testing only after we are convinced that the product is as good as we want it or when testing does not produce any further improvements in quality. Thus there is always an element of "past experience" in some of these decisions. Many projects, however, decide to stop testing prematurely due to schedule pressure or availability of resources. Shipping a product because you ran out of time or out of money will almost always result in a low-quality product. The direct effects of low-quality product are the pressure and cost placed on the postrelease support and maintenance team. Indirectly, the software product's reputation and the customers' sense of satisfaction will also suffer.

10.5   Inspections and Reviews

One of the most cost-effective techniques for detecting errors is to have the code or the intermediate documents reviewed by a team of software developers. Here, we will use the term *review* as a generic term to specify any process involving human testers reading and understanding a document and then analyzing it with the purpose of detecting errors, and reserve the term *inspection* for a particular variation that will also be described. These inspections are sometimes referred to as *Fagan inspections* in the literature.

Note that reviews for the purposes of finding errors are discussed here. There are many other techniques involving teams of people analyzing source code or other documents, including what is sometimes called a *walk-through*, which involves the author of a document explaining the material to a team of people for some other purpose such as knowledge-dissemination or brainstorming and evaluation of design alternatives. We will reserve the term *review* for analysis done by a team of people to detect errors.

Software inspections are detailed reviews of work in progress following the process developed by Michael Fagan at IBM. A small group of three to six people typically study a work product independently and then meet to analyze the work in more detail. Although the work product should be basically completed, it is considered as a work in progress until it has passed the review and any necessary corrections have been made.

The inspection process usually consists of the following steps:

1. *Planning:* An inspection team and a moderator are designated and materials are distributed to team members several days prior to the actual inspection meeting. The moderator makes sure the work product satisfies some entry criteria—for example, for code inspection, that the source code compiles or that it does not produce warnings when passed through a static analysis tool.

2. *Overview:* An overview of the work product and related areas is presented, similar to a walk-through. This step may be omitted if participants are already familiar with the project.

3. *Preparation:* Every inspector is expected to study the work product and related materials thoroughly in preparation for the actual meeting. Checklists may be used to help detect common problems.

4. *Examination:* An actual meeting is arranged where the inspectors review the product together. The designated reader presents the work, typically paraphrasing the text while everyone else focuses on finding defects. The author is not allowed to serve as the reader. Every defect detected is classified and reported. Typically, the meeting is dedicated only to finding defects; so no time is spent during the meeting on analyzing why defects occurred or how to solve them. Usually sessions are limited to one or two hours. As a result of the examination, the product is either accepted as is, corrected by the author with the moderator verifying the results, or corrected along with a reinspection.

5. *Rework:* After the meeting, the author corrects all defects, if any. The author is not required to consult with any inspector but is usually allowed to do so.

6. *Follow-up:* The corrections are checked by the moderator, or the corrected work is inspected again, depending on the result of the inspection.

Inspections are highly focused on finding defects, with all other considerations being secondary. Discussions about how to correct those defects or any other improvements are actively discouraged during such inspections in order to detect more defects. The output of an inspection meeting would be a list of defects that need to be corrected and an inspection report for management. The report describes what was inspected, lists the inspection team members and roles, and summarizes the number of and the severity of defects found. The report also states whether a reinspection is required.

Inspection teams are small groups of coworkers, usually of three to six people, with the author included. Usually all members of the inspection team are working on related efforts such as design, coding, testing, support, or training, so they can more easily understand the product and find errors. Their own work is usually affected by the artifact that they are inspecting, which means that the inspectors are motivated participants. Managers generally do not participate in inspections as this usually hinders the process. The inspectors would have a tough time behaving "naturally" with managers participating in the inspection meetings. An inspection team, besides the author, has the participants in the roles of moderator, reader, and scribe. Typically, authors are not allowed to assume any of these roles.

Inspections have proved to be a cost-effective technique to finding defects. A great advantage of inspection is that it can be applied to all intermediate artifacts, including requirements specifications, design documents, test cases, and user guides. This allows for defects to be detected early in the software process and corrected inexpensively. Although inspections are work intensive, their cost is usually much less than catching the errors in testing, where the cost of correcting them is much higher.

Although inspections are focused on finding defects, they do have a positive side effect in that they help disseminate knowledge about specific parts of the project and also about the best practices and techniques. Tsui and Priven (1976) describe positive experiences with using inspections to manage software quality at IBM as early as the 1970s.

10.6   Formal Methods

In a strict definition, formal methods are mathematical techniques used to prove with absolute certainty that a program works. A broader definition would include all discrete mathematics techniques used in software engineering.

Formal methods are more often used for requirements specifications. The specifications are written in a formal language, such as Z, VDM, or Larch, and then properties of the specifications are proved, through model-checking or theorem-proving techniques. Proving properties of formal specifications is probably the most popular application of formal methods. Formal methods can also be applied to prove that a particular implementation conforms to a specification at some level. Formal methods are typically applied to specifications and utilized to prove that the design conforms to the specification.

At the code level, formal methods usually involve specifying the precise semantics of a program in some programming language. Given this formalization, we can proceed to prove that given a set of preconditions the output will satisfy certain postconditions. Most programming languages need to be extended to allow for the specification of preconditions and postconditions. Once these are specified, there are tools that will, in many cases, produce a proof that the program is correct.

Considering that the other techniques cannot guarantee the absence of errors, the idea of proving the correctness of a program is very appealing. However, formal methods have several drawbacks:

- They require a considerable amount of effort to master the techniques. They require in-depth knowledge of mathematics and a measure of abstract thinking. Although most programmers and software engineers could be trained in these techniques, the fact is that most of them do not have training in this area. Even after training, formal methods require a substantial effort to be applied to a program. Gerhart and Yelowitz (1976) describe the difficulties related to using formal methods.
- They are not applicable to all programs. In fact, a fundamental theorem of theory of computation says we cannot mathematically prove any interesting property about programs in general. As a specific example, we cannot show, given an arbitrary program, whether it will halt or not. Either we restrict ourselves to a subset of all programs or there are some programs for which we cannot prove or disprove the property. Unfortunately, many practical programs would fall into this category.
- They are useful only for verification, not for validation. That is, using formal methods we could prove that a program evolved from and conforms to its specification but not that it is actually useful or that it is what the users really wanted, because that is a value judgment involving people.
- They are not usually applicable to all aspects of software development. For example, they would be very hard to apply to user-interface design.

In spite of their drawbacks, formal methods are useful and have been applied with success to some special real-world problems in industries such as aerospace or federal government. Learning formal methods can give much useful insight to a software engineer, and they can be applied to particular modules that need extremely high reliability. Even if specifications are not completely formal, the mental discipline of formal methods can be extremely useful. They can be applied selectively, so that critical or difficult parts of a system are formally specified. Informal reasoning, similar to formal methods, can be applied to gain more confidence about the correctness of a program. Preconditions and postconditions can also serve as documentation and help understand the source code.

10.7   Static Analysis

Static analysis involves the examination of the static structures of executable and non-executable files with the aim of detecting error-prone conditions. This analysis is usually done automatically and the results are reviewed by a person to eliminate false positives or errors that are not real.

Static analysis can be applied to the following situations:

- *Intermediate documents*, to check for completeness, traceability, and other characteristics. The particular check applied will depend on the document and how structured it is. At the most basic level, if you are dealing with unstructured data such as word-processing documents, you can verify that it follows a certain template, or that certain words do or do not appear.
- *If the document is in a more structured format,* be it XML or a specific format used by your tools, then more involved checking can be performed. You can automatically check for traceability (e.g., all design items are related to one or more requirements) and completeness (e.g., all requirements are addressed by one or more design items). Many analysis and design documents have an underlying model based on graphs or trees, which would make checks for connectivity, fan-in, and fan-out possible. Most integrated CASE tools provide some static analysis of the models created with them.
- *Source code*, to check for programming style issues or error-prone programming practices. At the most basic level, compilers will detect all syntactic errors, and modern compilers can usually produce many warnings about unsafe or error-prone code. Deeper static analysis can be done with special tools to detect modules that are excessively complex or too long and to detect practices that are probably an error. The specific practices that are considered error-prone will vary depending on the programming language, the particular tool, and the coding guidelines of the organization. Most tools provide an extensive set of checks that can be extended and provide ways to configure the tool to specify which checks to run. For example, in Java, there are two equality operations. You can use the = = operator, which checks for object identity (the two expressions refer to the exact same object) and the equals method, which checks whether the member variables of each object are equal. In the majority of the cases the intended semantics is to call the equals method, which means that the tool could warn about uses of the = = operator except for primitive values. Two popular open source tools to perform static checks on Java source code are PMD and CheckStyle. Both of them can detect more than 100 potential problems.
- *Executable files*, to detect certain conditions, with the understanding that much information is usually lost in the translation from source code to executable files. With the popularity of virtual machines and bytecode rather than traditional executables, an

executable may contain a substantial amount of information, allowing for many meaningful checks. For example, `java.class` files contain information about all the defined classes and all the methods and fields defined by the class. This information allows for the creation of call and dependency graphs, inheritance hierarchies, and the calculation of metrics such as cyclomatic or Halstead complexity. Warnings can be issued whenever the complexity metric or the inheritance depth is above a certain threshold, which would signal an excessively complex and error-prone module.

- *FindBugs* is an open source bytecode checker for the Java language that provides for more than 100 individual checks, and sample configuration files to verify consistency with Sun's Java coding guidelines.

Static analysis tools are extremely useful and are available for most of the popular programming languages, however we need to realize that these tools typically provide a very high number of false positives—that is, conditions that are flagged as error-prone by the tool but are not an actual error. It is not uncommon that 50% or more of the warnings correspond to valid usage. Conversely, there will still be many errors that are not caught by these tools.

The output of static analysis tools needs to be checked by experienced software engineers to verify whether the warnings correspond to actual errors or to correct code, and we should not gain a false sense of security by the fact that a program passes those checks.

10.8   Summary

The steps to achieving a high-quality product must be taken from the inception of the project; however, having ways to detect and later correct errors can help you achieve even higher quality. In this chapter we discussed the basic ideas of verification and validation. The basic techniques for verification, inspections and reviews, testing, static analysis, and formal methods were then introduced. Of those techniques, testing and inspections can be also used for validation. We have also discussed techniques for generating good test cases through equivalence classes, boundary value analysis, and path analysis as well as some fundamental concepts for setting criteria about when to stop testing.

Although all of these techniques have their cost, releasing a low-quality product is even costlier. All software engineers need to apply these techniques to their own work, and every project needs to apply them to the whole set of artifacts produced.

10.9   Review Questions

1. Consider the diagram shown in **Figure 10.8**.

   a. How many logical paths are there? List them all.
   b. How many paths are required to cover all the statements?
   c. How many paths are required to cover all the branches?

2. In code inspection, what would you set as the condition (e.g., how many discovered defects) for reinspection?

3. List the four techniques discussed to perform verification and validation.

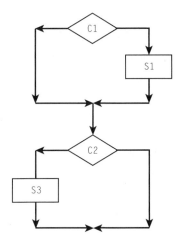

Figure 10.8 A logical flow structure

4. List two techniques you can use to perform validation—that is, to ensure your program meets user requirements.

5. Briefly explain the concept of static analysis, and to which software products it can be applied.

6. Briefly explain two different ways to decide when to stop testing.

7. Consider the simple case of testing 2 variables, X and Y, where X must be a non-negative number, and Y must be a number between -5 and $+15$. Utilizing boundary value analysis, list the test cases.

8. Describe the steps involved in a formal inspection process and the role of a moderator in this process.

9. What is the difference between performance testing and stress testing?

10.10   Exercises

1. Consider the seeded defect approach to creating a stop-testing condition and the example in this chapter.

   a. After reaching the 70% level, suppose that more and more (e.g., 20) unseeded defects are found without discovering a single new seeded defect. Explain what you think is happening.

   b. After reaching the 70% level, suppose that the remaining three seeded defects are found along with only four more real defects. Explain what you think is happening.

2. For the triangle problem described in Section 10.3.6, do the following exercises:

   a. Use test-driven development to define a method called Equilateral that returns true if the triangle is equilateral (and valid). An equilateral triangle is that for which all sides are of equal length.

b. Evaluate the coverage that the test cases you produced achieve. If you did not achieve full path coverage, create test cases to achieve path coverage.

c. Perform equivalence class partitioning, and create all necessary test cases.

3. Describe your level of comfort for quality if a group of software developers tell you that they utilized test-driven development. Explain why.

10.11   Suggested Readings

K. Beck, *Test Driven Development: By Example* (Reading, MA: Addison-Wesley Professional, 2002).

Checkstyle 4.1 tool, http://checkstyle.sourceforge.net, 2006.

E. M. Clarke and J. M. Wing, "Formal Methods: State of The Art and Future Directions," *ACM Computing Surveys* 28, no. 4 (December 1996): 626–643.

D. Coppit et al., "Software Assurance by Bounded Exhaustive Testing," *IEEE Transactions on Software Engineering* 13, no. 4 (April 2005): 328–339.

P. B. Crosby, *Quality Is Free* (New York: McGraw Hill, 1979).

M. E. Fagan, "Design and Code Inspections to Reduce Errors in Program Development," *IBM Systems Journal* 15, no. 3 (1976): 219–248.

FindBugs, http://findbugs.sourceforge.net, 2006.

S. L. Gerhart and L. Yelowitz, "Observations of Fallability in Applications of Modern Programming Methodologies," *IEEE Transactions on Software Engineering* 2, no. 3 (September 1976): 195–207.

Guide to the Software Engineering Body of Knowledge (2004 Version), http://www.swebok.org, 2005.

D. Hamlet, "Foundation of Software Testing: Dependability Theory," *ACM SIGSOFT Software Engineering Notes* 19, no. 5 (December 1944): 128–139.

P. C. Jorgensen, *Software Testing: A Craftsman's Approach* (Boca Raton, FL: CRC Press, 1995).

JUnit.org, http://www.junit.org/index.htm, 2006.

J. M. Juran and A. B. Godfrey, eds., *Juran's Quality Handbook*, 5th ed. (New York: McGraw Hill, 1999).

C. Kaner, J. Bach, and B. Pettichord, *Lessons Learned in Software Testing* (New York: Wiley, 2002).

A. M. Memon, M. E. Pollack, and M. L. Soffa, "Hierarchical GUI Test Case Generation Using Automated Planning," *IEEE Transactions on Software Engineering* 27, no. 2 (February 2001): 144–158.

G. J. Myers, *The Art of Software Testing* (New York: Wiley, 1979).

T. J. Ostrand, E. J. Weyuker, and R. M. Bell, "Predicting the Location and Numbers of Faults in Large Software Systems," *IEEE Transactions on Software Engineering* 13, no. 4 (April 2005): 340–355.

S. C. Reid, "An Empirical Analysis of Equivalence Partitioning, Boundary Value Analysis and Random Testing," *4th IEEE International Software Metrics Symposium* (November 1997): 64–73.

J. Rubin, *A Handbook of Usability Testing* (New York: Wiley, 1994).

F. Tsui and L. Priven, "Implementation of Quality Control in Software Development," *AFIPS Conference Proceedings*, National Computer Conference, vol. 45, (1976): 443–449.

D. A. Wheeler, B. Brykczynski, and R. N. Meeson Jr., eds., *Software Inspection: An Industry Best Practice* (Los Alamitos, CA: IEEE Computer Society Press, 1996).

J. A. Whittaker, "What Is Software Testing? And Why Is It So Hard?" *IEEE Software* (January /February 2000): 70–79.

CHAPTER 11

Configuration Management, Integration, and Builds

OBJECTIVES

- Describe the basic concept of configuration management.
- Analyze the relationship between the software artifacts and the development process.
- Discuss the configuration management framework.
- Describe the naming model of artifacts.
- Describe the storage and access model of artifacts.
- Describe the integration and build process.
- Discuss the various automation tools for configuration management.
- Analyze managing configuration management.

11.1 Software Configuration Management

Software configuration management is the process of managing all the pieces and parts of artifacts produced as part of software development and support activities. In this chapter, we will occasionally refer to software artifacts as software items or software piece parts and will sometimes drop the word *software* that precedes the word *artifact*. Software configuration management is itself composed of a multitude of activities:

- Understanding the policy, process activities, and the resulting artifacts that need to be managed
- Determining and defining the framework that needs to be used to manage these artifacts
- Determining and bringing in any tools that need to be brought in to facilitate the management of these artifacts
- Training and ensuring that the agreed-upon configuration management process is practiced and adhered to

Thus software configuration management is much more than just creating and keeping multiple versions of code or documents. Many organizations, both public and private, have guidelines on configuration management. The *IEEE Guide to Software Configuration Management* (Std. 1042–1987) and NASA's *Software Configuration Management Guidebook* are some examples. Software configuration management is also a key process of the Software Engineering Institute's Capability Maturity Model, which was introduced in Chapter 4. It is also often integrated with software change management process and the maintenance and support activities.

11.2 Policy, Process, and Artifacts

In order to determine which are the pieces or parts that need to be managed, it is important to understand the overall software development and support process and activities that will be utilized by an organization. A conservative and risk-averse organization that is developing large and complex software may choose to have a full waterfall process with inspections following every major activity such as requirements specification, design specification, coding, and test case generation. All documents and artifacts developed and inspected are codified and stored, providing a complete audit trail and tracing of all the material. Other organizations may have to adopt a full control of all the artifacts due to the type of industry they are involved in, such as the government or defense industry sector. These organizations would be more motivated to adopt configuration management of the software artifacts.

On the other hand, a small and agile process-oriented organization may choose a process that places emphasis on only a few activities, such as requirements specifications and coding. Such an organization may choose to control only the final version of requirements specification and code, without keeping all the intermediate versions.

The chosen process and the artifacts developed from the activities in that process will play a heavy role in the determination of what and to what level of detail we must manage. For example, an organization that adopts a process that moves from requirements through design and coding to multiple levels of testing before the final software product build may decide on managing all the following artifacts:

- Requirements specification
- Design specification
- Source code
- Executable code
- Test cases

Here, source code includes logic code, database tables, and user screen scripts. Similarly, test cases include test scenarios written in English and test scripts with the associated test data. Depending on the development and support process, different types of artifacts may need to be managed. For example, if formal design inspections are a part of the process, then design inspection results may also be considered as vital artifacts that need to be managed.

Managing versions of these artifacts as independent material is somewhat tedious but not very complex. The complexity increases when multiple artifacts and the relations among those artifacts need to be controlled. Consider the requirements specifications and the design specification. If we want to match these and control the interrelationship of each customer requirement with the resulting design elements to ensure traceability, then we must introduce a scheme that allows us to link the elements across two sets of artifacts. There are many other interartifact relationships such as the following that must be considered:

- Requirements and test cases
- Design elements and logic code segments
- Logic code segments and database tables
- User-interface screens and code segments
- Messages, help texts, and source code
- Test cases and logic code segments
- Database tables and initialization data

This set of relationships may be represented in a more thorough and clearer matrix form. As an example, consider the interartifact relationships shown in **Table 11.1**. This example shows how the artifacts may be related. One may use another matrix to show a slightly different relationship.

This relationship is further affected if different versions of each artifact must be considered. A software product may have several versions of requirements. For example, after an initial, general version of requirements is issued, there may then be a slightly different version for some special industry or customers that have different needs. Furthermore, there may have to be country-specific versions to handle, say, French, Japanese, or Brazilian requirements. Thus, we may need to handle the intra-artifact relationship.

When the intra-artifact and interartifacts relationships need to be simultaneously considered, we might be facing an extremely intricate web of associations. Consider the four sets of artifacts in **Figure 11.1**.

Table 11.1 A Matrix Showing Interartifact Relationships

	Requirements Elements	Design Elements	Code Logic	UI Screens	DB Tables	Initialization Data	Test Cases
Requirements Elements		X	X	X			X
Design Elements	X		X	X	X	X	
Code Logic	X	X		X	X	X	X
UI Screens	X	X	X				X
DB Tables		X	X			X	
Initialization Data		X	X		X		X
Test Cases	X		X	X		X	

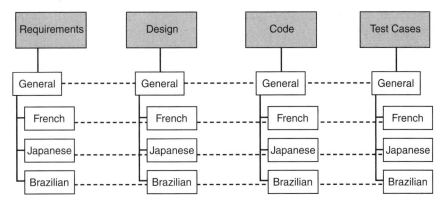

Figure 11.1 Intra-artifact and interartifact relationships.

Figure 11.1 shows the intra-artifact of different versions of requirements, design, code, and test cases respectively in a vertical fashion with solid lines. The interartifact relationship of, for example, French requirements to French design elements, to French coding elements, and French test cases respectively is shown horizontally with dotted lines.

If we trace a normal software product family that goes through multiple releases, covering multiple countries with different fix and service packages over a period of five or six years, the relationship diagram becomes completely unwieldy.

Consider the following example where a general software product with three country-specific versions goes through an annual new release through five years with an additional semiannual fix/upgrade service package. We will follow only a single artifact type, the design document, for the following illustration:

1. Original: The general version plus three country-specific versions add up to a total of four artifacts.

2. Annual releases: Each year there is a new release with its updated design artifacts. Thus there are 20 design artifacts (1 general + 3 country-specific = 4) after five years.

3. Semiannual (2 fix/updates) for five years: Each of the general releases has two fix/updates service packages associated with it annually. The first-year releases will have a total $5 \times 8 = 40$ service packages and thus will have 40 design update artifacts. The second-year release will have $4 \times 8 = 32$ service packages and will thus have 32 design update artifacts. The third-year release will have $3 \times 8 = 24$ design update artifacts. For five years, there will be a total of

$$\text{SUM}_{n=1,5} (n \times 8) = 120 \text{ service packages}$$

Thus, there will be a total of 120 design update artifacts associated with the 120 service packages.

Just tracing the design artifacts for the preceding example product, we see that the 4 original design artifacts expanded to a total of 20 new design artifacts plus 120 design fix artifacts, or 140 design artifacts in a span of 5 years. An organization that decides to control the related requirements documents, the related code, and the related test cases would find itself managing a horrendous number of interrelated artifacts.

11.2.1   Business Policy Impact on Configuration Management

The impact of a process decision on the management and control of artifacts can be further illustrated with the problem of allowing "branching" from intermediate artifacts. Consider the requirements documents in Figure 11.1. We can have a policy that allows only the following updates and modifications to requirements:

1. Only through the general version
2. Only to the latest version

The country-specific versions of French, Japanese, and Brazilian requirements are reviewed for appropriate updates as a result of the change to the general version. This policy enforces a sequential update process because the country-specific requirements are all successors to the general requirements. Now, let's consider a policy that allows a change to the French requirements version 2 after all the requirements artifacts have been updated to version 3. This is illustrated in **Figure 11.2**.

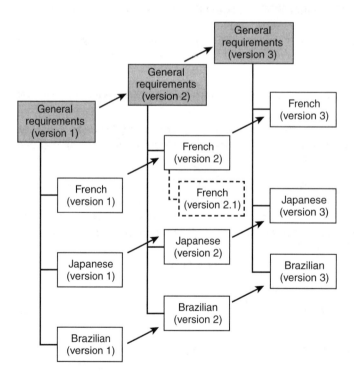

Figure 11.2 Allowing branching.

The branching from an intermediate artifact, French version 2 to French version 2.1, will require a reexamination of all the existing version 3 requirements to ensure that the change to French version 2 did not conflict with the existing version 3 requirements. The actual impact is much more if we include other artifacts such as the existing version 3 design and the version 3 code. We would need to examine for any conflict to all these existing artifacts. A business policy that allows customers not only to stay on French version 2 without migrating to the latest version 3 but also to update to French version 2, will impose a development policy and a process that greatly influences the management and control of the artifacts.

11.2.2   Process Influence on Configuration Management

Clearly the development and support process influences how the artifacts are managed. Consider the case of a large, complex software development that marches through three types of formal testing: (1) functional, (2) component, and (3) system. Only after all three formal testing activities are complete will the software product be built into a release, "golden" CD, which is then copied for distribution to the customers and users. **Figure 11.3** shows how unit-tested artifacts are first gathered and integrated for functional testing. The ones that have all of their problems fixed are considered to have passed. Only those that passed the functional testing are promoted to the functionally tested level. The code that passes the component test is then promoted to the component-tested level and eventually promoted to the system-tested "golden" copy. The concept of promotion of artifacts in a multilevel test process is to ensure that those codes tested at a certain level are locked and given no opportunity to be inadvertently degraded or regressed through some change. Along with the code, there are design material, test scripts, data, help texts, and other associated materials that must also be promoted from level to level until the final release.

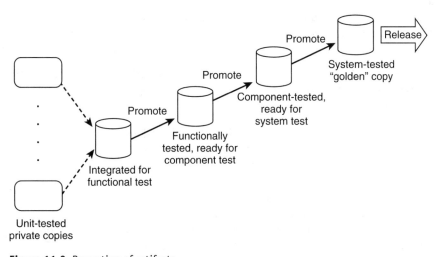

Figure 11.3 Promotion of artifacts.

Although Figure 11.3 does not explicitly show the promotion of all the associated artifacts that are stored in file libraries, these are indeed promoted with the code. It is just as important to ensure that all the artifacts at a certain tested level are promoted so that no regression or degradation occurs to them. The notion of artifact promotion in a test process requires certain capabilities, such as locking and access control, in configuration management.

11.3   Configuration Management Framework

In order to manage and control all the piece parts of the artifacts, software engineers must establish a framework to control these items. From the previous section, we can see that the software development and support policies and process will greatly influence the configuration management framework. We will discuss two main models that need to be included in the configuration management framework.

- Naming model
- Storage and access model

11.3.1   Naming Model

To properly control all the piece parts, there must be a way to uniquely identify each item or artifact and to be able to associate those items that are related. A sample naming model will be presented here. Depending on the business needs and process assumptions, different naming models may be created. The model here assumes the following:

- There is a unique software product name.
- There will be multiple types of artifacts (e.g., design documents, source code, executable code, requirements picture images, test scripts, test data).
- There may be multiple forms of artifacts (e.g., text, spreadsheets, picture images, audio sound bytes).
- There is a scheme that requires at least two levels of grouping. Software release level is the primary factor. Within a release level, there may be multiple levels of versions.
- There will be translated, multiple-country software releases.

For this set of assumptions, the following six-part naming model may be used. The periods are used as the delimiters to separate the naming components.

```
PP. CC. RRR. VVV. TT. FF
```

- Part 1—PP: The two-position slot of PP is the software product code. If P is allowed to be alphanumeric, then there are 36 legitimate characters for each position. Thus PP will give us 362, or 1296, possible product codes. For most software organizations that is more than sufficient.
- Part 2—CC: The next two positions, CC, represent the country code. Allowing 26 alphabet characters for each position, the two positions of CC will allow 262, or 676, countries. For most software products, the number of supported country versions is far fewer than 676. Most commercial products support English, French, German, Spanish,

Japanese, Chinese, Korean, and some Scandinavian countries. Unless the software product is for organizations such as the United Nations, 676 would be plenty. One may consider, for example, using the two-position ISO 3166 code for officially representing the countries.

- Part 3—RRR: The three-position RRR part represents the release number of the software. If we confine ourselves to just the numerical figures 0 through 9, then RRR can represent 103, or 1000, releases. Assuming the product takes on two releases per year, a three-positional numerical part will allow us to be in business for 500 years.

- Part 4—VVV: A three-positional versioning within each release, VVV is restarted for each release. Again, assuming only a numerical figure of 0 through 9, VVV would provide us with 1000 versions within each release. The artifact that will need a large number of versioning within a release is probably the code module. A code module may go through 1 to 100 versions of changes prior to release during the first year of development. Then, assuming a fairly error-prone or change-prone module, it may go through another 50 versions of changes per year during the maintenance and support period. This will allow for a program module life span of about 19 years, including the first year of development. In today's fast-paced technology world, a module life of 19 years should be quite sufficient.

- Part 5—TT: The two-positional type code describes the kind of artifact. It may be a requirements document, high-level design diagrams, database tables, test scenarios, test data, or source code. Here, T may be alphabetical and thus have 26 combinations. The two-positional code, TT, provides us with 262, or 676 different types of artifacts. This number of types of artifacts should be ample for even the most complex software development and maintenance.

- Part 6—FF: The format represents the form the artifact is represented. The artifact may be in a document form, in the form of a spread sheet, in executable code form, or in a jpeg image form. F may be a numeric figure between 0 through 9. Thus FF provides 100 different types of forms the artifact may be in.

Note that more combinations may be represented if we differentiate uppercase and lowercase letters. If necessary, pure numeric fields may also be changed to alphanumeric for expansion, and, of course, the number of positions for each part may be expanded. This six-part naming model may thus be used for a wide variety of software product development and support. The naming model is the key to uniquely identifying the items and to creating relationships among the items. In choosing tools, however, we need to pay special attention to the naming conventions that the tool may prescribe onto an organization. For example, compilers may require a special suffix or prefix for a source code file of different programming languages.

In addition to the naming model, a separate item-attribute description file, sometimes called an attribute model, may also be created. This attribute model essentially defines the characteristics associated with each of the artifacts, such as who the owner of the artifact is or when it was first created. It facilitates a richer artifact identification mechanism and may be included as a complementing companion to the naming model.

11.3.2   Storage and Access Model

The second key model to the configuration management framework is the storage and access model, which defines the facilities needed to store and to control the access of all the software artifacts. There are two fundamental functions in the model:

- `create`
- `delete`

The `create` function provides the capability to initially generate a new artifact and store it for configuration management. The `delete` function is the counterpart of `create`. The `delete` function destroys the artifact and eliminates it from configuration management.

There is also a set of access facilities in the model:

- `view`
- `modify`
- `return`

There are two types of retrieve functions. The `view` function allows the user to retrieve the artifact for reading purposes. The `modify` function allows the user to retrieve the artifact for the purpose of making changes to the artifact. The reason behind the differentiation is that when an artifact is retrieved by many users to be viewed only, there is no problem associated with contention. An artifact retrieved for the purpose of making changes can cause incompatibilities and conflicts. For example, users A, B, and C may all want to retrieve an artifact X to make their individual changes. Unless these three users communicate with each other while making their individual changes to artifact X, there is a strong possibility that the individual changes may conflict with each other. This possibility is greatly increased during test time when multiple changes may be occurring to a source code module. Thus a `modify` function, which is a controlled retrieval, is needed. The `modify` function allows only one user to retrieve the artifact for change purposes and prevents the conflict and contention problems. While the artifact is being modified the retrieval of that same artifact using the `modify` function is disabled for other users; however, others may still view that same artifact. The `return` function allows the modified artifact to be stored with the new modifications, and it reenables the `modify` function for that artifact. It is not possible to return an artifact unless that same person retrieved that artifact with the `modify` function. Thus the `modify` and the `return` functions are paired. In addition, the `return` function may also include an automatic incrementing of the version number of the artifact that is returned. These access functions with the automatic incrementing of version number provide a basic set of facilities for what is often called version control.

In many existing configuration management or version control products, the terms *check-in* and *check-out* are used. There are usually two forms of check-out. Check-out for read-only would be the same as the `view` function discussed previously, and check-out for edit would be the same as the `modify` function. Check-in would be the same as the `return` function.

There is also a set of control and service functions needed for the storage and access model. The extent of service functions required would depend on how much versatility is wanted for the configuration management. There are several examples of service functions:

- `import`
- `export`
- `list`
- `set` (release number or version number)
- `increment` (release number or version number)
- `change` (product code, country code, artifact type, or artifact form)
- `gather`
- `merge`
- `promote`
- `compare`

The `import` and `export` functions allow the artifacts to be brought into and moved out of the existing configuration management framework. The `list` function provides a listing of all the artifacts by product code, release number, or by some other identifier. The `set` function allows the establishment of a release number or version number of an artifact. Although the earlier described `return` function may include a version incrementing feature, the `increment` service function allows the release number or the version number to be explicitly incremented by the desired amount. It may also allow decrementing through incrementing by a negative amount. The `change` function provides the service to alter the product code or the country code or any part of the artifact name. The `gather` function may specify and link all the related artifacts by product code or by release number. For example, we may gather all the related artifacts by a product and country code and then export them to another organization. The `merge` function combines a change in one artifact into another artifact. This function may be useful if a set of fixes or changes is made to an existing, released artifact and that same set of changes needs to be incorporated into another artifact that is being prepared for the next release. Thus the `merge` function is helpful for multiple, parallel development. The `promote` function allows the designated artifacts to be moved to a different status. The usage of the *promote* function was earlier explained in the example of promoting tested code to different status levels prior to release. Often, especially in service and maintenance of a module, we would like to see what previous changes were made. A compare function will allow us to see the differences between two artifacts or two versions of the artifact.

Many more service functions may be incorporated into the storage and access model if needed. An example of an additional function may be a `locking` and `unlocking` mechanism. Another example would be the `where-used` or `where-referenced` function. It would allow us to find all the artifacts that reference a given artifact. The `where-used` function was extensively utilized several years ago when we were searching for all modules that contained or used the date field in order to solve the year 2000 problem.

The configuration management framework described here would certainly be easier to implement if we could automate some or most of the activities through an automated tool.

There is a very important activity called *integration and build* related to the configuration management framework. It is a must for large software development. The amount of related code and data that must be processed into one set of executables can be a daunting process without formal control. This activity will be discussed separately in the next section.

11.4   Build and Integration and Build

The build process is a set of activities associated with the integration and conversion of source files to a set of executable files targeted for a specific execution environment. The execution environment includes both the hardware and the software system that runs the software that was constructed during the build process.

The build cycle for a single program is a fairly simple one that every programmer is familiar with. The activities involve two major steps:

- Compile
- Link

The source code is compiled first. Any compilation error is then fixed and resubmitted for recompile. As soon as the source code is successfully compiled, it is linked with all the needed, externally referenced items that are relatively limited in number. Once the link activity has been successfully completed, the program is ready for testing, debugging, fixing, and so on.

Now consider a large, complex software application that has hundreds of source files that may undergo integration. These interrelated artifacts must be properly controlled or the build process may fail after several hours of processing. A common mistake in a multimember development team is to have a change made to a source code without the knowledge of other members. The other modules that depend on this changed module have a high probability of a reference mismatch that will cause the build activity to crash. As the build process becomes longer and more complex, a special build file, sometimes called a descriptor file or configuration file, is used to manage and control the build activities. A popular build file from the C and UNIX system days of the 1970s and 1980s is the makefile used by the `Make` function. The build file controls the order of the following activities of a software build cycle:

- Dependency and cross-reference checking
- Compilation of source code into executables
- Linking the executables
- Generating any required data file

With an automated tool, the build process of a complex software system can be greatly alleviated. After a build file is defined, the automated tool will then process the build cycle according to the build file. For large, complex software, the complete build cycle may take more than 6 or 7 hours. Because of the lengthy time needed for these builds, they are often performed at night. You may hear the term *nightly builds* used for this process.

Our experiences with large software development have also taught us to ensure that if the current build process fails, we are not left with nothing. That is, the previously built system is always kept as a backup. Should the current build cycle fail, then the system from the last build remains as the most recent system and may still be used to continue activities such as testing. Having a build file will certainly help us trace and correct some of the build process errors. The build file can serve as an audit mechanism for the build process. Because the build cycle for a large system is so long, we often break it into parts. This allows us to check to see that each step is completed properly before going on to the next step; it prevents us from having to restart and repeat a long build cycle when something fails at the end due to a mistake in one of the earlier steps.

When the software is in the test phase of the development cycle, bugs are found and fixed on a daily basis. Not all the source code is affected by these fixes and changes. Often only a small number of source programs are modified. In such cases, there is no need to perform a complete rebuild, but extreme care must be observed in these partial builds. Finally, when the total development cycle is completed and the final release is ready to be developed, a complete rebuild from the entire source should be performed. One last caution: the final build must ensure that the software system built is for the run-time environment of the targeted users, not just for the developers' environment. There have been cases where everything executes well on the developers' system, but due to some differences in the environments such as an old version of an executable in some library the software will not run properly on the users' environment.

11.5 Tools for Configuration Management

As mentioned earlier, software configuration management is a set of activities related to controlling the piece parts resulting from software development and support. In large software projects, these activities can be tedious and complex, and thus very prone to error. It thus makes sense to automate as many of these activities as possible.

These configuration management tools may be viewed in three tiers. The first basically performs version control and change control, processes that are often available without any change. Some of the earlier and more popular ones applied mostly to controlling source code are the Revision Control System (RCS), which was written by Walter Tichy at Purdue University, and the Source Code Control System (SCCS), which was provided with most of the UNIX systems. Today, GNU (which is an acronym that stands for "GNU's Not UNIX") and the Free Software Foundation (FSF) make a clone of SCCS known as CSSC available. Other tools include Concurrent Versions Systems (CVS); Project Revision Control System (PRCS), which is a tool like CVS and RCS with an easier-to-use front end that has been developed by Paul Hilfinger of the University of California, Berkeley; and Subversion, a CVS replacement tool sponsored by Tigris.org, another open source community focused on tools for collaborative software development. The Suggested Readings section at the end of this chapter provide references to these tools.

The second tier of configuration management is to include the build function. One of the popular earlier build tools was the Make utility that came with the UNIX systems, created by S. I. Feldman of AT&T Bell Labs in the mid 1970s. This function uses a descriptor or configuration file, such as the makefile, as its direction to find all the source files and the dependencies among them in generating the final executable file. Other build tools that are free of charge include Odin, Cons, SCons, and Ant.

Odin is a build tool much like the Make utility. Although it is more advanced and runs faster than Make, its descriptor file is not compatible with the makefile, which made it less attractive as an immediate replacement for Make. Cons is another build tool, released in 1996 by Robert Sidebotham and now maintained by Rajesh Vaidheeswarren. It is meant to be an improvement over the Make tool and works on several platforms, including AIX, FreeBSD, HPUX, Linux, Windows NT, and Solaris. It is distributed under the GNU General Public License as published by the Free Software Foundation. SCons is based on the architecture of Cons and is a result of the competition in 2000 sponsored by Software Carpentry. It was first released in 2001 under the nonrestrictive MIT license. Apache Ant (Another Neat Tool), distributed by the Apache Software Foundation, is a Java-based Make-like build tool started by James Davidson, a freelance software developer, to help build Tomcat, which is an Apache web server engine. Because it is XML based, Ant configuration file is different from the UNIX shell-based commands of Make.

The third tier of software configuration management tools to integrate the configuration management activities with the development and support process activities. This is a feature that is not included in most of the free wares. Only a limited number of commercially available configuration management tools have integrated with some of the development and support process activities. For example, the requirements and versions of requirements artifacts developed using a requirements tool will often remain within that requirements tool. The requirements artifacts are rarely "tied" to the related design document, source code, and test cases. The procedure that is most often supported by the more sophisticated configuration management tools is the change management process. There is not yet a complete development process–integrated third-tier software configuration management tool.

There are, however, several commercial configuration management tools available for large software development and support that are attempting to cover more than simply the source code artifacts. Because of their relatively richer functionality, these commercial tools are much more complex. The following three tools are probably the most prevalent ones at the writing of this text:

- ClearCase
- PVCS (Serena ChangeMan)
- Visual SourceSafe

ClearCase is a family of software configuration management tools that operates with multiple development environments such as the Microsoft Visual Studio.Net, open source Eclipse, IBM WebSphere Studio, and Rational Application Developer. It also provides an extensive build capability. Initially released by Atria, it was then bought by Rational, which in turn was acquired by IBM. Made for large, complex, multiteam software development and support, it is now known as IBM Rational ClearCase.

PVCS is also a family of software configuration management tools. It started as a tool set more appropriate for medium-sized development. In 2004, its owning enterprise

Merant was acquired by Serena Software. The PVCS family of tools is now converted and integrated into the Serena ChangeMan family of tools.

Visual SourceSafe started as a simple code version control tool developed by One Tree Software. Since its acquisition by Microsoft in 1994, the tool has grown considerably and is integrated with the Microsoft development environment. However, it still predominantly focuses on version control. It is suited for teams that are small and geographically distributed.

Currently, there is no single configuration management tool that can manage all the different artifacts and their interdependencies, and it may be necessary to cobble several tools together. In deciding which tools are a best fit for your particular organization, consider the following questions:

- What artifacts are important to the organization and how are they related? Should those artifacts be managed under some type of automated tool and for how long?
- Does the specific automation tool have all the (1) necessary and (2) desired configuration management functions?
- Does the specific automation tool run in the development and support environment of the organization and handle all the different types of artifacts (e.g., supported programming language, design language, configuration file script language)?
- Will the existing naming model work with the automation tool or does the naming model need to be modified? If the names need to be modified, is there any conversion tool to help?
- Does the specific automation tool generate the artifacts that will run in the users' environment without any change to that environment?
- Can the tool accommodate geographically separate, multisite development?
- How many resources are required to run the specific automation tool (e.g., CPU speed, memory)?
- Is the specific automation tool supported? How is it supported (e.g., on a 24/7 schedule)?
- How often is the automation tool updated and new releases made available?
- Does the tool vendor provide any formal education? In what form?
- Are there documentations such as user and reference manuals?
- Are there current reference accounts that you may either visit or call?

Finally, unless the automation tool is free, you should check the price of both the product and the support service of the tool. Many tools are priced and licensed by the number of users or by an enterprise-wide agreement.

11.6   Managing the Configuration Management Framework

Software configuration management is considered one of the successful areas that benefited directly from the contributions made in software engineering practices and research. We cannot assume though that it is able to operate automatically by itself. There continues to be a need for overt emphasis in software configuration and release management. Software configuration management should be brought into an organization in a planned fashion, possibly in stages.

In its simplest form, we have to make sure that all the source code materials are properly compiled and linked to form a releasable package that users can simply install and execute. Of course, in order to ensure that all the source materials are the right source materials during and throughout the development stages, we must introduce and implement the discipline of configuration management. The fundamental discipline involves keeping clear account of the multiple versions of source material and being able to deliver any one of those versions for integration and build, which generates the desired software release for users. As the number of coding artifacts and the frequency of changes increase, a person, called the configuration management administrator, along with some automation, must be introduced.

After mastering the fundamental software configuration management discipline in development, we can then branch into support activities. Making multiple changes to modules at a fairly frequent pace is an inherent part of software support and maintenance. Applying software configuration management to the support process is a natural extension from development.

Once all the code and code-related artifacts are placed under configuration management, the organization is ready to include other artifacts, such as requirements, design, or test case artifacts. Keeping all the other artifacts and maintaining the proper relationships require an additional level of sophistication. The configuration management administrator needs to be brought in to help design a broader system that will allow us to store, access, trace, control, and relate all these artifacts. We should be able to generate a complete software product package that includes all the requirements, associated design documents, inspection/review results, change requests, source code, executable code, data, test cases and scripts, test data, test reports and results, reference manuals, and marketing brochures. This level of sophistication requires the organization to have a clearly stated development and support process, a well-defined set of artifacts generated from the process activities, and an integrated configuration management system.

A key to success in any system is having knowledgeable and motivated team members, clear goals, and good process and tools to help users. Software configuration management is no different. The participating software development and support engineers must all be trained and knowledgeable in configuration management, in the reasons and goals behind configuration management, in the process involved, and in the usage of the associated tools. These management steps should be taken before, or at least at the very early stages of, the actual software development and support activities.

11.7   Summary

A large, complex software project requires the proper management of all the artifacts that are generated. In addition, these artifacts have a set of complicated relationships that must be accounted for in order to produce a release and to be able to support that release.

A configuration management framework is composed of two main parts:

- Naming model
- Storage and access model

Coupling these two models with the integration and build process, we can manage the software piece parts that are generated and can produce different software releases for users. Various tools are discussed for different levels of sophistication in automating configuration management. These range from version control to integration and build, interartifact management, and process control. The introduction of configuration management to an organization should also be brought in with a good plan and possibly in stages.

11.8   Review Questions

1. What is a naming model used for?

2. List the four major activities associated with software configuration management.

3. What are check-in and check-out?

4. List three concerns you may need to look into before choosing a configuration management tool.

5. What are the build steps of a single program?

6. What is linking and what are we linking in a build process?

7. Explain the difference between the `view` and the `modify` functions in the storage and access model of configuration management.

8. Name a tool from each of the three tiers of automating the configuration management activities.

11.9   Exercises

1. How would you use the naming model to trace a design artifact to its requirements? Show an example.

2. Consider the situation where your naming model allows a two-position artifact type and a three-position artifact format. Compare this with source code naming conventions for C++ or Java source code files. Discuss the problem that may occur during build.

3. Discuss the activity of promoting artifacts to the next level.

4. In version control, why do we need to worry about multiple accesses for modification purposes? Show an example of what can happen to a source code when it is not under version control.

5. How does allowing branching from an intermediate artifact in an existing sequence of artifacts that is under version control create more complexity?

6. In version control, there has been debate on how to implement the internal storage of the different versions of an artifact. One argument is to keep the complete copy of each version. Another is to keep only the delta changes from version to version, with the first version being the only complete copy.

    a. Give one reason why you may want to keep a complete copy of each version.

    b. Give one reason why you may want to keep only the delta.

    c. What would be the drawback of each of these approaches?

11.10   Suggested Readings

Apache Ant, http://ant.apache.org, 2005.

Atria Software, ClearCase User's Manual, Natick, MA, 1992.

M. E. Bayes, *Software Release Methodology* (Upper Saddle River, NJ: Prentice Hall, 1999).

S. P. Berczuk and B. Appleton, *Software Configuration Management Patterns: Effective Teamwork, Practical Integration* (Reading, MA: Addison-Wesley, 2003).

Cons (A Software Construction System), http://www.gnu.org/cons/stable/cons.html, accessed 2012.

CSSC (GNU's clone of SCCS), http://gnu.org.software/cssc, accessed 2012.

CVS (Concurrent Versions System), www.gnu.org/software/cvs, 2005.

S. Dart, "Concepts in Configuration Management Systems," *Third International Software Configuration Management Workshop* (New York, NY: ACM Press, 1991).

———, "The Past, Present, and Future of Configuration Management," *Software Engineering Institute Technical Report*, CMU/SEI -92-TR-8, 1992.

J. Estublier et al., "Impact of the Research Community for the Field of Software Configuration Management," *Proceedings of the 24th International Conference on Software Engineering*, 2002, pp. 643–44.

A. M. J. Hass, *Configuration Management Principles and Practices* (Reading, MA: Addison-Wesley, 2003).

A. van der Hoek, A. Carzaniga, D. Heimbigner, and A. L. Wolf, "A Testbed for Configuration Management Policy Programming," *IEEE Transactions on Software Engineering* 28, no. 1 (January 2002): 79–99.

IBM Rational ClearCase, http://www-01.ibm.com/software/awdtools/clearcase, accessed 2012.

International Workshop on Software Configuration Management, *Workshop Proceedings from Springer, Lecture Notes in Computer Science* (LNCS) 1005 (SCM 4 and SCM 5-1995), 1167 (SCM 6 -1996), 1235 (SCM 7-1997), 1439 (SCM 8- 1998), 1675 (SCM 9-1999), and 2649 (SCM 10 and SCM 11 – 2001 and 1003).

A. Leon, *A Guide to Software Configuration Management* (Norwood, MA: Artech House, 2000).

Microsoft Visual SourceSafe, http://msdn.microsoft.com/en-us/library/3h0544kx%28v=vs.80%29.aspx, 2013.

NASA Software Configuration Management Guidebook, http://ntrs.nasa.gov/archive/nasa/casi.ntrs.nasa.gov/19980228473_1998393844.pdf, 2013.

C. Nentwich, W. Emmerich, A. Finkelstein, and E. Ellmer, "Flexible Consistency Checking," *ACM Transactions on Software Engineering and Methodology* 12, no. 3 (January 2003): 28–63.

PRCS (Project Revision Control System), http://prcs.sourceforge.net, 2005.

PVCS (Serena ChangeMan), http://www.serena.com, 2005.

RCS (Revision Control System), http://www.gnu.org/software/rcs/rcs.html, 2005.

T. Roche, *Essential SourceSafe* (Milwaukee, WI: Hentzenwerke Publishing, 2001).

SCons, http://www.scons.org, 2004.

Subversion, http://subversion.apache.org, accessed 2012.

W. Tichy, "Software Configuration Management Overview," http://www.ida.liu.se/~petfr/princprog/cm.pdf.

B. White, *Software Configuration Management Strategies and Rational Clear Case: A Practical Introduction* (Reading, MA: Addison-Wesley, 2000).

E. J. Whitehead Jr. and D. Gordon, "Uniform Comparison of Configuration Management Data Models," *Proceedings of 11th International Workshop on Software Configuration Management* (SCM-11), 2003, 70–85.

CHAPTER 12

Software Support and Maintenance

OBJECTIVES

- Describe postrelease product support and customer service activities.
- Discuss product defect and nondefect support tasks.
- Analyze a sample customer support and service organization.
- Describe product-fix releases, which contain only product defect fixes, and maintenance releases, which contain small product enhancements and defect fixes.

12.1   Customer Support

Large software products go through a very lengthy and expensive development process. However, the postrelease product support and maintenance cycle is several times longer than the original development cycle. The software product life span after the initial release lasts many years. The success of the product is dependent on the real users' experience with the software. Despite developers hopes to have "user friendly" and "high-quality" software, many large software products are complex and contain defects at product release time. Furthermore, due to a variety of reasons such as resource and schedule constraints, the first release of a product may not include everything in the requirements list. Thus it is extremely important that there is a good understanding of and extensive preparation made for postrelease customer support. The customer support and services include two main types of activities:

- Product defect support
- Product nondefect support and services

In addition, most of the customer support and service for large software products charges a fee. Many software organizations charge as much as 10% to 20% of the original product price for one year of postrelease product support and customer service. Some charge a fee on a "per-call" basis where each telephone call to the customer support service requires the caller to pay for the support/service effort. These paying customers and users clearly expect a professional level of services and product maintenance updates. A number of the product support and customer service models extend the support and service into a customer consulting practice. The consulting service will include customer product education and mentoring as well as performing product extensions and customizations. In general, once a software product is modified and customized, that portion is not covered by the general product support contract and must be supported by the consulting service contract. We will not discuss the extended model of consulting services in this text except to mention that it is a growing but difficult business. Companies such as IBM and Wipro of India have made IT consulting a global business.

For those using or planning to use open source software, product support and customer service may be a problem. Because the software product is free, there is no legal obligation to support it. For some open source software, there may be a commercial support provider, but usually it is for a popular product that is in demand. For example, Red Hat is a company that provides support for Enterprise Linux, which is a free operating system, and for JBoss Enterprise Application Platform.

12.1.1   User Problem Arrival Rate

Once a software produce is released, there is usually a surge of question and problem reports from users as the early usage rate picks up. It is well known that the problem discoveries and reports arrivals follow an exponential curve much like the Rayleigh curve shown in **Figure 12.1**. However, the real data are not as smooth as what is depicted in Figure 12.1.

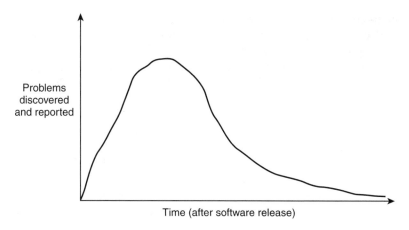

Time (after software release)

Figure 12.1 A Rayleigh curve illustrating problem arrival.

The problem arrival rate increases very quickly in the beginning as users try a new software product. In the beginning, the users are exercising the main paths and finding all the easy "low-hanging fruit" problems. As these major problems get fixed and user sophistication increases, the problem reporting rate will also decrease to a lower rate. Sometimes a software product may be mistakenly thought to be of high quality when the initial problem reports come in very slowly. When this happens, it is important to check the actual usage rate of the product because many customers may not immediately use newly released software. Some software engineers assign the term _usage-time_ to the time axis in Figure 12.1 and thus expand strict calendar time to depict the problem arrival curve. A usage-time unit is often defined as follows:

> Usage month = (Number of users actively using the software) × (Number of months of usage)

This formula ensures that both time and usage are included when depicting the problem arrival rate. Kan (2003) contains an extensive discussion on the Rayleigh model and defect arrival rates. These defect arrival rates also resemble the test defect discovery rates and reliability models during testing. (See Musa, Iannino, and Okumoto [1990] for additional details on reliability models.)

The preparation for customer support must start before the software is released. The support and service workload and the number of support personnel required are estimated from the problem arrival curve. Therefore, it is vital that there is some way to accurately estimate the problem arrival rate. For those organizations having a history of usage data, the estimation of problem arrival rate of a similar situation is quite feasible. The difficulty occurs when a new product to the organization is being released. The subject of estimation and reliability modeling is beyond the intent of this text. (See the Suggested Readings section for references.) Estimating the number of required support personnel is only a first step. The support personnel need to be educated on the software product. Often this is accomplished through education in both the software and the usage environment. Sometimes the support personnel are included in the testing effort as part of the education and transition activities. Other times an original developer or a tester is seeded in the support team to mentor the support team during the first six months or so of the product support period.

In experienced support organizations, detailed accounts of usage and problem reports are constantly and carefully analyzed. The data from the first several months are sometimes used as a checkpoint to see if defect discovery and arrival projections are tracking to projection. During the early support period, a renegotiation of support resources may be needed, especially if more problems are coming in than were originally projected.

The actual cost of maintenance and subsequent releases would depend on the marketing and financial situation of each software product. Those successful software products that have large user communities tend to stay in the market for years with multiple updates and releases. Even then, eventually, the product will enter a sunset period and be taken off the market. The product sunset period may take a year or two and usually go through the following sequence:

1. Stop any product's new feature or functional enhancement release.
2. Fix only very high-severity problems related to the old product.
3. Announce a new replacement product.
4. Encourage existing users and customers to migrate to the new product.
5. Notify users remaining on the old product of the planned termination of product support.
6. Provide customers who are still remaining on the old product with names of possible software vendors willing to continue the old product support.
7. Terminate customer support on the planned date and withdraw the software product from the market.

Sometimes, a software product is withdrawn, but there is no new replacement product. In such situations, the sunset period may be a lot longer in order to allow users to find an alternative solution.

12.1.2   Customer Interface and Call Management

A typical customer support organization has several layers of personnel performing different types of activities. **Figure 12.2** is an example of a software support organization with two layers of support and service functions. There is an outer layer handling the interfaces with the customers, and there is an inner layer of technical experts diagnosing and fixing the more difficult problems, including changing the code.

The outer layer is composed of the service and support representatives who represent the software product and the service functions to customers and users. At the same time, these service and support representatives are advocates for the customers and represent the customers' view of how the product needs to be fixed or modified. These representatives must possess exceptionally good communication skills and application domain knowledge. The inner layer is composed of more technical and product-knowledgeable personnel whose main task is to develop code fixes of the customers' problems. These two groups work very closely and, most of the time, jointly maintain a frequently asked ques-

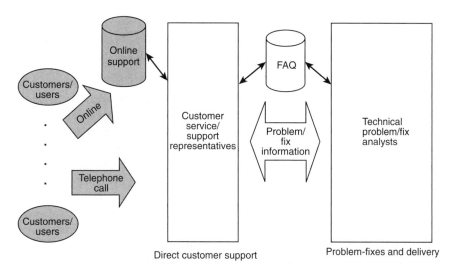

Figure 12.2 A typical customer service and support organization.

tions (FAQ) database. This database contains a history of past, known problems and the associated fixes, and it may also contain work-around for problems that do not yet have fixes. There are also frequent communications concerning customer problems and fix status between the two groups.

The customer support/service representatives handle customer problems in two major forms:

- Customer telephone calls
- Online submissions

When a customer or user encounters a problem, the traditional mode of operation is to call the customer support representatives. Depending on the size of the support/ service organization, there may be an automatic call management tool that directs the incoming calls to different service representatives, based on the type of problem and the availability of the representatives. The support/service representative who receives a call follows a sequence of activities such as the following:

1. Take the customer's name and identification to ensure that this is a qualified customer (e.g., a customer who has paid for the software service).
2. Listen to and record the description of the problem.
3. Perform a scan of the FAQ database to check for similar problems and solutions.
4. Provide the answer if it is a previously reported and already resolved problem.
5. Provide an expected fix date if it is a previously reported but unresolved problem.

6. If it is a new problem, provide a work-around if possible. If there is no work-around, agree on a priority level for the problem with the customer. Based on this agreed-upon priority level, provide an estimated fix time to the customer.

7. Record the problem and issue a report to the technical fix team.

Call management is the process of dealing with customer calls and ensuring that they are handled smoothly. The customer support/service representatives are encouraged to resolve only those problems that are short and easy to handle over the phone and do not require code fixes. The automated call management tool also aids supervisors in collecting data on the call traffic, call queue length, call response and process time, number of missed calls, and other relevant information. The number of representatives that are required to support the product and to service the customers depends on the expected call volumes, which in turn depend on the height and shape of the expected problem arrival curve shown in Figure 12.1. At times, customers may not be satisfied with a particular service representative's attitude or that person's answer. In such cases, there must be a backup process to handle the unsatisfied customers. In the past, many of these services have been outsourced to off-shore countries; however, companies such as Dell have moved them back close to the corporate home office to improve the support services.

In addition to direct and synchronous call support, support/service representatives are also asked to maintain an online website for asynchronous customer support. Many of the telephone call activities are automated with this asynchronous interface. The support/service website begins by asking for the customer's name and identification and automatically checks the qualification of the customer. The customer's reported problem is automatically checked against the FAQ database and a response is automatically generated, based on whether there is a match. If it is a new problem, the request is automatically reported and later viewed by a customer support/service representative. A response is then communicated to the customer, along with the representative's assessed problem priority level and estimated fix date. This response may be a direct email or a posting that the customer may check later, or both. There may also be a customer escalation facility, which handles dissatisfied customers. Some support organizations will post some product marketing announcements and future release announcements on the support/service website. Others will post versions of the actual code fixes on the site, allowing the customers to directly download the fixes and install them themselves.

All experienced customers know that the way to receive fast and quick consideration is to have the problem priority assessed as high as possible. They are keenly aware of the relationship between the problem priority level and the problem-fix response time. An example of this relationship is demonstrated in **Table 12.1**. Many experienced customers will ask for this type of service agreement before signing up and paying for the customer support/service contract. A particular concern will be finding out if the customer call center operates 24 hours a day for 7 days a week. Today, most customers expect this level of responsiveness.

12.1.3   Technical Problem/Fix

If a problem is beyond the ability of the support/service representative, then the technical problem/fix analyst is brought in. There may be a work-around or a temporary fix that may be passed to the customer. In that case, both the problem description

Table 12.1 Sample Problem Priority Levels

Priority Level	Problem Category	Fix Response Time
1	Severe functional problem with no work-around	As soon as possible
2	Severe functional problem but has work-around	1–2 weeks
3	Functional problem that has work-around	3–4 weeks
4	Nice to have or to change	Next product release or earlier

and temporary solution is logged in the FAQ database to help other customers who encounter a similar problem. Meanwhile, a formal change request is created so that a more permanent fix, which may involve code change, is generated. Based on the change request, the solution to the problem is designed, coded, and tested. A very high priority fix will be packaged and made available to customers immediately. It will also be integrated into a fix release, which is a collection of problem-fixes that is released periodically. The non-high-priority fixes are all integrated and packaged into periodic fix releases.

The technical problem/fix analysts are usually well-qualified engineers who are experts in designing coding, and testing. However, different from development software engineers, these problem/fix analysts have neither the support of the product require-ments analysts nor the original product designers. Thus they have to possess both the product-specific, industry knowledge as well as general technical knowledge. While this is a management problem, the appreciation and recognition of these technical problem/fix analysts has been long overdue. Their special value is just starting to be recognized.

The process of passing a customer problem from the support/service representative to the technical problem/fix analyst and getting the solution back to the customer is almost the same as the one used between testers and developers. The following is a high-level summary of such a process:

1. Problem description, problem priority, and other related information is recorded in a problem report that is submitted to the problem-fix-and-delivery group.
2. The problem-fix-and-delivery group will explore and analyze the problem, includ-ing the reproduction of the problem.
3. The problem-fix-and-delivery group either accepts or rejects the problem.
4. If the problem is rejected, the direct customer support group is immediately notified; if the problem is accepted, then a change request is generated and the problem enters a fix cycle of design, code, and test.
5. Depending on the priority and nature of the problem, the fix may be individually packaged and released immediately to the customer or the fix may be integrated into a fix release package.
6. The FAQ database is updated to reflect the status of all the problems so that the customer support/service representatives may quickly and accurately advise the customers on the problem resolution status.

The design, code, and test cycle of a problem-fix is not very different from the design, code, and test activities of the development cycle. The danger is that the fix cycle may not utilize the same level of software engineering discipline because many of the problem-fixes may involve only one or two lines of code fix. It is so tempting to just fix the code and go on to the next problem. For an organization that is handling multiple software product releases across multiple countries, as mentioned in Chapter 11, the discipline of keeping all the requirements, design, coding, and testing documentations updated is imperative. A code fix to a problem often needs to be propagated to other releases and also to multiple country versions. The tasks and activities of the problem-fix-and-delivery group require the same software engineering methodologies and techniques as those described in the earlier chapters of this text. In addition, there is more awareness of the need for measurements as customers are starting to demand contractual agreements on service levels with penalty clauses if the agreement is not met. This is especially true with hardware system availability where most of the system is expected to be available between 99% and 100%. Fortunately, the customer demand on software has not yet reached such a level.

The problem/fix process for life-threatening situations is very different from the normal condition. It is not uncommon to see support personnel physically on site at a customer's system to fix and resolve the problem in such emergency situations. In fact, depending on the particular case, even the original designer or programmer sometimes participates in supporting the customer. In such situations, the changes and fixes made at the customer site still need to be documented and the fix code integrated back into a general fix release later for other customers. A word of caution: Support is only for problems originating from the original software product, not for any modified or customized code problem. Today, most software product organizations provide only executable object code and do not release source code anymore to evade the issue of supporting customer-modified code.

12.1.4   Fix Delivery and Fix Installs

The deliveries of fixes follow two major paths. There are the regular and periodic fix releases that are on a quarterly or semiannual cycle. These are the different code fixes that have been accumulated since the last fix release. A fix release, in general, does not contain the complete product. It is not a total product refresh but contains only those modules and code that are affected by the problem-fixes. The fix code is packaged in a sequential order. The fix releases are also sequential, and the customers are expected to install the fix releases in sequential order. All fix releases are made available to all the customers that have a valid support/service contract. These fix releases, sometimes called patches, are downloadable from an online site or are shipped to the customers on CDs.

Not all customers will apply (or install) the fix releases immediately. These are customers who have achieved a "working" state and do not want to risk their working software with any new fix releases. They may, however, encounter a problem later and want a particular problem-fix. These customers must be reminded to apply all the fix releases in sequence since they last fully applied a fix release. Such a retroactive application of all the fix releases can be very time consuming and frustrating when the customer wants only one problem fixed or a single patch. However, in order to keep the support service effort at a reasonable level, customers are always encouraged to apply the fix release as soon as possible after it becomes available.

The other path of fix delivery is for the high-priority emergency fixes. In such a situation, a single fix may be delivered to the customer whose system may be down and whose business is suspended. The customer will immediately apply the fix upon receiving it. The customer's system is brought up and business resumes. However, those customers who applied this emergency fix must be cautioned when the next regular fix release is made available. They should not perform a partial install of the fixes in the fix release, figuring that they already have the emergency fix applied. It is possible that some of the fixes in the accumulated fix release may impact the emergency fix that was already applied. At times, the customers who have applied the emergency fix may have to back out that emergency fix first and then apply the complete fix release. **Figure 12.3** depicts a fix release (n+1) that contains three accumulated fixes.

Suppose there is an emergency problem and an emergency fix is delivered to those customers who are at Fix Release n level in Figure 12.3. Assume that the emergency fix sent to the customer at Fix Release n level touches code statements 3, 4, and 5. Meanwhile there is already a new, next code fix, Fix 1, for problem 1 that is placed into the integration bucket for the next fix release, Fix Release n+1. Furthermore, suppose that because of the Fix 1 which affected the Fix Release n (Statements 3, 4, 5, and 6), the already delivered emergency code fix must now be altered to Fix 2 because it touches the same area. Then any subsequent problem-fix, Fix 3, must be based on this altered emergency fix, Fix 2. This is an example of why an emergency fix cannot be left in the code and why customers cannot just blindly apply the fix release.

The delivery group of the customer support/service organization must keep track of the delivery status and customers' fix apply status. When a new fix release is available, an information document that contains the list of problems and corresponding fixes is included along with advice to customers who may be at different release, version, or fix release

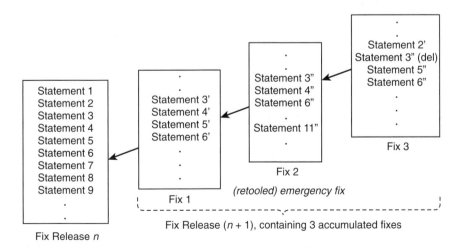

Figure 12.3 Fix overlay problem.

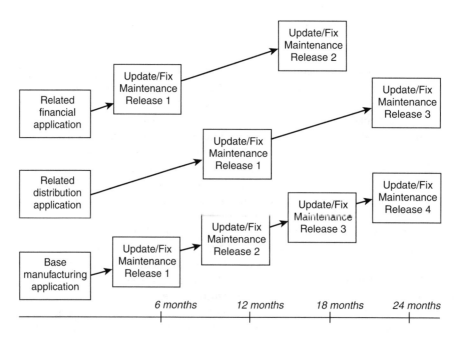

Figure 12.4 Multiple-product fix releases.

levels. In addition, there are times when software applications may be so intertwined that a fix release of one must be coapplied with a fix release of another software product. For example, an operating system fix release may be related to a fix release of a database system and of a network system. These three fix releases are corequisites of each other and must be applied together for all the fixes to work. This corequisite situation is discussed more in the next section and is shown in **Figure 12.4**. The various fix release information is also shared with the customer service support representatives so that when a customer reports a problem, it is clear what level the customer is at with which product.

12.2   Product Maintenance Updates and Release Cycles

In the previous sections we discussed the customer support/service activities and the concerns of fix releases and applying emergency fixes. Aside from product defect problems, there also are small, functional enhancements provided to customers as maintenance updates. Usually, when there is a major functional enhancement or a new platform supported, the software product will be newly priced as a different product release. These new product releases are also developed by the product development organization as opposed to the customer support/service organization. However, these small, incremental changes are not treated as a new product release. They are often included as a part of the customer support/service contract. An example is the addition of the support of a new device, such as a new printer. Another example, for a payroll application, may be the changes needed to accommodate the annual tax law changes. These product updates are usually integrated with the product defect fixes release and delivered as a product maintenance update.

Different software application products will require different product maintenance cycles. Some applications will go through a maintenance update every six months, and others will have an annual update to match legislative updates. Figure 12.4 illustrates three separate but related commercial software applications that are releasing their updates at slightly different periods. Each product organization can have their separate release plans, except when there are product linkages. For example, if a new feature modification in the manufacturing application is related to some area in the distribution application, then their respective update/fix maintenance releases must match and be made available simultaneously. The Update/Fix Maintenance Release 2 of Manufacturing may be related to the Distribution application's Update/Fix Maintenance Release 1. Then these two maintenance releases must be timed to come out at the same time, and the updates/fix maintenance releases for the two software products must list each other as corequisites in their respective documentations, which are shipped along with the code. The customers must apply both of these at the same time. Otherwise the new feature may not work. Cross software applications planning is a complex and vital set of activities that involves both technical and business knowledge. Its significance is gaining more attention as different software companies strike up business alliances and partnerships, not to mention corporate merger and acquisitions. It is also clear that configuration management, discussed in Chapter 11, and an automated configuration management tool are necessities in order for customer support and service to succeed.

12.3   Change Control

In addition to the need for configuration management, a large customer support/service organization must have a well-established change control. Just as development organizations must have good change control or risk scope creep and blown schedules, the customer support and service organization must control all the changes, whether the change originated from a customer problem or a planned small, incremental, feature enhancement. The scheduling of changes based on the number of anticipated problems and change requests is usually resource gated. There may be special situations when an unexpectedly large volume of change requests can drive a customer support/service organization to increase their staffing with temporary help personnel. Due to the dynamic nature of many of the customer support/service organizations, it is even more crucial to have a good change control process.

Change control is a process that manages the flow of the following activities:

- Origination of a change request
- Approval of a change request
- Acting on a change request
- Tracking and closing a change request

Along with the activity flow, there is also certain information that must be passed through the flow. The information relevant to a change request is usually captured in a change request form. A sample of such a form is shown in **Figure 12.5**.

For easy identification and tracking purposes, each change request is given a request number. The date of the initial request and the requestor name are also needed, and the change request should include a priority indication of high, medium, or low. The priority

```
┌─────────────────────────────────────────────────────────────────────────┐
│                                                                           │
│   Change request number: _____        Request date: _____     │
│                                                                           │
│   Requestor name: _____                                        │
│                                      Request   Accepted date:_____   │
│                                      status:   Rejected date:_____    │
│   Requestor priority: High, Medium, Low        Processing start date:_____ │
│                                                Completion date:_____   │
│                                                                           │
│   Brief change request description: _____ │
│   _____  │
│   _____  │
│   _____  │
│                                                                           │
│   Areas impacted by the change request: _____ │
│   _____  │
│   _____  │
│   _____  │
│                                                                           │
│                                                                           │
│   Estimated effort: _____   Inclusion in maintenance Rel.#: _____  │
│                                                                           │
└─────────────────────────────────────────────────────────────────────────┘
```

Figure 12.5 Sample maintenance change request form.

level provides the information for the decision process of which maintenance release should the solution to the change request be placed in; thus it serves not only as a priority for the work order but also as a priority for making the solution available to customers. The request status allows the tracking and managing of the change request. Note that not every change request is approved. Some are rejected. Although not included in Figure 12.5, a more sophisticated form would include a field for a rejection reason code. The request may be in the process of being worked on, and the process start date would be used for tracking. When the change request is fulfilled, the completion date is filled in. There is an area for a brief description of the change request. If more space is needed, an attachment may accompany the request form. In order to ensure sufficient analysis has been performed, the request impact analysis field is included. The impact analysis should include the names of all the modules, database tables, and so on, that are affected. The impact analysis makes it possible to determine all the corequisite and prerequisite changes that must accompany this change request. The tighter the coupling among components, the more prerequisite and corequisite relationships will exist. The decisions made at the design stage may come back and adversely affect the product support and maintenance cycle. Work effort estimation is also needed for the change request to be evaluated for planning the required resources and scheduling a potential completion date. In addition, there needs to be an estimate of which upcoming release the change request would be included in.

There are more comprehensive change request forms for organizations that desire to manage the change request more thoroughly. For example, the estimated effort field may be modified into two fields that capture the initial effort estimate and the actual effort expended. Also, there may be a field that shows the actual modules, database, and so on, that were impacted by the change request. However, it is important that the form is not made more complex than necessary. There must be a good reason to have a field included in the form. The information such as the brief change request description and impact areas, besides serving as information for accepting or rejecting the request, are all rolled into a customer support newsletter that either precedes or is sent together with the maintenance/fix release code.

Many software organizations perform extensive studies over these change request forms to better understand their product shortcomings, customer needs, and future product directions. An experienced customer support and services group can greatly enhance the customer's perception and sales of the product. Those who have extended the support and services group into a consulting service have also seen some outstanding revenue opportunities. The customer support/service organization performs a wide variety of activities related to both product defect and nondefect support. Some even perform marketing-related activities such as customer opinion surveys.

12.4 Summary

This chapter describes both defect and nondefect support and services. The support activities start as soon as a software product is released. The customer problem reports that come into the support and service organization are found to follow an exponential track that resembles a Rayleigh curve. The workload and resource effort estimation is often based on the accuracy of this problem arrival curve.

A customer support/service organization is usually composed of two major groups:

- Customer service/support representatives who readily interact with the customers either through telephone calls or online websites.
- Technical problem-fix analysts who work on deeper problem-fixes, including design, code, test, and release.

Various problems associated with applying code fixes and releases are described—from emergency problems to regular and periodic maintenance releases.

Finally, all maintenance changes must be controlled with change requests as done in the product development cycle. A maintenance change request form is discussed in terms of its usage in controlling change requests.

12.5 Review Questions

1. List three customer support functions that a customer support/service organization performs.

2. Explain the customer problem arrival curve in terms of customer usage of the product and the fixes.

3. What is the formula for usage month?

4. What is a prerequisite/corequisite relationship of product maintenance and fix releases?

5. What is a problem priority level? What is it used for?

6. Describe the steps involved when a customer problem is passed from the customer service/support representative to the technical problem/fix analyst until the problem is resolved.

7. Give an example of a problem that may occur if a customer stays on a particular release, skips several maintenance/fix releases, and then applies a fix release.

8. What is the estimated effort field on the change request form used for?

12.6   Exercises

1. Visit the online customer support site of a software product company and compare the list of support functions they offer against your list from Review Question 1.

2. Explain what the problem arrival curve may look like if a software product that is released does not get installed and used until six month later.

3. In addition to prioritizing the work order itself, what is the change request priority information on the change request form used for?

4. Consider a situation where an important customer has installed a generic software application and also customized some parts of the application. Explain the effect that would have on supporting this customer if under the following circumstances:

   a. The customized code is only in interfacing to an application that the customer wrote in-house.

   b. The customization is only in adding an entry in a database table.

   c. The customized code is in the main logic of the purchased software application.

12.7   Suggested Readings

V. Basili et al., "Understanding and Predicting the Process of Software Maintenance Releases," *Proceedings of the 18th International Conference on Software Engineering*, March 1996.

S. Dart, A. M. Christie, and A. W. Brown, "A Case Study in Software Maintenance," Software Engineering Institute, CMU/SEI-93-TR-8, Carnegie Mellon University, 1993.

S. H. Kan, *Metrics and Models in Software Quality Engineering*, 2nd ed. (Reading, MA: Addison-Wesley, 2003).

T. Kilpi, "New Challenges for Version Control and Configuration Management: A Framework and Evaluation." In *Software Engineering: Selected Readings*, edited by E. J. Braude (Piscataway, NJ: IEEE, 2000): 307–315.

J. D. Musa, A. Iannino, and K. Okumoto, *Software Reliability* (New York: McGraw Hill, 1990).

Red Hat, http://www.redhat.com, 2005.

G. Ruhe and M. O. Saliu, "The Art and Science of Software Release Planning," *IEEE Software* (November/December 2005): 47–53.

Software Support and Maintenance FAQ, http://faq.gbdirect.co.uk/support/, 2006.

CHAPTER 13

Software Project Management

OBJECTIVES

- Analyze the four phases of project management:
  - Planning
  - Organizing
  - Monitoring
  - Adjusting
- Discuss three specific project effort estimating techniques:
  - COCOMO
  - Function point
  - A simple technique for object-oriented environment
- Describe two more techniques of project management:
  - Work breakdown structure for task scheduling
  - Earned value management for project monitoring

13.1   The Necessity of Project Management

We have spent several chapters of this text discussing software design and the software development process and methodologies. Why can't we just follow these processes and methodologies and complete a project? What if a project requires only two or three people? On the surface it may seem that a small project can just follow a development process and be left alone to complete a project without any project management. However, we may question how it is determined that a project needs only two or three people. Is there a software development process that these people all agree on and have experience in? Furthermore, how does anyone, including the project team members, know if a project is progressing properly unless someone is monitoring it?

Even small and fairly simple software projects need project management. What differs among the various software projects is in the degree of management efforts. A large and complex software project would require some sophisticated project management skills and considerable effort, along with tools to aid the management tasks. The key is to strike a balance between lean project management and excessive project management, never letting it become too meager or too overbearing.

13.2   The Project Management Process

Many software engineering students, as well as some professionals, confuse software project management with the software engineering process and development life cycle. Software project management follows a management process to ensure that the appropriate software engineering process is implemented, but it is not itself a software engineering process. **Figure 13.1** depicts the high-level flow of a software project management process and the four major sets of activities (known as POMA) that are involved:

1. Planning
2. Organizing
3. Monitoring
4. Adjusting

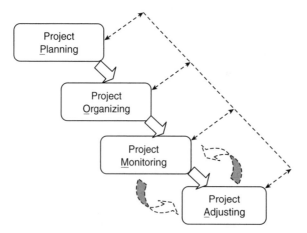

Figure 13.1 Software project management process.

These four activities of POMA may sometimes overlap. Most of the major portions of the activities are performed in sequence, a flow depicted by the large arrows in the figure. The curved arrows in Figure 13.1 show how the monitoring and adjustment phases of project management not only overlap but heavily interact in a cyclic fashion. As the project status information is gathered and reported, it is often necessary to adjust and make changes to the project. The combination of monitoring and making the proper adjustments is what dictates proper project control.

The dashed arrows in Figure 13.1 depict that the needed adjustments may affect some of the previously set plans, methodologies, organizational policies, reporting structures, and so on, that were established in earlier phases. While the four POMA phases appear to be in sequence, there will be incidents in each phase that may cause what was completed in a previous phase to be altered. Software project management, like other project management, often requires an iterative process. Tsui (2004) provides additional information on managing software projects and the concept of POMA.

Project management ensures that the following goals are met:

- The end results satisfy the customer's needs.
- All the desired product/project attributes (quality, security, productivity, cost, etc.) are met.
- Target milestones are met along the way.
- Team members are operating effectively and with high morale.
- Required tools and other resources are available and effectively utilized.

It is important to remember that a project manager cannot do this alone but has to work through the team members to accomplish these management targets.

13.2.1 Planning

Planning is a natural first phase of any project. The success and failure of the project rides heavily on the results of proper planning. Yet so many software projects tend to rush and minimize this phase citing schedule and cost constraints. Even with a well-planned project, it is not unusual to still see many changes and modifications. Some will use this reason to develop a poor plan or even totally skip planning. Having a well-conceived and documented plan, however, will help facilitate the anticipated modifications that often occur in a software project.

During the early planning phase, the answers to the following questions will contribute to the formulation of a project plan:

- What is the nature of the software project, who is sponsoring the project, and who are the users?
- What are the needed requirements and what are the desired requirements?
- What are the deliverables of the project?
- What are the constraints of the project (schedule, cost, etc.)?
- What are the known risks of the project?

Notice that these are very close to the same questions asked during the requirements gathering and analysis activities. Software engineering's requirements methodologies and process provide the directions on how to perform information gathering and analysis. Project management must ensure that there are qualified resources, proven methodology, and ample time set aside to perform the tasks related to answering these questions. The problem of who funds this part of the planning phase has always been a difficult business question. Sometimes customers and users are asked to fund these activities separately; other times the software project organization will sponsor the activities as costs of doing business and fold them into the cost of the total project. Today, large, sophisticated organizations realize the importance of this planning phase and are willing to pay for part of the activities.

Once the basic project requirements are understood, the rest of the project planning activities are much easier to perform and complete. The following activities are the major parts of project planning:

- Ensure that the requirements of the project are accurately understood and specified.
- Estimate the work effort, the schedule, and the needed resources/cost of the project.
- Define and establish measurable goals for the project.
- Determine the project resource allocations of people, process, tools, and facilities.
- Identify and analyze the project risks.

There are skills and techniques involved in each of these activities. Some will be further explained in separate sections of this chapter. Based on the proper completion of requirements gathering and analysis, the total work effort is estimated. This estimation is then used to establish a project schedule and cost. The schedule milestones are set according to the chosen process, tools, skills, and so on.

One of the most difficult tasks during this phase is defining realistic and measurable goals. We are used to making grand claims about software products—superior quality, easy to use, easy to maintain. We also like to claim that we have the most efficient and productive team members or most effective methodology. Unless these claims are well defined and measurable, they cannot serve as project goals because there will be no way of monitoring them. As happens in requirements gathering and analysis, a project manager will not be defining these goals alone. It usually is, and should be, a team effort. The success of a project is determined by whether the jointly planned and agreed to goals are achieved. Therefore, the project team members should all understand these goals and measurements. For example, if one of the project goals is to have a high-quality product, the term *high quality* must be defined, or no one will know if the goal has been achieved. But simply defining the term alone is not enough. A common mistake would be to define *high quality* as a product that satisfies customer requirements—a definition that becomes circuitous and useless and does not include and allow quantitative analysis. A goal or definition must be measurable so that as we are monitoring the project we can ascertain if the product will achieve the high quality expected. The quality goal may thus be restated more precisely as follows.

> The product quality goal is that 98% of the listed functional requirements in the approved requirements specification document are all tested and have no known problems at the product release time. The remaining 2% of the listed functional requirements are also all tested and have no known severity 1 problems at the product release time. Severity 1 problems are those that cause the function not be completed and there is no manual workaround to complete the required function.

Although not perfect, this goal specification provides us with ways to measure the progress toward the final attainment of a goal. We can quantitatively count the number of total functional requirements, the number of tested functional requirements, the number and severity of problems found during the test, and the number and severity of problems remaining at product release time. With these we can determine whether we have achieved the quality goal.

Similarly, the goal of meeting project schedule should be stated with more than just a single date. It must be divided into multiple elements that can be measured along the way. For example, a schedule goal may be divided into a set of milestone dates and have a stated goal of meeting 95% of all the milestones along the way as well as meeting the final completion date. If only the final completion date is stated as the goal, then it would be very difficult to measure the project's progress or have any early warning sign of schedule problems. Very little corrective action can be taken if there is no input on schedule status until the schedule problem has surfaced on the night before the final completion date. The goals need to be quantitatively measurable and monitored throughout the project. Nonmeasurable goals are often said to be nonmanageable. The concept of measurement and metrics is discussed further in a later section of this chapter

Another part of planning activities is the identification and analysis of risk items. There are very few projects with no risk. Software projects are fraught with cost overruns and schedule delays. Risk management thus becomes an integral part of software project management, and all risks must be considered during the planning phase. Risk management itself is composed of three major components:

1. Risk identification
2. Risk prioritization
3. Risk mitigation

How do we identify risks? Some fertile areas to look for risks include new methodology, requirements new to the group, special skills and resource shortage, aggressive schedule, and tight funding. It is important to consider all possible items that might have a negative impact on the project. Of course, such a list may be huge and impossible to work with, so it will be necessary to prioritize the risks and perhaps decide to consider and track only the high-priority problems. After a prioritized list of risks is agreed on, the planning process must include an activity set to mitigate these prioritized risks and to take some action. Hoping that some external force will magically appear and reduce the risks would be foolishly optimistic. A plan to mitigate these risks must thus be included during the project planning phase.

The activities in a project planning phase all contribute to developing an overall project plan. Depending on the projects, some project plans may be quick and short while others may be very extensive and lengthy. The content of a project plan must include the following basic items:

- Brief description of the project requirements and deliverables
- Set of project estimations
  - Work effort
  - Needed resources
  - Schedule

- Set of project goals to be achieved
- Set of assumptions and risks

The plan may be expanded to include a discussion of the problems to be resolved, differentiating between those problems that must be fixed and those that it would be nice to fix. A user and customer profile may be included. A detailed description of all the major requirements and deliverables may be placed in an appendix portion of the plan. The work effort estimate may be explained and shown in detail. The required resources and cost may be broken into major categories of human resources, tools and methodologies, and facilities. The schedule may be divided into sets of major and minor milestones. The project goals may be expanded to include multiple project attributes, more than just meeting schedules and costs. The definition and measurements of all the goals need to be clearly developed. In addition, a list of assumptions, major risks, and minor risks may be included. These risks and assumptions may be accompanied with a discussion of how these risks will be contained throughout the project.

Although it is true that there will always be many unknowns during the planning stage, the more thorough the project planning phase is, the higher the chance that project will be successful. This does not mean that there will be no change to the project or to the plan. Even the best planned project will face some changes as the earlier unknowns become clearer. There will also be some justifiable change of heart as the project progresses. All project managers and project team members should be prepared for such changes. The authors and proponents of the Agile process discussed in Chapter 5 understand this so well that they plan only for short iterations of development and caution against excessive planning.

13.2.2 Organizing

Once a project plan has been formulated or even before it has been completed, the organizing activities must be initiated. For example, as soon as we have the estimated resources planned, hiring and placement may begin. **Table 13.1** shows how some of the planning and organizing activities may be paired and overlapped.

As soon as a specific planning activity such as risk planning is complete, we can establish the mechanism for tracking and mitigating the risks. The project manager does not need to wait for every planning activity to be finished before starting the organizing phase.

Table 13.1 Pairing Planning And Organizing Activities

Planning	Organizing
Project content and deliverables	
Project tasks and schedule	Set up tracking mechanisms of tasks and schedules
Project resources	Acquire, hire, and prepare resources such as people, tools, and processes
Project goals and measurement	Establish mechanism to measure and track the goals
Project risks	Establish mechanism to list, track, and assign risk mitigation tasks

The organizing phase requires more than broadband management skills. For example, the setting up of tools or the establishment of process and methodologies all require resources. Software projects, more so than many other types of projects, are still very people intensive. Thus one of the first activities in the organizing phase, for the project manager, is the recruiting, hiring, and organizing of the software development and maintenance teams.

Because software development and maintenance projects are more human intensive than most of the projects in other industries, it is vital that the project manager pay special attention to the personnel requirements and ensure that there is an organizational structure built in a timely manner and based on the project plan. Having a great plan and not being able to execute it due to a lack of, or a wrong grouping of, personnel is not always openly acknowledged because issues with people, organizations, and skill sets are often the most uncomfortable and emotional items to discuss.

During the organizing phase, other resources such as tools, education, and methodologies need to be scheduled, and preparations need to be made so that they are available at the correct time. Even though the plan may contain the appropriate financing for the resources, this is the phase when all problems related to procurement or financing of resources are rooted out and resolved.

In addition, all the mechanisms required for monitoring the project need to be defined and set up. In particular, the project goals that will be tracked during the monitoring phase need to be revisited, and all modifications to them should be made at this time.

13.2.3   Monitoring

After the project plan is set and organized, the project still cannot be expected to just coast to a successful completion by itself. No matter how thoroughly the plan is prepared and how carefully the project is organized, the process is never perfect. Inevitably, some part of what was planned and organized will face a change. Two simple examples would be the departure of a skilled person or a nonconformance with the agreed-upon test procedure. Either of these will require some adjustments to be made. However, if the project is not constantly monitored, the information may arrive too late and the result will be costly.

Clear mechanisms must be put in place to regularly and continuously gauge whether the project is progressing according to plan. There are three main components involved in project monitoring:

1. Collection of project information
2. Analysis and evaluation of the collected data
3. Presentation and communication of the information

The monitoring mechanism must collect relevant information pertaining to the project. The first question is what constitutes relevant information. At a minimum, the planned and stated project goals must be monitored. The second question is how the information will be collected. These two issues should have been addressed during the planning and the organizing phases. Data collection comes in two modes. Some data are gathered through regular and formal project review meetings. In these reviews, preestablished project information must be available and presented without exception. If any exception does occur, it should be viewed as a potential problem and will deserve at least a quick look by the project manager. Other data are collected through informal channels such as management walk around—a process of informal socializing that should be a natural part of the manager's behavior. In today's global economy and distributed software development, the collection of data through indirect and informal channels is becoming increasingly difficult in spite of the advances in technology. Direct human contact is a costly proposition for geographically distributed organizations. As a result, many managers will cut on travel expenses and opt to spend on equipment or some other directly visible item. Software project managers need to be especially sensitive to this because the software industry is still a human-intensive business.

The information collected through the regular and formal project review meetings are analyzed in a variety of ways. Most project managers will attempt to perform the analysis themselves. In large and complex projects that involve several organizations and a long time frame, there may need to be a small staff group that performs the data analysis with established techniques such as the following:

- Data trend analysis and control charts
- Data correlation and regression analysis
- Moving averages and data smoothing
- General model building for both interpolating and extrapolating purposes

Of course, none of these activities are free. They have to be part of the plan and part of the organizing activities. If no fund has been allocated and no qualified personnel have been recruited for these activities, they cannot be done. This area is also fertile ground for outsourcing to other countries where the cost of data analysis is cheaper, where there are many qualified resources, and where the data can be quickly transported through electronic channels.

The collected and analyzed information must be communicated, reported, and acted upon. Otherwise, the entire monitoring process may be construed as nothing more than a superfluous bureaucratic exercise. Information reporting requires different presentation styles and awareness of the fact that the way some information is presented and visualized can certainly sway the receivers of the information. For example, we all love to see the revenue chart showing a curve that goes upward from left to right. The following are some of the more popular ways to visualize and report this information:

- Pie chart to show proportions of different categories
- Histogram to show relative frequencies of different data value ranges in bar chart form
- Pareto diagram (a modified histogram) to show data in ascending or descending order
- Time chart to show the values of data through time
- Control chart (a modified time chart) to show the values of data through time in relationship to acceptable bounds
- Kiviat diagram to show multiple metrics

All of these forms are shown in **Figure 13.2**. The control chart and the Kiviat chart may require a little explanation. The control chart has established upper and lower bounds.

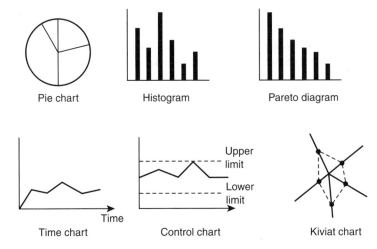

Figure 13.2 Visualization and reporting of information.

The attribute of interest is tracked as data through time, and the situation is reviewed whenever the tracked information falls outside of the upper or lower limits. The Kiviat chart shows the data points for multiple attributes or dimensions of interest; the example in Figure 13.2 shows five attributes of interest and the data points representing these areas.

In reality, we often find that the resources required to perform the monitoring is underestimated. Running regular project meetings is a very time-consuming activity. The analysis of gathered information may require some skilled statisticians. The very tasks of project monitoring themselves may require the first project adjustment as we realize the shortage of skilled data analysis resources.

Based on the monitored information, the project manager and the team would then collectively make decisions on whether the observations indicate a need for a change.

13.2.4   Adjusting

Making adjustments is a crucial step in project management. As mentioned earlier, the chance that a project requires no change is very small. If the monitoring process indicates any need for adjustment, then the project management team must take timely actions. The areas that need change may be many and varied. However, the most likely instruments for adjustment that are available to the project management are the following:

- Resources
- Schedule
- Project content

There is usually a trade-off decision that needs to be made among these three items, which are tightly coupled. The resources are directly under the control of the project management. For the most part, projects are usually in need of more resources. When more resources are added to the projects, the timing of such additions is very important. As was well explained in Frederick Brooks' *The Mythical Man-Month* (1995), adding human resources to rescue schedules may often result in the reverse effect. New employees may slow down the existing, experienced workers on the project because of the amount of time the experienced people would have to take away from their assigned work to explain and bring the new person on board. Similarly, introducing a new tool or a new process at the wrong time can produce the reverse effects of elongating the time and cost. This does not mean that project adjustments that call for more resources should be ignored. The more the tasks are independent, the easier it is to add resources because there are fewer coupling concerns to consider. The project management team only needs to analyze the timing and the type of resource addition.

In contrast, there are times when resources are reduced. An example of human resource addition and reduction that often happens in a software project would be temporary testers who are brought on board to perform well-planned and scripted tests but are released after the testing has been completed. This is a planned increase and decrease of human resources. The more familiar cases are the nonplanned situations where a schedule crunch or an unexpected change in project content forces the project team to consider adjustments in resources. Assuming the schedule crunch means that the schedule must be maintained but other parameters may change, then adding resources is one possible solution and must be seriously considered. There are times when a crucial human resource may drop off from the project. Then the project management team must consider the possibilities of adjusting either the schedule or the project content or both. Doing nothing and just asking the remaining people to bear the brunt may only work once or only for a short period of time. For the most part, the project management team must consider some actions against the schedule or against the project content when there is a resource change.

Another scenario is that a schedule needs to be kept intact or even shortened but lost resources cannot be replaced or added quickly enough. That leaves only the option of a reduction of project content. Reducing project content late in the project cycle, much like adding human resources, is not trivial. A designed and coded functional area that has some level of coupling to other parts of the software cannot easily be taken out without careful consideration of the other interrelated areas. The time and effort spent in reducing the project content in order to keep or shorten a schedule may in fact create additional work and increase the schedule. In the event that more skilled resources can be added very quickly and in time, then that may be a better solution than reducing project content. There are times when customers flatly ask for a schedule reduction due to increased competition, or when the upper management of a software development organization may request an earlier product release than planned due to unplanned external events. In such cases, a change in schedule will affect and most likely require adjustments to resources or to product content or both. Again, schedule changes are often unplanned and require that an appropriate adjustment is made quickly.

Often there are also changes in project content that occur after the project requirements are set and the project is organized to start. Inevitably, it is the customer or the user who asks for a change or an addition. Sometimes it is just human error or the result of seeing some prototype function and having a better understanding. We have already discussed possible effects of late reduction of the project contents. Additions or changes to project content are also time sensitive. In any case, most of the changes in project content would require an adjustment in either schedule or resources or both.

These three parameters—resources, schedule, and project content—are often the three key factors that project managers focus on during the monitoring and the adjusting phases. Changing one usually affects the other two. Notice that another familiar attribute in software engineering, software quality, has not been brought into the adjustment and trade-off discussion. This is because software quality level, once agreed upon, should be tracked but should rarely be an element offered in the adjustment and trade-offs of the software project. Software engineers and management should be extremely careful not to trade quality for schedule or for other parameters.

13.3   Some Project Management Techniques

There are many specific techniques involved in each of the four POMA phases. Some require extremely deep technical knowledge and others demand great social skills. In this section, we will focus on four commonly needed project management skills: (1) project effort estimation, (2) work breakdown structure, (3) project status tracking with earned value, and (4) developing measurements and metrics. The first two of them are techniques needed in the planning and organizing phases, and the third is needed in the monitoring phase. The fourth is needed for part of planning and for monitoring. Additional details on software project management techniques can be found in Kemerer (1997).

13.3.1   Project Effort Estimation

Estimating the software project effort has always been a difficult task, especially for the new managers who come up from the ranks of technical positions. Many would still say that while more rigor is needed, effort and cost estimation is an art that requires a lot of past experience. This experience relates to knowing what to consider, how much extra buffer needs to be put in, and how much buffer can be tolerated by the business.

In estimating software project effort, there must be some inputs that describe the project requirements. The accuracy and the completeness of these inputs is a significant problem. Because the inputs themselves are mostly estimates, it becomes necessary to convert them into a single numerical number expressed in some unit of measurement such as person-months. After the effort has been expressed in some units, the problem of uniformity must be faced. In other words, one person-month may vary dramatically depending on the skill level of the assigned person. In spite of these problems, it is still necessary to estimate the project effort and put a plan together. With so much uncertainty, it is not difficult to see why monitoring and adjustment phases are crucial to project management.

In general, the estimation may be viewed as a set of project factors that may be combined in some form to provide the effort estimate. The following general formula can be used:

$$\text{Units of effort} = a + b(\text{size})^c + \text{ACCUM(factors)}$$

The units of effort are often person-months or person-days. There are several constants and variables that are estimated. The constant, a, may be viewed as the base cost of doing business. That is, every project has a minimum cost regardless of the size and the other factors. This cost may include administrative and support costs such as telephone, office space, and secretarial staff. This constant is attained after some amount of experimentation. The variable *size* is an estimate of the final product size in some units, such as lines of code. The constant b is a figure that linearly scales the *size* variable. The constant c allows the estimated product size to influence the effort estimation in some nonlinear form. The constants b and c are derived through experimentation with past projects. The term *ACCUM(factors)* is an accumulation of multiple factors that further influence the project estimation. The function ACCUM may be an arithmetical sum or an arithmetical product of a list of factors, such as technical, personnel, tools, and process factors, and other constraints that influence the project. We will discuss two specific approaches to effort estimation that may be viewed as some derivative of this general formula. A third effort-estimation technique addresses only a limited portion of the general formula and will be introduced for the object-oriented development paradigm later in this chapter.

COCOMO Estimation Models   The first estimation model we will look at here is the constructive cost model (COCOMO) approach, which originated in the work of Barry Boehm. Boehm has modified and extended his original COCOMO to COCOMO II (Boehm 2000). Here we will provide only a summary discussion of COCOMO. The original COCOMO includes three levels of models: a macro, an intermediate, and a micro. We will utilize the intermediate level here as an illustration and show the overall COCOMO estimation process. The following is a summary of the steps in COCOMO estimation.

1. Pick an estimate of what is considered as three possible project modes: organic (simple), semidetached (intermediate), and embedded (difficult). The mode is picked based on a consideration of eight project characteristics, which are discussed later. The choice of mode will determine the particular effort estimation formula, which will also be discussed later in this section.
2. Estimate the size of the project, in thousand lines of code (KLOC). Later models in COCOMO II allowed other metrics such as function point.
3. Review 15 factors, known as cost-drivers, and estimate the amount of impact each factor will have on the project.
4. Determine the effort for the software project by inserting the estimated values into the effort formula for the chosen mode.

The mode of the project is chosen based on the following eight parameters:

1. The team's understanding of the project objectives.
2. The team's experience with similar or related projects.
3. The project's need to conform with established requirements.
4. The project's need to conform with established external interfaces.
5. The need to develop the project concurrently with new systems and new operational procedures.

6. The project's need for new and innovative technology, architecture, or other constraints.
7. The project's need to meet or beat the schedule.
8. Project size.

This first step of choosing the mode is a nontrivial task because no software project falls neatly into a single category. The three modes of organic, semidetached, and embedded may be roughly equated to simple, intermediate, and difficult projects, respectively. Most of the projects will have a mix of project characteristics. For example, the eighth parameter, "project size," may be small, but the seventh parameter, "need to meet or beat the schedule," may be very stringent for the specific software project. Even just considering these two characteristics, it would be difficult deciding whether a project is simple or intermediate. Imagine the difficulty of making a decision on the project mode when a software project has a mixture of eight characteristics. After considering all of them, a project mode has to be determined. Here again some past experience would come in handy. Also, within an organization that has a history of project management data, a new project manager may be able to consult the organization's project database. Once the project mode is determined, an estimation formula needs to be chosen. The following are the corresponding estimation formulas for the three modes, with the effort unit indicated in person-months:

Organic: $\text{Effort} = [3.2 \times (\text{size})^{1.05}] \times \text{PROD} (f\text{'s})$

Semidetached: $\text{Effort} = [3.0 \times (\text{size})^{1.12}] \times \text{PROD} (f\text{'s})$

Embedded: $\text{Effort} = [2.0 \times (\text{size})^{1.20}] \times \text{PROD} (f\text{'s})$

Thus, based on the eight parameters, if we decide that the project is simple (organic), the effort for the organic mode will be estimated with the equation *Effort = 3.2 × (size)^{1.05}*. This estimation equation provides the basic estimation of project effort in person-months, and it is the first level of estimation.

The next level of estimation in COCOMO is to consider 15 additional project factors, called cost-drivers. PROD (f's) is an arithmetic product function that multiplies the 15 cost-drivers. Each of these 15 cost-drivers has a range of numerical values, ranging from very low to extra high. These 15 cost-drivers may be categorized into four main groups:

- Product attributes
    1. Required software reliability
    2. Database size
    3. Product complexity
- Computer attributes
    4. Execution time constraint
    5. Main memory constraint
    6. Virtual machine complexity
    7. Computer turnaround time
- Personnel attributes
    8. Analyst capability

9. Applications experience
10. Programmer capability
11. Virtual machine experience
12. Programming language experience
- Project attributes
13. Use of modern practice
14. Use of software tools
15. Required development schedule

Table 13.2 shows the values that these 15 cost-drivers may take on. The project manager or the person given the responsibility of project estimation would review all 15 cost-drivers and the range of values for each one. Note that different cost-drivers have different ranges of values. For example, consider cost-driver 1, required software reliability. The lowest value is 0.75 and the highest is 1.40. If this cost-driver is deemed to be very low or less than 1, it will lower the PROD (f's), and if it is deemed to be very high or greater than 1, it will increase the PROD (f's). The nominal value 1.0 will not affect the overall arithmetic product PROD (f's). Note that cost-driver 8, analyst capability, has 1.46 as its lowest value because low analyst capability would require more effort. The highest value for analyst capability is 0.71 because high analyst capability would lower the effort. Thus PROD (f's) may be viewed as the mechanism that allows another level of adjustment to the initial project estimate provided by the earlier organic, semidetached, and embedded effort estimation equations.

Table 13.2 COCOMO Cost-Driver Values

Cost-Drivers	Very Low	Low	Nominal	High	Very High	Extra High
1	0.75	0.98	1.0	1.15	1.40	—
2	—	0.94	1.0	1.08	1.16	—
3	0.70	0.85	1.0	1.15	1.30	—
4	—	—	1.0	1.11	1.30	1.65
5	—	—	1.0	1.06	1.21	1.66
6	—	0.87	1.0	1.15	1.30	1.56
7	—	0.87	1.0	1.07	1.15	—
8	1.46	1.19	1.0	0.86	0.71	—
9	1.29	1.13	1.0	0.91	0.82	—
10	1.42	1.17	1.0	0.86	0.70	—
11	1.21	1.10	1.0	0.90	—	—
12	1.14	1.07	1.0	0.95	—	—
13	1.24	1.10	1.0	0.91	0.82	—
14	1.24	1.10	1.0	0.91	0.83	—
15	1.23	1.19	1.0	1.04	1.10	—

The difficulties with COCOMO include the choosing of the particular project mode based on the 8 parameters, the estimation of product size, and the considerations of the 15 cost-drivers. These all require some past experience. Therefore, almost all experienced managers would attach some amount of buffers to the estimate.

While the basic principles are still the same, the early 1980s version of COCOMO has been significantly modified and has evolved into COCOMO II. In the past 20 years, the development process has changed from the traditional waterfall model to more iterative processes, the development technology has moved from structured programming to object-oriented programming, and the usage operational environment has evolved from batch to transactional to highly interactive online web. The development tools have also grown from simple compilers and linkers to a fully integrated toolkit that combines design and programming logic, database, network middleware, and user-interface development. COCOMO II has been modified to include these changes. We will only provide a brief update of COCOMO II here. It has three models for estimating at different stages of the software project:

- Creating early estimates during prototype stage
- Making estimates after the requirements are captured, during the early design stage
- Making estimates after the design is complete and coding has started

COCOMO II does still ask for an estimate of the size, which can now take on one of the three metrics:

- Thousand lines of code (KLOC)
- Function point
- Object point

Like lines of code, function point is an estimation of the size of the software project; it is discussed in the next section. Object point is another estimation of the project size, much like function point.

COCOMO II has 29 factors to consider instead of the 3 modes and 15 cost-drivers. Much like the previous 15 cost-drivers, these 29 factors are grouped into the following 5 categories:

- Scale factors
- Product factors
- Platform factors
- Personnel factors
- Project factors

Within each of these, there are five scale factors, five product factors, three platform factors, six personnel factors, and ten project factors.

Research on software project estimation and, specifically, COCOMO II research and tool development, are heavily pursued at the University of Southern California. (See the reference to its website in the Suggested Readings section.)

Function Point Estimation   The lines-of-code unit of measure has dominated the software size-estimating arena for many of the early software engineering years. But it has had its share of problems, and many different metrics have been proposed along the way. Function point was first introduced by Albrecht and Gaffney (1983) in the 1980s. It has gained popularity and is an alternative to the lines-of-code metric for size of a software project. While many improvements and extensions have been made to this technique, we will describe the original version here.

Five components of software are considered in the function point estimation process:

1. External inputs
2. External outputs
3. External inquiries
4. Internal logical files
5. External interface files

Each component is assigned a weight, based on three possible descriptions of the project:

1. Simple
2. Average
3. Complex

Table 13.3 shows the weights that would be assigned to each of the components based on the assumed complexity of the project. Thus if a project is assumed to be a simple one, the number of estimated external inputs would be multiplied by the weight 3 and the estimated number of external outputs would be multiplied by the weight 4 and so on. The unadjusted function point (UFP) for a simple project would be the arithmetic sum of these weighted components as follows.

UFP = (number of inputs $\times$ 3) + (number of outputs $\times$ 4) + (number of inquiries $\times$ 3) + (number of logical files $\times$ 7) + (number of interface files $\times$ 5)

The unadjusted function point estimate hinges on how accurately the numbers of each of the five components are estimated and the project complexity assumption. Here again, some past software project experience would be very helpful.

Once again, as in COCOMO, there are a number of factors influencing decision. There are 14 technical complexity factors that need to be considered, with each taking on a value of 0 through 5:

1. Data communications
2. Distributed data

Table 13.3 Function Point Weights

Software Components	Simple	Average	Complex
External inputs	3	4	6
External outputs	4	5	7
External inquiries	3	4	6
Internal logical files	7	10	15
External interface files	5	7	10

3. Performance criteria

4. Heavy hardware usage

5. High transaction rates

6. Online data entry

7. Online updating

8. Complex computations

9. Ease of installation

10. Ease of operation

11. Portability

12. Maintainability

13. End-user efficiency

14. Reusability

The sum of these 14 technical complexity factors has a value ranging from 0 (0×14 = 0), to 70 ($5 \times 14 = 70$). If the technical complexity factor is judged to be nonessential, then it would be given a value of 0; if it is thought to be extremely relevant, it is given a value of 5. A total complexity factor (TCF) is then calculated based on the sum of these 14 technical complexity factors:

$$TCF = 0.65 + [(0.01) \times (\text{sum of 14 technical complexity factors})]$$

Thus TCF may have a value ranging from 0.65 to 1.35. Finally, the function point (FP) is defined as the arithmetic product of unadjusted function point (UFP) and total complexity factor:

$$FP = UFP \times TCF$$

Note that because TCF may vary between 0.65 and 1.35, TCF provides the adjustment factor for the initial estimation, which is the UFP. Again, if we believe that there needs to be more buffering than what TCF's 1.35 allows, then extra buffering may be added.

Function point is only an estimation of the size. To convert the function points into an effort estimate, we need to have some idea of the productivity of the group. That is, we still need to convert function points into some form of person-month. Assuming that there is an organizational database that allows us to state that the productivity figure may be estimated at 25 function points per person-month, we can calculate the effort estimation, in person-months, for a project estimated at ZZZ function points as follows:

$$Effort = (\text{ZZZ function points}) / (25 \text{ function points/person-month})$$

As in other estimation techniques, it is very difficult to have consistency across different organizations and estimators with function points. A total of 100 function points should mean the same regardless of who stated it. In order to achieve such consistency within the software engineering field, there is an organization called International Function Point Users Group (IFPUG), which provides both education and information exchanges on function points. Since the inception of this estimation technique, the field of software engineering has evolved considerably. Similar to COCOMO II, there are many FP extensions proposed and tried by various groups.

A Simple OO Effort Estimation   Lorenz and Kidd (1994) introduced a very simple technique for those who want to estimate with object-oriented (OO) objects. This technique has some resemblance to the function point approach in that it is based on an estimated number of components or classes that would be in the final software product and associating some weight to the classes. The number of estimated OO classes may be viewed as the size parameter in the general formula introduced earlier. The process for this estimation technique is summarized in the following four steps:

1. Estimate the number of classes in the problem domain. This may be done by studying and analyzing the requirements.

2. Categorize the types of user interfaces and assign weights as follows:

No user interface (UI)	2.0
Simple, text-based UI	2.25
Graphical UI (GUI)	2.5
Complex GUI	3.0

    These weights are derived from past experiences with many OO projects and from examining the effects the type of UI had on numbers and types of classes.

3. Multiply the estimated number of classes in Step 1 by the weight associated with the type of user interface that is projected for this project. Add this arithmetic product to the original estimate of classes to get a new estimate of total classes that may be in the final product.

4. Multiply the estimated total number of classes from Step 3 by a number between 15 and 20, a productivity estimate of the number of person-days required to develop a class.

In order to carry out these four steps, there are several assumptions that must be made—for example, the estimated number of classes in Step 1 or the number of person-days needed to develop a class. Such decisions would require not only prior project experience but a certain amount of design in mind. The project manager thus needs to sit down with the designers and agree on the estimated number of classes and the projected user-interface category.

For example, let's assume that the initial estimate is 50 classes and the user interface is considered to be complex GUI. We then would multiply 50 by a factor of 3.0, which gives us 150 additional classes. Adding the 150 to 50, we have a new estimate of total final classes of 200. Assuming the productivity is 18 person-days per class, the effort estimate would then be $200 \times 18 = 3600$ person-days. The person-day unit for effort may be converted to a person-month unit, if desired.

The important thing to remember is that all of these effort estimates are indeed just estimates. Project managers must apply some intelligence and appropriate amount of buffer to these calculations before conveying any effort estimates to the customers or the users or even to their own management.

13.3.2 Work Breakdown Structure

Estimating a complete project work effort is an important but difficult task. It can be made a little easier if the overall project is divided into smaller portions that provide a basis for the rest of planning activities such as scheduling and staff assignments. The work breakdown structure (WBS) is a depiction of the project in terms of discrete subactivities that must be conducted to complete the project. WBS first looks at the required deliverables of the software project. Then, for each of the artifact that needs to be delivered, a set of high-level tasks that must be performed to develop the deliverable is identified. These tasks are also presented in an ordered fashion so that task scheduling can be accomplished from the WBS. The following is a framework for performing WBS:

1. Examine and determine the required external deliverables of the software project.
2. Identify the steps and tasks required to produce each of the external deliverables, including the tasks that would be required to develop any intermediate internal deliverable needed for the final external deliverable.
3. Sequence the tasks, including the specification of tasks that may be performed in parallel.
4. Provide an estimate of the effort required to perform each of the tasks.
5. Provide an estimate of the productivity of the personnel that is most likely to be assigned to each task.
6. Calculate the time required to accomplish each of the tasks by dividing the effort estimate by the productivity estimate for each task.
7. For each external deliverable, lay out the timeline of all the tasks needed to produce that deliverable and label the resources that will be assigned to the tasks.

For example, let's consider an external deliverable of test scenarios for a small software project that is estimated to be around 1000 lines of code or involve approximately 100 function points. As part of the WBS, we need to first list the tasks that are required to produce this deliverable. Such a list may look as follows:

- Task 1: Read and understand the requirements document.
- Task 2: Develop a list of major test scenarios.
- Task 3: Write the script for each of the major scenarios.
- Task 4: Review the test scenarios.
- Task 5: Modify and change the scenarios.

These five tasks appear to be sequential, and they are at a macro level. However, we can probably gain some speed if some of the major tasks can be subdivided into smaller pieces and be performed in parallel. It would also seem that as some of the test scenarios are developed they can be reviewed and fixed. So, we may consider some overlapping of subtasks when we are ready to convert the WBS to a schedule. For illustration purposes, we divide Task 3 into Task 3a, Task 3b, and Task 3c to represent three equally divided subtasks of the script-writing activities. Task 4 can be decomposed to Task 4a, Task 4b, Task 4c to match the three Task 3 subactivities. Similarly, Task 5 can be subdivided into Task

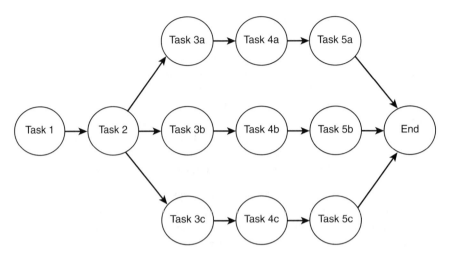

Figure 13.3 A WBS network of tasks.

5a, Task 5b, and Task 5c to match the three subactivities of Task 4. **Figure 13.3** shows what the WBS network of tasks for this deliverable would look like. Clearly illustrating the WBS and the sequence along with which tasks may be carried out in parallel, this figure can become a very convenient tool when the number of tasks and sequences is large.

The next step is to estimate the effort required to complete each of the tasks. For Task 1, we need to estimate the effort required to read and understand the requirements of a project that is about 1000 lines of code or about 100 function points. For Task 2, we need to estimate the number of test scenarios that would need to be developed and how long it would take to come up with such a list. For Tasks 3a, 3b, and 3c, we need to estimate the effort needed to develop the test scripts for one-third of the scenarios. Similarly, we need to estimate the effort required to review one-third of the scenario scripts for Tasks 4a, 4b, and 4c. Estimating effort needed for Tasks 5a, 5b, and 5c would be very difficult because they depend on how many modifications are required as a result of Tasks 4a, 4b, and 4c. Nevertheless, all these initial estimates must be done. Fortunately, we do get to adjust our project because, as discussed in Section 13.2.4, adjustment is an intricate part of the four phases of project management. After these initial estimations have been made, we need to make an assumption and estimate the level of competency or the productivity of the people who will be assigned to all of these tasks. Then the estimated time for each of the tasks in Figure 13.3 can be computed by dividing the estimated effort by the estimated productivity. **Figure 13.4** shows the same WBS tasks with the estimated time units required to perform these tasks and the order of the tasks. From this information, we can establish the preliminary schedule as shown in **Figure 13.5**. Note that there are three main parts to the schedule: (1) the tasks, (2) the human resource assignment, and (3) the time units.

The transformation from WBS task network to an initial schedule directly moved two items: the tasks and the time units. The middle column in Figure 13.5 lists the presumed staff resource assignment, an important consideration that is the source for the produc-

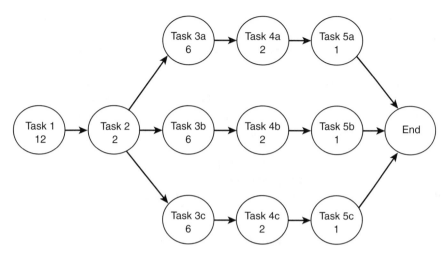

Figure 13.4 Task network with estimated time units.

Tasks	Person	Time
1	X, Y, Z	12 units
2	X, Y, Z	2
3a	X	6
3b	Y	6
3c	Z	6
4a	Z	2
4b	X	2
4c	Y	2
5a	X	1
5b	Y	1
5c	Z	1

Figure 13.5 Initial schedule estimate.

tivity assumptions used to compute and estimate the time units required to complete the task. Earlier, it was also mentioned that the tasks may overlap. Once the initial schedule is formulated, the project management may look for the possibilities of overlapping the tasks, besides the already shown parallel tasks. In this example, the end of Task 1 and the beginning of Task 2 may overlap. The overlapping of subtasks, Task 3a, 3b, and 3c with Task 4a, 4b, and 4c would be a lot trickier because a different person—a person who is committed to writing test scripts but may not have completed the writing task—must perform the review. Without including the column on resource assignment in the initial schedule, these kinds of subtleties may escape the project planners. In our example here, we have chosen to keep everything simple and showed no overlap of tasks in the initial schedule.

Considering all the different types of estimations that went into the task network of Figure 13.4, we should anticipate that the first schedule shown in Figure 13.5 will need to be modified as the project proceeds. This initial schedule should be reviewed by as many of the project constituents as possible before the schedule may be regarded as a planned schedule.

Work breakdown structure is an important and necessary input to the creation of the initial schedule. Unfortunately, many software project schedules are constructed without developing a thorough WBS, and the result is an unattainable and unrealistic project schedule.

13.3.3   Project Status Tracking with Earned Value

Keeping track of or monitoring project status is the activity that compares what was planned against what actually took place. There are multiple attributes of the project that need to be tracked. Most of these are identified in the set of goals stated in the project plan. We are constantly and periodically comparing the actual status of the attributes expressed as project goals against what was planned. In this section we will discuss the tracking of project efforts using the concept of earned value (EV), which was first developed by organizations inside the U.S. government. Fleming and Koppelman (2000) provide an extensive discussion on EV.

When using the earned value management technique, the fundamental concept is to compare the status of how much effort has been expended against how much effort was planned to have been expended at some point in time. First we will need to understand some basic terminology, and then an example will be provided to clarify these definitions.

- Budgeted cost of work (BCW): The estimated effort for each of the work tasks.
- Budgeted cost of work scheduled (BCWS): The sum of the estimated effort of all the tasks that were scheduled to be completed at a specific status-checking date. (This is the sum of all the BCWs that were scheduled, according to the plan, to be completed at a specific status-checking date.)
- Budget at completion (BAC): The estimate of the total project effort; it is the sum of all the BCWs.
- Budgeted cost of work performed (BCWP): The sum of the estimated efforts of all the tasks that have been completed at the specific status-checking date.
- Actual cost of work performed (ACWP): The sum of the actual efforts of all the tasks that have been completed at a specific status-checking date.

A factor that should be remembered is that BCWS, BCWP, and ACWP are all stated in terms of a specific status-monitoring date. Thus those values will change relative to the status date.

Table 13.4 shows an example of estimated efforts and actual efforts expended as of a specific date, which is 4/5/2012. The date format used here is month/day/year. The

Table 13.4 Earned Value Example   Date: 4/5/2012

Work Tasks	Estimated Effort in Pers-days	Actual Effort Spent So Far in Pers-days	Estimated Completion Date	Actual Completion Date
1	10	10	2/5/2012	2/5/2012
2	15	25	3/15/2012	3/25/2012
3	30	15	4/25/2012	
4	25	20	5/5/2012	4/1/2012
5	15	5	5/25/2012	
6	20	15	6/10/2012	

efforts are measured in person-days (Pers-days). Each task has a budgeted cost of work, and the BCWs for the six tasks are shown in the column showing estimated effort. For example, for Task 4 the BCW is 25 Pers-days. The sum of this column, or the sum of the BCWs, is the budget at completion:

BAC = 10 + 15 + 30 + 25 + 15 + 20 = 115 Pers-days.

Now let us look at the three values that are computed relative to the status taking date, which in this case is 4/5/2012. By examining the column showing the estimated completion date, the BCWS as of 4/5/2012 includes Tasks 1 and 2. The BCW for Tasks 1 and 2 respectively are 10 and 15 Pers-days:

BCWS = 10 + 15 = 25 Pers-days

We next look at how much of the estimated work is completed on 4/5/2012. This can be found by examining the actual completion date column. We see that tasks 1, 2, and 4 have been completed. These three completed tasks had been estimated to take 10, 15, and 25 Pers-days:

BCWP = 10 + 15 + 25 = 50 Pers-days

The actual effort expended for those tasks that were completed on 4/5/2012 is found by looking at the actual completion date and taking the effort values for those completed tasks from the column entitled "Actual Effort Spent So Far in Pers-days." The actual effort for completed Tasks 1, 2, and 4 are 10, 25, and 20 Pers-days respectively:

ACWP = 10 + 25 + 20 = 55 Pers-days.

The next step is to define earned value in terms of the earlier definitions. Earned value is an indicator that will tell us how much of the estimated work is completed on a specific date. It compares the sum of all the estimated efforts of the completed tasks as of the status date against the sum of the estimated efforts of all the tasks:

EV = BCWP / BAC

In terms of our example, EV = 50 / 115 = 0.43. We may interpret this to mean that the project is 43% complete as of 4/5/2012.

There are two more status indicators that can be derived from the definitions. These are variance indicators that, once again, compare the planned or estimated value against the actual value. The first one is a schedule variance (SV) indicator, which is defined as the difference between estimated efforts of the tasks that have been completed by the status date and the estimated efforts of the tasks that were scheduled or planned to have been completed by the status date:

$$SV = BCWP - BCWS$$

In our example, on 4/5/2012, BCWP is 50 Pers-days, and BCWS is 25 Pers-days. Thus SV = 50 − 25, or 25 Pers-days. We may interpret the project status as 25 Pers-days ahead of schedule from an effort perspective.

The second variance indicator is the cost variance (CV), which is defined as the difference between the estimated efforts of the tasks that have been completed at the status date and the actual efforts expended for the tasks that have been completed at that status date.

$$CV = BCWP - ACWP$$

In our example, on 4/5/2012, BCWP is 50 Pers-days, and ACWP is 55 Pers-days. Thus CV = 50 −55, or −5 Pers-days. In this case, on 4/5/2012, we have 5 Pers-days of effort cost overrun.

The earned value management system provides us with a concrete way to monitor project status from a cost/effort perspective. However, the schedule variance is not an indicator of calendar time schedule but an effort schedule. Clearly more indicators may be constructed from this basic set of definitions, but we will not include them here. We have found that the set EV, SV, and CV provide a good indicator of project status, but we must still remember to look beyond the numbers, ask questions, and delve into other parameters when monitoring a software project. As a final reminder, if the monitored information indicates potential project problems, then adjustments must be made. Do not wait for some project-saving event to occur on its own. Project managers rarely have such luck.

13.3.4   Measuring Project Properties and GQM

We have discussed the need to set goals for a software project during the planning stage so that these goals can be tracked and checked to see if they have been met. The goals are stated in terms of such properties as schedule, cost, productivity, maintainability, defect quality, and so on. Clearly, the specific characteristics of interest must be well defined before any measurement of can take place. Besides setting and tracking goals, the reasons for measurement include the following:

- *Characterization:* Allows us to gather information about and intelligently describe a property.
- *Tracking:* Allows us to gather information about a property through such parameters as time or process steps.
- *Evaluation:* Allows us to analyze the property via gathered information.
- *Prediction:* Allows us to correlate properties and to extrapolate or conjecture about the property based on the gathered information.
- *Improvement:* Allows us to identify areas of improvement based on an analysis of gathered information.

It is critical for software engineers to join the rest of the engineering communities to adopt measurement and quantitative analysis. Measurement is a vital part of quantitative management. Software (product or project) measurement is a mapping of an attribute of a software product or project to some set of numeric or symbolic entities. It can be deceivingly tricky to come up with good measurements. The following is a short guideline to assist you:

1. Conceptualize the entity of interest such as the software product or project, the members of the project team, etc.
2. Clearly define the specific attributes of interest such as product design quality, programmer productivity, and project cost, etc.
3. Define the metrics to be used for each attribute of interest such as defects per class in a UML class design diagram, lines of code developed per programmer month, dollars expended per project month, etc.
4. Devise the mechanism to capture the metrics; this could include manually counting the number of defects in each designed class in the UML diagram.

Basili and Weiss (1984) introduced the Goal-Question-Metric (GQM) approach to software metrics. GQM has been used quite successfully by many organizations. This approach defines a measurement model based on three levels:

- *Conceptual level:* Establish a goal. For instance, "Improve the time to locate a software code problem."
- *Operational level:* Develop a list of questions related to the goal. For example, "How does the program complexity influence software debugging time?"
- *Quantitative level:* Develop metrics. These could include the number of control loops in the program for control complexity and the number of person-minutes spent on debugging efforts.

Next, we will briefly touch on the theory of metrics to further guide us in the establishment of valuable metrics. The extensive detail regarding the mathematic mapping theory of metrics is too large in scope to cover in this text. We will, however, discuss the four scale levels of metrics: nominal, ordinal, interval, and ratio.

The nominal level allows us to distinctively categorize a property. For example, consider the case of measuring the number of software defects by source categories such as design, code, test, integration, and packaging. The danger with this set of categories as a metric is that a defect may originate from both design and coding. We must ensure that every defect is assigned only to a unique category for the metric to be nominal.

The ordinal level provides an ordering of the property. For example, when one is measuring customer satisfaction with categories of very satisfied, satisfied, neutral, not satisfied, and very dissatisfied. This metric is more than just nominal because it also provides an ordering of very satisfied to very dissatisfied.

The third level of metrics is the interval level. The interval level allows us to describe equal intervals. For instance, program A has 200 function points, which is 20 function points more than program B. This difference is the same as program C with 70 function points, while program D has 50 function points. The difference, 20 function points, is considered to have equal intervals. Note that we could not have performed this type of operation with ordinal-level metrics. Consider the difference between very satisfied and satisfied and the difference between satisfied and neutral in the ordinal metric example. These two differences are not necessarily of equal intervals.

The final metric, ratio, allows us to compare the ratio of two measurements because it has a defined 0 in the metric. For example, it makes sense to say program A, which has 100 lines of source code, is 4 times the size of program B, which has 25 lines of source code. This is a result of the established 0 line of code as minimum size. The ratio scale is the highest metric level.

13.4   Summary

We first introduced the four POMA phases of software project management: (1) planning, (2) organizing, (3) monitoring, and (4) adjusting. POMA is shown to be sequential at the macro level. However, the phases may overlap and may actually iterate among themselves, especially between the monitoring and adjustment phases. The complex and time-consuming planning phase is the key to project success. The monitoring phase is also important, and all projects must be monitored until the end. When necessary, the project manager must take actions and make the appropriate adjustments.

A general formula for effort estimation that involves several parameters is first shown. Then the following three specific techniques related to this general formula for effort estimation are discussed:

- Constructive cost model (COCOMO) approach
- Function point estimation
- Simple OO effort estimation

The principles behind the original COCOMO estimating methodology are explained and then its extensions and modifications into COCOMO II are introduced. The function point estimation technique for project size is shown as an alternative to the line-of-code estimation technique. How function point size effort may be converted to effort estimation is also discussed. The OO effort estimation technique is involved with estimating the number of key classes and the assumed productivity level of the software engineers.

Another important planning technique, work breakdown structure, is demonstrated with a network of tasks and their respective estimated efforts. The significance of WBS to developing an initial project schedule, in a bar chart form, is explained with an example.

Project monitoring involves the ongoing comparison between what is planned and what is actual. Based on this observation, project managers would have to decide on whether any action, or adjustment, needs to be taken. Earned value management is introduced as a viable technique for monitoring the project effort and project schedule. This process essentially compares the planned or estimated project task efforts against those project task efforts that were actually expended. We have explained the need for setting goals and tracking the goals as part of project management. In order to accomplish those tasks, measurement is needed. GQM is introduced as a methodology, and the scales of metrics are also discussed.

13.5   Review Questions

1. List and discuss the elements of a project plan.

2. What are the fours phases of project management?

3. What are the three components of risk management?

4. What is a Kiviat chart, and when would you use it?

5. What are the three attributes of a software project that are most often considered for trade-off decisions for project adjustment?

6. Consider the COCOMO project effort estimation methodology.

    a. What are the three project modes?

    b. What are the eight project characteristics that you need to consider in order to decide the project mode?

    c. How do the 15 cost-drivers influence the initial effort estimate?

    d. Consider a software project that you have estimated at 2 KLOC in size. You believe that it should be in organic mode and that the arithmetic product of the 15 cost-drivers or PROD (f's) is 1.2. What is the estimated effort in person-months?

7. Using function point methodology, compute the unadjusted function point for an average project that has 10 external inputs, 7 external outputs, 5 external inquiries, 3 internal logical files, and 4 external interface files.

8. Assume that the total complexity factor for the software project in the previous question is 1.1 and the productivity figure is 20 function points per person-month. What is the function point for the project? What is the estimated effort in person-months for the project?

9. What is WBS, and what is it used for?

10. What are the three key project status indicators, EV, SV, and CV, in earned value project status tracking methodology?

11. What are the four scale levels of metric?

12. What is GQM?

13.6   Exercises

1. Compare and contrast a software development process with the software project management (POMA) process.

2. Describe one activity that belongs to the organizing phase.

3. Consider a software project that asks you to track the grades of the entire fresh-man class at your college, by major, by gender, and by geographical region. Pull together a plan for this software project, including the work needed to clarify the requirements and deliverables.

4. When would you utilize the control chart for monitoring and why? Give an example.

5. Discuss the perils of increasing resources as a part of project adjustment.

6. Compare the list of factors considered in the effort estimation techniques of COCOMO and of function point.

7. When we perform the arithmetic multiplication of TCF to UFP, what is the range of adjustment (in a percentage) made to the unadjusted function point (UFP)?

8. Consider the task network illustrated in **Figure 13.6**, with the estimated effort shown in units of person-months. Make the appropriate assumptions to convert it into a project schedule.

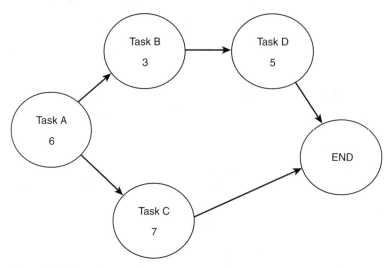

Figure 13.6 A task network.

   a. Explain what assumptions you need to make.

   b. Use these assumptions and convert the task chart to a schedule bar chart.

9. We saw in the earned value example shown in Table 13.4 that there is more actual effort spent than what the BCWP indicates on 4/5/2012 because that calculation only includes the completed tasks. Suppose we invent another term called all actual efforts spent (AAES) to include all the efforts spent as of the status date and then use it to compute a new formula: EV′ = AAES / BAC.

   a. Discuss your opinion of utilizing EV′ instead of EV.

b. Because AAES is just a redefined and expanded BCWP, do you believe the SV and CV figures will be more representative of the true project status if we use AAES in computing SV and CV? Why?

10. In the effort estimation of OO projects, we arithmetically multiply the counts of estimated classes by an estimated 15 to 20 person-days per class.

a. Do you believe this is a wide enough range for the development of a class? What would be some of the parameters you would consider about the class or the developer before assigning a productivity figure?

b. If you were to come up with a productivity number to develop a class, what activities (design, code, test, etc.) would you include in that estimated figure?

13.7 Suggested Readings

A. J. Albrecht and J. Gaffney, "Software Function, Source Lines of Code, and Development Effort Prediction: A Software Science Validation," *IEEE Transactions on Software Engineering* (November 1983): 639–648.

V. R. Basili and D. Weiss, "A Methodology for Collecting Valid Software Engineering Data," *IEEE Transactions on Software Engineering* 10, no. 6 (November, 1984): 728–738.

B. W. Boehm, *Software Engineering Economics* (Englewood Cliffs, NJ: Prentice Hall, 1981).

——, "Software Risk Management: Principles and Practices," *IEEE Software* (January 1991): 32–41.

—— et al., *Software Cost Estimation with COCOMO II* (Upper Saddle River, NJ: Prentice Hall, 2000).

F. P. Brooks Jr., *The Mythical Man-Month: Essays on Software Engineering*, anniversary edition (Reading, MA: Addison-Wesley, 1995).

P. F. Drucker and N. Stone, eds., *Peter Drucker on the Profession of Management* (Cambridge, MA: Harvard Business School Press, 1998).

Q. W. Fleming and J. M. Koppelman, *Earned Value: Project Management*, 2nd ed. (Newton Square, PA: Project Management Institute, 2000).

A. J. Hayter, *Probability and Statistics for Engineers and Scientists*, 2nd ed. (Pacific Grove, CA: Duxbury Press, 2002).

International Function Point Users Group (IFPUG), http://www.ifpug.org

S. H. Kan, *Metrics and Models in Software Quality Engineering*, 2nd ed. (Reading, MA: Addison-Wesley, 2003).

C. F. Kemerer, *Software Project Management: Readings and Cases* (Boston, MA: Irwin McGraw-Hill, 1997).

M. Lorenz and J. Kidd, *Object-Oriented Software Metric* (Upper Saddle River, NJ: Prentice Hall, 1994).

S. McConnell, *Software Project Survival Guide* (Redmond, WA: Microsoft Press, 1998).

A. D. Meyer, C. H. Loch, and M. T. Pich, "Managing Project Uncertainty: From Variation to Chaos," *MIT Sloan Management Review* (Winter 2002): 60–67.

I. Myrtveit, E. Stensrud, and M. Shepperd, "Reliability and Validity in Comparative Studies of Software Prediction Models," *IEEE Transactions on Software Engineering* 31, no. 5 (May 2005): 380–391.

R. R. Patrashkova-Volzdoska, S. McComb, S. Green, and W. Compton, "Examining a Curvilinear Relationship Between Communication Frequency and Team Performance in Cross-Functional Project Teams," *IEEE Transactions on Engineering Management* 50, no. 3 (August 2003): 262–269.

M. Rene, "Risk Management for Testers," *Software Quality Professional* (June 2005): 24–33.

J. Ropponen and K. Lyytinen, "Components of Software Development Risk: How to Address Them? A Project Manager Survey," *IEEE Transactions on Software Engineering* (February 2000): 98–111.

M. Shepperd and D. Ince, *Derivation and Validation of Software Metrics* (Oxford, England: Clarendon Press, 1993).

Standish Group, The Chaos Report (1994), http://net.educause.edu/ir/library/pdf /ncp08083b.pdf, accessed 2012.

F. Tsui, *Managing Software Projects* (Sudbury, MA: Jones and Bartlett Publishers, 2004).

University of Southern California, Center for Software Engineering, http://sunset.usc.edu /csse/research/COCOMOII/cocomo_main.html

H. Weihrich, "Management: Science, Theory, and Practice." In *Software Engineering Project Management*, 2nd ed., edited by R. H. Thayer (Los Alamitos, CA: IEEE Computer Society, 1997): 4–13.

C. Zucchermaglio and A. Talamo, "The Development of a Virtual Community of Practices Using Electronic Mail and Communicative Genres," *Journal of Business and Technical Communication* 17, no. 13 (July 2002): 259–284.

CHAPTER 14

Epilogue and Some Contemporary Issues

In this text, we have discussed most of the main topics of software engineering. It has been our intent to provide a broad introduction to the subject and yet to be concise enough to allow the material to be covered within a semester time frame of 15 to 16 weeks. Although many "favorite" topics in software engineering may not be included, readers will be directed to the Suggested Readings section at the end of each chapter.

It is clear that the main topics of today will also evolve and change. What is now considered new and exciting in software engineering may be old and irrelevant in a few years. However, there are some topics that will remain important, and we hope we have captured those. This book emphasizes the need for software engineering by starting with the implementation problem of a program by a single person and by demonstrating the tremendous increase in complexity when the problem is changed to building a system such as a commercial payroll system. The traditional software engineering activities of requirements analysis, designing, implementation, testing, and system integration are discussed with mostly large and complex systems in mind. The supporting activities of configuration management, process management, and project management are also presented with large teams and complex systems in mind. There is recognition that not all projects, especially those that are small, need the same process or the same management approach or even the same set of activities. For example, we expect a continued pendulum swing toward Agile processes in the next few years (see Chapter 5). There are many topics that need to be covered in much more detail in a follow-on course. Each of the software engineering activities that contributes directly to the development of the product—such as requirements gathering, analysis, testing, or designing—deserves a complete course.

With software becoming a ubiquitous element in the engineering curriculum and in many other disciplines, topics such as reuse, copyright, ownership, certification, and ethics are also gaining our industry's attention. These are topics future software engineers will need to wrestle with. We gave only a cursory coverage to these in Chapter 3. As quality continues to be a recurring theme in software engineering, it should be a natural part of the basic fabric of software engineering. As such, we have pointed to quality as a motivator to perform activities such as design and implementation as thoroughly and as well as possible. Thus, we did not dedicate a separate chapter to quality but do realize its ongoing significance in our industry.

A growing and an important area related to quality is the notion of measurement and metrics. It is very difficult to know if we are gaining ground in software engineering unless we can measure some of the characteristics of the software product, software process, software methodology, and software management. This is a fairly important topic, and we have covered only a part of it in Chapter 8, where design characteristics and the associated metrics are discussed. We expect more emphasis will be placed in this area as our industry starts to ask more critical questions: How do we know a design is complete and good? What is the basis for making release decisions?

Most of the large commercial software products undergo multiple versions and usually last many years. The area of maintenance and support will continue to be a growing area. For many software engineers, it is not the case that their projects will dutifully march through the traditional software life cycle depicted in this text. Many software engineers will be engaged in developing and maintaining existing systems. They may be engaged in service and support of customers much more than in developing a complete, new system. This area, covered in Chapter 12, will require more emphasis in the future as software service businesses continue to expand and grow.

Finally, the Internet and related new software tools have placed additional opportunities and constraints on our field. As mission-critical applications become Internet-based and e-commerce continues to grow, we need to be much more aware of the issues related to security, integrity, and recovery. We will provide a short definition and discussion of security in the following section. We did not cover the other issues here but expect that it will be a growing field that future software engineers will have to keep an eye on. The topic of user-interface characteristics (as discussed in Chapters 7 and 8) is evolving quickly as new tools such as Macromedia's Dreamweaver and Flash gain popularity. The software engineers interested in this area would need to include skills and knowledge from fine arts and communications disciplines in addition to their technology skills.

Software engineering was born during an era when software project schedules were regularly missed and cost overruns were constantly recurring. Since then we have learned to place more effort in planning and in controlling projects. Newer and better techniques and methodologies have been introduced. Productivity-related tools helped us not only reduce complexity and effort but also improve on product and process quality. This field is more disciplined today, and we expect it to evolve into one that will have better defined and substantiated laws and principles for all of us to follow.

In the next few sections we will delineate some of the more recent concerns and progresses in software engineering. The topics covered, by definition, are the authors' choices and thus reflect some of the authors' biases.

14.1   Security and Software Engineering

Today, the functionalities provided by software applications are moving to the Internet as online business services, and Service Oriented Architecture (SOA) is rapidly gaining popularity. (See Finch [2006] and Zimmermann [2005] in the Suggested Readings section.) As computer networks have become more pervasive—almost every software system is connected one way or another to the Internet—the opportunities for malicious users to exploit errors to gain unauthorized access to a system has also increased tremendously. At any moment, there is a high probability that somebody is thinking of how to hack into a system. As professionals, we need to design software to withstand these attacks. Security issues also spawn discussions in other related topics such as privacy and trust.

Although there are particular techniques to make software more secure, most software security–related problems are really software defects that can be avoided or fixed with standard software engineering techniques. In fact, most software security problems, such as buffer overruns and SQL and HTML injection, may be categorized as input validation errors.

One issue that compounds security problems is that most modern applications are not completely written in statically typed languages, but rather a combination of statically and dynamically typed languages. Most web applications are developed in HTML that is then interpreted by a web browser. Also, most applications send SQL strings to a DBMS for interpretation. We need to make sure that the inputs we are processing do not change meaning when interpreted by a DBMS or a browser, and we cannot rely on static typing to help us; we need to make sure that every input is valid.

Following the traditional patterns in computing, researchers are actively exploring the theoretical aspects of computer security, and practitioners are incorporating these techniques into programming. However, we need to popularize the inclusion of security practices into software development processes. We are working on theory and coding practices but have yet to engineer secure systems. It will take time before security thinking becomes pervasive and most development processes incorporate security as one of its most important elements. Many leading companies such as Microsoft, IBM, and others have started to embrace development life cycles that include security as an integral part of the cycle.

See Howard and Lipner (2006) in the Suggested Readings section for a description on Secure Development Life Cycles. Also, BSI (2009), an initiative of the National Cyber Security Division (NCSD) of the U.S. Homeland Security in conjunction with the Software Engineering Institute (SEI), has developed processes and technologies for software developers to utilize and incorporate in their development life cycle.

14.2   Reverse Engineering and Software Obfuscation

With the advent of cloud computing and software as a service model and its increasing popularity, application software are frequently moved across the Internet. Application software code is often exposed, and the opportunity for sabotage or reverse engineering is much higher. In contrast to the earlier desire in software engineering to simplify software to improve on complexity and quality, software engineers are now experimenting with software obfuscation to further increase complexity to diminish human understandability. Software obfuscation is a new area in software engineering where the goal is to make reverse engineering uneconomical for the perpetrators. It is achieved through some form of transformation to the original software, preserving the functionality but altering the source code.

It has been shown that a "generalized black-box" software obfuscator is not possible (Barak et al. 2001). However, there are still many practical software obfuscation techniques worth considering for slowing down reverse engineering. Some of the more popular ones include the following categories of techniques:

- Lexical obfuscation
- Data obfuscation
- Control obfuscation
- Call-flow obfuscation

As an example, lexical obfuscation has been practiced by many earlier programmers who purposely named program variables out of context to confuse the readers. The more the readers were confused, it was thought erroneously, the brighter the author was. This practice is now deemed bad software engineering, especially for software understandability, testing, and future maintenance. However, with the recent need for software protection, this same technique is used for software obfuscation. This technique is relatively limited and weak. It clearly does not provide sufficient protection.

More sophisticated techniques include data obfuscation and control obfuscation. Data obfuscation transformation targets the data and the data structures in the program via complicating the data structure, data operations, and data usage. Popular techniques include splitting an array structure or modifying the inheritance relationship. Control obfuscation techniques include the altering of the control flow by inserting irrelevant, but innocuous, predicates or by harmless reordering of some of the program statements. While lexical, data, and control obfuscation techniques focus on the micro level, call-flow obfuscation techniques concentrate on the macro level of control flow across modules.

The effectiveness of software obfuscation techniques may be viewed or measured in different ways. We may ask (1) how potent the technique is, (2) how resilient the technique is, (3) how expensive the technique is, or (4) how surreptitious the technique is. At the moment of this writing, there is no universally agreed upon set of measurement attributes for software obfuscation. Besides software obfuscation, there are other areas engaged in software prevention techniques, such as watermarking and tamper-proofing, from malicious perpetrators. Interested readers should consult Collberg and Thomborson (2002). Other, more recent sample articles on software obfuscation by Balachandran and Emmanuel (2011) and Tsui, Duggins, and Karam (2012) are also included in the Suggested Readings section.

14.3   Software Validation and Verification Methodologies and Tools

In this section we discuss some of the recent progress that has been made in the area of software validation and verification. Validation implies that the software has been shown to be acceptable to the customer and is correct, while verification implies that the software is properly developed from the requirements and abides to the specifications given. Both development process and test process experts have been investing in software methodologies and tools to improve these areas.

We have described several software processes, leading into the currently popular iterative and incremental Agile process of Scrum (see Chapter 5). In the Agile processes, software is developed in small increments by small teams. Thus, with Agile processes, there is frequent unit testing of the completed code to ensure that what is developed is of good quality and satisfies the customer/user needs. In Chapter 10, we introduced Test-driven development (TDD) with JUnit tool. A more recent approach to improving unit testing is the usage of formal assertions with a run-time assertion checker to decide whether the coded software methods are working correctly. This new approach to unit testing uses a combination of formal specification language called Java Modeling Language (JML) and the JUnit testing framework (Cheon and Leavens 2004).

JML is heavily influenced by the Eiffel language and the concept of "programming by contract" professed by Bertrand Meyer (1988). The key to this approach is using the traditional notion in program correctness proofs by specifying precondition, postcondition, and the invariant characteristics of the software to help in unit testing. JML is a language that allows one to specify the pre-, post-, and invariant conditions without requiring the deep formalism in past specification languages such as Z or Larch. A tool called JMLUnit generates JUnit test classes from these JML specifications. During execution, the tool checks that if the specified preconditions for a software method hold, the specified postconditions for that method will also hold. Clearly, with JML and the associated tools, the better the person who specifies these conditions, the more effective the methodology and the more valuable the tool will be. Although JML is tailored to Java programming development, which is fairly easy to use for Java programmers, it still requires technically sophisticated people to develop these pre-, post-, and invariant assertions. Through checking the assertions and ensuring that the pre- and postconditions match and that the invariant condition holds, this relatively new approach provides a marked improvement in software verification. Refer to Chalin et al. (2006) and Burdy et al. (2005) in the Suggested Readings section for more on JML and the associated tools.

A similar approach to improving unit testing in the Agile process environment, originating directly from the test-driven development methodology, is the behavior-driven development (BDD) approach. BDD was first introduced by Dan North in 2006. The basic idea here is to use the language of the business domain, as opposed to technical specifications in JML, and involve the users and the stakeholders of the software. Involving the stakeholders and users during unit testing and ensuring that the delivered software functionality is acceptable to them is an excellent way to validate the software. Thus BDD moves unit testing closer to validation of software functionality beyond software verification. The natural language of the users is used to express the features and functionalities through scenarios. A scenario is just a set of natural language assertions that describes the conditions that the software feature must satisfy. Users can easily understand and validate if the unit testing satisfied their needs expressed by them in their own normal language. The previously mentioned pre-, post-, and invariant conditions in JML are tucked into these scenarios expressed with natural domain languages. Thus this approach is much more inclusive and allows nontechnical stakeholders to participate in the development of unit tests and acceptance criteria. There is a guideline to expressing a scenario. The standard guideline, in the Cucumber tool described by Wynne and Hellesoy (2012), is to express a scenario with three major segments as follows:

- Given
- When
- Then

A scenario is thought of in terms of what the "given" state or condition for the feature to function is. The "when" segment of the scenario describes the stimulus, and the "then" segment describes the result. For example, for the functionality of adding a student into a course, one may describe the scenario as follows:

Scenario: Enrolling a student into a course.

Given: The course has not reached its student limit.

When: Enroll a student into a course.

Then: The student is added to the course's student list.

Clearly, this scenario may be expressed and understood by both technical and nontechnical people. Using this approach, the BDD methodology, along with a tool such as Cucumber, becomes more inclusive and allows the functional and feature validation to be accomplished within unit testing. The Cucumber tool will assist in the development of the unit test and the code for this functionality.

The development and generation of the actual test case itself, in the form of code, still requires programming knowledge. The Cucumber tool is based on another popular language platform, Ruby on Rails. Refer to Tate and Hibbs's (2006) description of Ruby on Rails in the Suggested Readings section.

We are seeing more and more automation and methodology improvements in software development today. As we mechanize more of the development activities, the chance of software project success in terms of cost, schedule, quality, and customer acceptance should also improve.

14.4 Suggested Readings

V. Balachandran and S. Emmanuel, "Software Code Obfuscation by Hiding Control Flow Information in Stack," International Workshop on Information Forensics and Security Iguacu, Brazil (November 2011).

B. Barak et al., "On the Impossibility of Obfuscating Programs," Proceedings of the 21st Annual International Cryptology Conference on Advances in Cryptology, Santa Barbara, California (August 2001): 19–23.

Build Security In (BSI), https://buildsecurityin.us-cert.gov/daisy/bsi/home.html, 2009.

L. Burdy et al., "An Overview of JML Tools and Applications," *International Journal on Software Tools for Technology Transfer* 7 no. 3 (June 2005): 212–232.

R. A. Caralli, "Sustaining Operational Resiliency: A Process Improvement Approach to Security Management." Technical Note CMU/SEI-2006-TN-009 (April 2006).

P. Chalin, J. R. Kiniry, G. T. Leavens, and E. Poll, "Beyond Assertions: Advanced Specifications and Verifications with JML and ESC/Java2," In *Formal Methods for Components and Objects* (Springer Verlag, 2006).

M. T. Chan and L. F. Kwok, "Integrating Security Design into the Software Development Process for E-commerce Systems," *Information Management Computer Security* 9, no. 3 (2001): 112–122.

Y. Cheon and G. T. Leavens, "The JML and JUnit Way of Unit Testing and Its Implementation," Technical Report #64-02, Department of Computer Science, Iowa State University (2004).

C. S. Collberg and C. Thomborson, "Watermarking, Tamper-Proofing, and Obfuscation—Tools for Software Protection," *IEEE Transactions on Software Engineering* 28, no. 8 (August 2002): 735–746.

C. Finch, "The Benefits of the Software-as-a-Service Model," *Computerworld,* http://www.computerworld.com/5/article/107276/The_Benefits_of_a_Software_as_a_service_Model, January 2, 2006.

S. Garfinkel, "Privacy Requires Security, Not Abstinence," *MIT Technology Review* 112, no. 4 (2009): 64–71.

M. Howard and D. Leblanc, *Writing Secure Code,* 2nd ed. (Redmond, WA. Microsoft Press, 2003).

M. Howard and S. Lipner, *The Security Development Lifecycle* (Redmond, WA: Microsoft Press, 2006).

B. Meyer, *Object-Oriented Software Construction* (Cambridge, UK: Prentice Hall International, 1988).

D. North, "Introducing BDD," http://dannorth.net/introducing-bdd/, 2006.

B. A. Tate and C. Hibbs, *Ruby on Rails* (Sebastopol, CA: O'Reilly Media, 2006)

F. Tsui, S. Duggins, and O. Karam, "Software Protection with Increased Complexity and Obfuscation," 49th ACM SE Conference, Tuscaloosa, Alabama (March 2012).

M. Wynne and A. Hellesoy, *The Cucumber Book: A Behaviour-Driven Development for Testers and Developers* (Dallas, TX: The Pragmatic Book, 2012).

O. Zimmermann et al. "Service-Oriented Architecture and Business Process Choreography in an Order Management Scenario: Rationale, Concepts, Lessons Learned." OOPSLA 05, San Diego, CA (October, 2005).

APPENDIX A

Essential Software Development Plan (SDP)

A. Product Description

Describe the product and the client in general.

   i. Work for hire: Include the Request for Proposal (RFP) from the client. Document any product ambiguities with proposed questions to ask the client, user, or to research. Consider any constraints the product has and technical capabilities needed. Can include the organization structure/chart for clarity on personnel.

   ii. Non-work for hire: Provide a description of the potential audience and what goals are to be satisfied with this product, including a list of major product functionalities and salient features.

B. Team Description

Describe the strengths/skills needed for the team members of this product. Is there need for subject matter experts (SME)?

C. Software Process Model Description

Describe the model (e.g., iterative Scrum, XP, or modified waterfall) to be used for this project. Include justifications for the process model choice.

D. Project Definition

Describe the users and the user environment. Include novice/expert descriptions. Consider creating different personas with different needs and motivations. For the user environment include the software used previously, other software used in conjunction, and the look and feel of the contemporary software genre. Can include use cases of the product, work flow diagrams, and/or business flow.

E. Project Organization

Include work breakdown structure (WBS) of the project: the schedule of the team's tasks; dependencies of the tasks; estimated time for each task; and PERT and Gantt charts with critical time, budget, and BID to the client with signature required.

F. Validation Plan

Create some draft input and output screens as low-level prototype to validate the initial understanding of the product.

G. Configuration/Version Control

Specify the process and attributes for version control of all project and product artifacts.

H. Tools

Provide a list of major system, subsystem, and tools required for development.

Appendix B

Essential Software Requirements Specifications (SRS)

Following are three examples of Essential SRS. The IEEE guideline 830 discussed in Chapter 6 Section 5 is the foundation for the SRS.

Example 1: Essential SRS—Descriptive

A.   System Overview

This section should contain a brief description of what the software system will do. It is intended as an introduction and should be informal and concise.

B.   Technical Requirements

This section should describe the operational parameters of the software product. It should contain information (if applicable to the product) such as:

    i.   Functional requirements (this part could be done with use cases)

    ii.   Nonfunctional requirements such as performance and other constraints

    iii.   User-interface specification

    iv.   User task flow

    v.   Input/output and other data specifications

    vi.   Interface specifications to other systems

C. Acceptance Criteria/Interaction Scenarios

This section should define the functionality the software must implement. It can include interaction scenarios. The scenarios consist of the user inputs and system responses. The low-fidelity prototypes are included. The type of questions that should be asked include:

    i.   How-to: Questions ask how some action is performed.

    ii.   Who: Questions ask who is responsible for a task.

    iii.   What-kind-of: Questions request further refinements of some concepts.

    iv.   When: Questions ask about timing constraints.

    v.   Relationship: Questions ask how one requirement is related to another.

    vi.   What-if: Questions ask about cases in which an action could go wrong or its preconditions.

    vii.   Follow-on: Questions stem from other pending questions.

D. Validation/Verification

This section will describe requirements for the system validation/verification. The requirements and scenarios should help in this process. Validation will determine whether the software satisfies the customer needs as were specified in the requirements and the scenarios. Verification will determine if the software is functionally correct.

E. Requirements Considerations

This section should contain the following:

    i.   Assumption made about the software.

    ii.   End users: Describe each type of user.

    iii.   Existing systems: State any existing system and/or other related entities.

    iv.   Environment: State the environment in which the system will operate.

    v.   Limitations: State what the system will not do.

    vi.   Rationale: Describes how the requirements meet or exceed the needs of the customer.

F. Other Information

Any pertinent information can be added to this document.

Example 2: Essential SRS—Object Oriented

1.0 Initial Requirement Modeling

  1.1. Usage model

  1.2. Initial domain model

  1.3. Initial user-interface model: Develop screen sketches or a user-interface prototype

  1.4. References

2.0 Modeling Requirements

  2.1 System environment

  2.2 Major usage requirements specification: Explore how users will work with the system. Contains a collection of use cases on a Rational Unified Process (RUP) project, a collection of features for a Feature Driven Development (FDD) project, or a collection of user stories for an Extreme Programming (XP) project.

    2.2.1 XXXX Use case

      Use case: Search XXXX

      Preconditions; Postconditions; Actions

    2.2.2 YYYY Use case

      Use case: Submit YYYY

    2.2.3 ZZZZ Use case

      Use case: Update ZZZZ

      Use case: Receive ZZZZ

      Use case: Assign ZZZZ

      Use case: Receive review

  2.3 User characteristics

  2.4 Nonfunctional requirements

3.0 Requirements Specification

  3.1 External interface requirements

  3.2 Functional requirements such as:

    3.2.1 Search

    3.2.2 Communicate

    3.2.3 Add

    3.2.4 Modify

    3.2.5 Update

    3.2.6 Status

    3.2.7 Report

    3.2.8 Assign

Example 3: Essential SRS—IEEE Standard

Example 4: Essential SRS—Narrative Approach

A. Introduction

Contains an overview of the software development project and the planned new product or upgrade. For upgrades, this section may be condensed to focus on the purpose and objectives of the upgrade. For new software, this section typically includes:

    i. Purpose and objectives: Describes the main objectives of the SRS.

    ii. Software product overview: For both new software and upgrades, lists the most important features and functional capabilities of the planned software. For a software upgrade, lists the principal objectives of the upgrade, and the added features and capabilities to be implemented.

    iii. Business and financial objectives: For software with commercial potential outside the company, includes the key business objectives that customers expect the software to address, and financial objectives such as market share, unit shipments, and revenues.

B. Description of the Problem

For new software, describes why the software is needed, and identifies important unresolved questions. For software upgrades, this section may be condensed to focus on open issues and questions.

    i. Why software is needed: Gives reasons in terms of both management and user needs.

    Describes the existing current work practices used by customers, including alternative software products or manual processes. Explains from a management perspective the benefits to be provided by the software, such as how it will solve or improve a business problem. Examples:

        a. Reducing inventory levels

        b. Reducing time to process and ship an order

        c. Achieving competitive advantage

        d. Improving customer satisfaction

    This section also explains from a user perspective how the software will improve existing business processes such as data entry, report generation, decision making, calculations, and usability issues.

    ii. Open issues and questions: Lists the customer workflow processes, technology, financial issues, and business concerns that must be addressed before the software upgrade can be successfully developed and used.

C. Description of Software Solution

Summarizes the proposed software product: its capabilities and attributes. For both new software and upgrades, this section typically includes:

    i. Enhancement requests: Lists and prioritizes requests received regarding software capabilities and features, such as from management, client, end users, or user groups. These needs have been collected through meetings, interviews, and other means.

ii. Features and functional capabilities: Often presented as a table listing and prioritizing features and their descriptions, with sufficient detail that developers will easily understand how the software must work.

iii. Software attributes and general considerations: Lists items other than features or functionality. Examples here are the need to interface with certain other software, and the software or hardware platforms to be supported.

iv. Operational requirements: Lists other requirements that the software will meet as it is used. Examples are business or decision rules, user workflows, usability attributes, installation requirements, or required training for users.

v. Standards and regulatory considerations: Names any applicable standards that the software will meet. Industry examples include EPA, IEEE, NRC, ASTM, ANSI, and ISO. Company-specific examples include forms, work procedures, or data formats.

vi. Long-term plans for future releases and features: Includes items such as future customer needs and desires, and accommodation of future hardware or software platforms.

vii. Maintenance and support costs: Describes plans for items such as customization, patch releases, and ongoing support for users.

Appendix C

Essential Software Design

The examples provided below follow two different methodologies in design. Example 1 is an object-oriented design using a UML approach, and Example 2 is a structural design approach.

Example 1: Essential Software Design—UML

A. Architectural Design

High-level architectural pattern: Layered, MVC, client server, and so on. See Chapter 7.

B. Use-Case Scenarios

Expand the previous documentation of the initial use-case diagram into use-case scenarios.

C. Sequence Diagrams (in concert with steps D and E)

The use-case scenarios developed in Step B would be developed into the sequence diagram with the invention of the many classes needed to support the action in the scenario. In parallel, the class diagram begins to incorporate the classes invented in the sequence diagram and the methods are added to the class diagram as they are thought out by the team members.

D. Class Diagram

A class responsibility collaborator (CRC) model can also be developed.

E. Collaboration Diagram

When a class needs another class to perform a substep, those classes are associated in the collaboration

F. Relational Database Design

G. State Modeling (may be optional until detail design)

The major objects of the product are represented as the many states involved with the state transitions for them.

H. User-Interface Design

Interaction screens are developed from the use cases. Navigation for the different screens are specified.

I. Design Validation—Customer Acceptance of the Low-Fidelity Prototypes

The initial screens drawings and navigational flow are presented to the client or client's specified user for acceptance, modification, and/or complete revision.

NOTE: Steps C, D, and E are done in parallel.

Example 2: Essential Software Design—Structural

A. Architectural Design

High-level architectural pattern: Layered, MVC, client server, and so on.

B. Context Diagram

This is the level 0 of the data flow diagram (DFD). It shows the system (without decomposition) and the external entities. The system has flows of data to the external entities. The scope of the product is defined with this diagram.

C. DFD Level 1

This diagram is the first decomposition of the entire system. Usually the processes are numbered 1.0, 2.0, 3.0, and so on, and they are called *subsystem*. For example:

1.0 Interface subsystem

2.0 Management subsystem

3.0 Error handling subsystem

4.0 XXX process subsystem

5.0 Report generator

D. DFD Level 2

These diagrams are the explosion of each of the subsystems in Level 1. Their numbering will expand from their parent; so the Level 2 for 1.0 Interface subsystem could be

1.1 Interface interaction

1.2 Input validations

1.3 Interface management

E. DFD Level 3 to N

Continue to explode each of the processes into the next level.

F. Process Specification (PSPEC)

When a process does not need to explode, give the logic to the process.

Appendix D

Essential Test Plan

A test plan is a roadmap that allows some feasibility check of the following items:

- Resource/cost
- Schedule
- Goals

A test plan contains the following major components:

A. Goals and Exit Criteria
   i. Quality goals that need to be met for test phase to exit
   ii. Robustness goals of the product
   iii. Schedule goals of the project
   iv. Performance and efficiency goals of the product

B. Items to Be Tested/Inspected
   i. Executables such as modules and components
   ii. Nonexecutables such as requirements specification or design specification

C. Test Process/ Methodologies

    i. Unit test/ Functional test/ Acceptance test/ Regression test/ and so on, methodologies

    ii. Inspections/reviews methodologies

    iii. Black-box testing (e.g., Input domain test, boundary value testing)

    iv. White-box testing (e.g., control path testing, data flow testing)

    v. Test metrics (e.g., code coverage, branch coverage, number of problem by severity)

    vi. Test—bug report—fix—retest process

D. Resources

    i. People (number of, skills, etc.)

    ii. Tools (for measurement, defect management, etc.)

    iii. Systems (test execution platform, test case development, etc.)

E. Schedule

    i. Test-case development

    ii. Test execution

    iii. Problem reporting and fixing

F. Risks

    i. Missing goals

    ii. Back-up resources needed

G. Major Test Scenarios and Test Cases

    i. Boundary value and input domain test cases

    ii. Control path and dataflow test cases

    iii. Integration and intermodular test cases

Glossary

Architectural design phase The period during which the high-level overview of the system is developed.

Black-box testing A testing methodology where the test cases are mostly derived from the requirements statements without consideration of the actual code content.

Cohesion An attribute of a unit of high- or detail-level design that identifies the degree to which the elements within that unit belong or are related together.

Coupling An attribute that addresses the degree of interaction and interdependence between two software units.

Data slice All the data tokens in a slice that will affect the value of a specific variable of interest.

Data token Any variable or constant.

Design constraints Statements that constrain the ways in which the software can be designed and implemented.

Detailed design phase The phase in which the architectural components are decomposed to a much finer level of detail.

Error   A mistake made by a software engineer or programmer.

Failure/problem   The inability of a system to perform a function according to its specifications. It is a result of the defect in the system.

Fault/defect   A condition that may cause a failure in a system. It is caused by an error made by the software engineer. A fault is also called a bug.

Functional requirements   What a program needs to do.

Glue tokens   The data tokens in the procedure or program that lie in more than one data slice.

High-fidelity prototype   A detailed mock-up resembling and behaving close to the final product.

Low-fidelity prototype   A simple mock-up sketch of the target product.

Nonfunctional requirements   The manner in which the functional requirements need to be achieved.

Object-oriented design   A technique that models a design with classes, their relationships, and the interactions among them.

Principles of software engineering   The rules and assumptions in software engineering derived from extensive observations.

Program or procedure slice   All the statements that can affect the value of some specific variable of interest.

Program requirements   Statements that define and qualify what the program needs to do.

Refactoring   A change made to the internal structure of software to make it easier to understand and cheaper to modify without changing its observable behavior.

Requirements   The statements that describe what the software system should be but not how it is to be constructed.

Requirements engineering   A set of activities related to the development and agreement of the final set of requirement specifications.

Software development process   The set of tasks, the sequence and flow of these tasks, the inputs to and the outputs from the tasks, and the preconditions and postconditions for each of the tasks involved in the production of a software.

Software engineering   A broad field that touches upon all aspects of developing and supporting a software system.

Superglue tokens   The data tokens in the procedure or program that lie in every data slice in the program.

UML sequence diagrams   Diagrams that illustrate the flow of messages from one object to another and the sequence in which those messages are processed.

UML state diagram   A diagram representing information concerning the states of an object and the allowed state transitions.

Unified Modeling Language (UML)   An object-oriented modeling language that provides the elements and relationships to model software requirements and design.

Use case   A sequence of actions that a system should perform within the business flow context of the user or the actor.

User interface   What the user sees and hears from the system.

Viewpoint-oriented requirements definition (VORD)   Both a requirements elicitation and a requirements analysis methodology.

White-box testing   A testing methodology where the test cases are mostly derived from examining the code and the detailed design.

Index